REVELATION

Published by
The Bible Reading Fellowship
First Floor, Elsfield Hall
15–17 Elsfield Way, Oxford OX2 8FG
ISBN 1 84101 363 3

First edition 1997
Revised edition 2005
10 9 8 7 6 5 4 3 2 1 0

Acknowledgments
Unless otherwise stated, scripture quotations are taken from
The New Revised Standard Version of the Bible, Anglicized
Edition, copyright © 1989, 1995 by the Division of Christian
Education of the National Council of the Churches of Christ in
the United States of America, and are used by permission. All
rights reserved.

Scripture quotations taken from The Revised Standard Version of
the Bible, copyright © 1946, 1952, 1971 by the Division of
Christian Education of the National Council of the Churches of
Christ in the United States of America, are used by permission.
All rights reserved.

Scripture quotations taken from the Holy Bible, *New International
Version*, copyright © 1973, 1978, 1984 by the International
Bible Society. Used by permission of Hodder & Stoughton
Limited. All rights reserved. 'NIV' is a registered trademark of
International Bible Society. UK trademark number 1448790.

A catalogue record for this book is
available from the British Library

Printed in Singapore by Craft Print International Ltd

REVELATION

THE PEOPLE'S BIBLE COMMENTARY

MARCUS MAXWELL

A BIBLE COMMENTARY FOR EVERY DAY

Introducing the
People's Bible Commentary
SERIES

Congratulations! You are embarking on a voyage of discovery—or rediscovery. You may feel you know the Bible very well; you may never have turned its pages before. You may be looking for a fresh way of approaching daily Bible study; you may be searching for useful insights to share in a study group or from a pulpit.

The People's Bible Commentary (PBC) series is designed for all those who want to study the scriptures in a way that will warm the heart as well as instructing the mind. To help you, the series distils the best of scholarly insights into the straightforward language and devotional emphasis of Bible reading notes. Explanation of background material, and discussion of the original Greek and Hebrew, will always aim to be brief.

- If you have never really studied the Bible before, the series offers a serious yet accessible way in.

- If you help to lead a church study group, or are otherwise involved in regular preaching and teaching, you can find invaluable 'snapshots' of a Bible passage through the PBC approach.

- If you are a church worker or minister, burned out on the Bible, this series could help you recover the wonder of scripture.

Using a People's Bible Commentary

The series is designed for use alongside any version of the Bible. You may have your own favourite translation, but you might like to consider trying a different one in order to gain fresh perspectives on familiar passages.

Many Bible translations come in a range of editions, including study and reference editions that have concordances, various kinds of special index, maps and marginal notes. These can all prove helpful in studying the relevant passage. The Notes section at the back of each PBC volume provides space for you to write personal reflections, points to follow up, questions and comments.

Each People's Bible Commentary can be used on a daily basis, instead of Bible reading notes. Alternatively, it can be read straight through, or used as a resource book for insight into particular verses of the biblical book.

If you have enjoyed using this commentary and would like to progress further in Bible study, you will find details of other volumes in the series listed at the back, together with information about a special offer from BRF.

While it is important to deepen understanding of a given passage, this series always aims to engage both heart and mind in the study of the Bible. The scriptures point to our Lord himself and our task is to use them to build our relationship with him. When we read, let us do so prayerfully, slowly, reverently, expecting him to speak to our hearts.

CONTENTS

PBC REVELATION: INTRODUCTION

For those who don't read introductions

If you are one of those people who tend to skip the introduction, welcome. There are just three things I'd like to tell you about this book before you begin.

Firstly, it is not a verse-by-verse commentary, and it doesn't have the text of Revelation in it. It will make sense if it is read on its own, but it assumes that you have the appropriate passage fresh in your memory while you read. The best way to use it is to read the passage, then read the comment. The version it is based on (except in a very few places) is the New Revised Standard Version (NRSV), though any version will do.

Secondly, it takes the view, along with that of most scholars, that the book of Revelation would have been perfectly well understood by its first-century readers, and is therefore not a detailed blueprint of the plan of God for the second coming. It primarily addresses the churches of the Roman province of Asia Minor, and has to be understood as a message to them. At the same time, it is intended to carry a message for all the Church, and is highly relevant to today's Christians, carrying a timely message to the world of the 21st century.

Finally, it certainly does not claim to be definitive! The broad thrust of Revelation's message is agreed by the vast majority of scholars, but there is a wealth of diverse opinion on its details. In a book of this size it is impossible to give every view, or even to argue in detail for the interpretations given here. It is simply offered as a way into the book of Revelation, and an antidote to the idea that this book of the Bible is beyond anyone other than an expert scholar.

Introducing Revelation

It's very tempting, when we pick up a commentary (even a fairly simple one like this), to miss out the introduction. We want to get to grips with what the Bible says, or to prepare a Bible study or sermon, and the introduction is full of boring stuff about dates, authorship, geography, literary style and so on. Sometimes these details are quite important, however, and help us to understand what the writer was trying to say, and how it may apply to us. This is especially the case with Revelation, which has been interpreted in many different ways, some of them so weird as to give the impression that it is either irrelevant to today's Christians or the preserve of specialists.

In this introduction I want to set out very briefly the approach taken in this short commentary and explain why I think it is the best one. There will also be a few comments on dates, who wrote it, why, and how the book is put together. If it is your first encounter in any depth with the strangest book in the New Testament, you will probably find these comments helpful. If you want more detail on technical matters of dating, authorship and so on, you will find them in the introductions to the commentaries mentioned in the reading list at the end of this section.

What sort of book is Revelation?

At one time, many people thought that Revelation, the second half of Daniel, and to some extent the visions of prophets such as Ezekiel and Zechariah were a unique type of writing found only in the Bible. It was easy, then, to see them as a coded message about the future. This way of interpreting Revelation is still popular in some circles, which see it as a detailed prediction either of the history of the world as a whole or of the Church in particular. It is then usually seen as dealing mainly with the period immediately before the return of Christ. The symbolic language it uses is interpreted in the light of current events. For instance, the beast from the sea which we meet in chapter 13 is seen as the Pope, or Martin Luther, or Hitler, or Stalin, or Ming the Merciless, or whoever the interpreter's enemy might be.

The good point about this way of looking at the book is that it does stress that Revelation is applicable to the Church of the present. It also reminds us that Christians look to the future and the coming of God's kingdom. The big problem with it is that it assumes that John, the writer, was writing about specific events and people in the far future from his own time. This would mean that most of the book was irrelevant to the churches to which it is specifically addressed (chs. 2—3). It also means that it is in fact impossible to know who and what these future people and events are. Although writers throughout history have seen Revelation as portraying the events of their own time (the Thirty Years War, the First World War, the formation of the European Union), history has carried on without Jesus' return. It seems strange that the Bible should contain a book which is so impenetrable.

Another way of looking at the book is to see it as a collection of powerful, poetic images that stimulate Christian imagination and devotion. This is true as well, but there must be more to it than that. Otherwise, our imagination can run riot, and we can read into it anything we like. It seems strange that someone should write a book which he claims is a message from Jesus himself (1:1–2) but which can mean anything the reader wants it to mean.

In the last hundred years or so, scholars have realized that Revelation belongs to a particular style of writing which was popular in Jewish and Christian circles for about a hundred years before and after the time of Jesus. These books are known as 'apocalypses' from the Greek word *apokalypsis*, which simply means 'revelation'. They take various forms, but between them they have certain recognizable characteristics. They are often written in the name of a famous teacher or prophet of the past, as though he had predicted the events of the real writer's time. The book of Daniel falls into this category. It was most probably written to encourage Jews of the second century BC but in the name of a famous figure of the exile to Babylon in the sixth century BC. This may seem dishonest to us, but was a recognized literary convention in the ancient world.

Apocalypses often claim to show the history of the world from the viewpoint of heaven. They tend to be given to the writer in the form of a message or vision brought by an angel, and they promise the mighty intervention of God, who will act to bring about his rule and to save his people in a miraculous manner. Sometimes they are highly symbolic, though few are as laden with strange images as Revelation is. Many such apocalypses still exist, and provide an important insight into Jewish and Christian thought in the period of the early Roman empire.

In recent years, some scholars have begun to argue that the images of cataclysmic change in apocalyptic language are not really about 'the end of the world'. Instead, they should be seen as predicting, or even calling for, great changes in the social order. On this view, apocalyptic writing is as much a call for action by its readers as a prediction of God's intervention. It seems to me that, to a great extent, both views can be held together. Certainly we shall see that as far as Revelation is concerned, it does deal with the end times and the return of Christ, followed by the last judgment. It does not do so by providing a detailed timetable, or even a description of actual future events.

Rather it affirms, in powerful poetic and pictorial language, that the final victory of God is indeed coming. It also makes a powerful call to the Church to live in the light of the coming Christ, and implies a call to model the present world on the coming kingdom.

It is clear, then, that Revelation belongs to the apocalyptic style of writing, and would have been understood as such by its first readers. So it was definitely written to the churches in the Roman province of Asia Minor. At the same time, the writer makes it clear that he is writing a book for all the Church, and one which will have a lasting relevance to Christians. Of all the books of the New Testament, Revelation comes closest to being written consciously as scripture. Its detailed interconnections with the Hebrew scriptures, the construction that deliberately aims to repay detailed study, and its repeated claim to be the very message of God himself suggest that John comes close to putting his work on the same level as the Old Testament. To say that it is a first-century apocalypse does not rob it of its significance. It gives us the key to understanding it.

The claim that Revelation is a carefully constructed piece of literature, which takes its inspiration from the Old Testament and falls into a well-known genre, may be a little disturbing to some readers. If John has constructed it so thoughtfully, what are we to make of his claim that it came as a revelation of Jesus? Can we really call it revelation at all? The brief answer is that we can, but that needs some explanation.

Firstly, Revelation is no more or less inspired than any other book of scripture, all of which are claimed by Christians to be part of God's revelation of himself, and bear witness to the supreme revelation in Jesus Christ. This means that the sort of literature represented by a particular book doesn't affect its being God's word. History, legend, poetry, biography and apocalyptic all bear testimony to the revelation of God.

Secondly, when John claims to have had visions, there is no need to doubt him. He also claims, however, to be a prophet, and a characteristic of the great Old Testament prophets such as Isaiah, Jeremiah and Ezekiel is their careful reflection on God's word and their imaginative use of scripture. A good example would be Jeremiah's bold picture of God breaking his own law out of love for his people (Jeremiah 3:8 and 12; compare Deuteronomy 24:1–4). John also uses the scriptures creatively. In fact, there is not a single direct quotation from the Old

Testament in Revelation, but any single verse carries an echo of or clear allusion to scripture.

John has clearly taken his visions, reflected deeply on them, re-worked them in the light of scripture, and produced an apocalypse of unrivalled colour and vigour, which he presents to the Church as a clarion call from its risen Lord.

In this commentary we will therefore treat it as a message to the churches of John's own time, dealing with the difficulties and temptations facing Christians in the Roman empire. We will discover John's visionary use of scripture and his deep conviction that the Old Testament bears witness to, and is fulfilled in, Jesus Christ. We will also discover that it has a great deal to say to Christians in the world at the beginning of the 21st century.

Date and author

It is hard to decide exactly when the book was written, but the best guess is probably near the end of the first century, about AD95, during the reign of the emperor Domitian. Because of Revelation's stress on persecution, it used to be said that Domitian was one of the great persecutors of the church, but there is little independent historical evidence to support this claim. When John wrote, many would remember Nero's persecution of the Christians of Rome in AD64, and there would have been local and sporadic outbreaks of persecution. John warns that worse is to come.

We know nothing about John except what we can guess from Revelation. He is probably not the same John who wrote the fourth Gospel and the letters of John, though he came from the same area and the same group of churches.

The symbolism of Revelation

John is steeped in the Hebrew scriptures, which he probably knew in Hebrew, since his references to it sometimes seem to be his own translation, although he also uses the published Greek version of the day, known as the Septuagint (usually abbreviated to LXX). In his book, he seeks to tie together his vision of the role of the Church, and Jesus' message to it, with the messages of the prophets of the Old Testament. He draws heavily on Daniel, Ezekiel, Zechariah, Isaiah and the themes of Exodus. Most of the symbols he uses are his reinterpretation of the symbols of the Old Testament. He could expect his readers to be familiar with their Bibles (our Old Testament) as well as with the stories and sayings of Jesus. Unlike most writers of apocalypses, he rarely explains the meaning of his symbols, leaving it to his readers' knowledge of the Bible. For this reason, we will make frequent references to the Old Testament, though not as many as a detailed study would require.

John's failure to explain the symbols in detail is quite deliberate. It allows them to carry several meanings, each of which can speak to the Church in different situations and at different times, though the overall message of the book is clear.

Revelation is very carefully written, though in a rather rough and ready Greek, which seems intended to give the book a 'biblical' feel. Detailed study shows that John was adept at the styles of biblical interpretation which were popular in his day, especially among Jewish writers. For those with a good grasp of the Hebrew scriptures, there are hidden layers of meaning within his writing. There is, however, no secret message for those with deep knowledge. John's clever biblical cross-references make exactly the same point as the book as a whole —that the Church is called to witness faithfully to Jesus and to resist the temptation to compromise with the world.

The structure of Revelation

John not only uses his biblical references carefully, he also puts a lot of effort into the way the book is constructed. To anyone who has read several commentaries on Revelation, this may seem a strange statement, since almost every commentator has his or her view of exactly what the structure is. This is because we tend to think of books as having a straightforward progression from the beginning, through the middle, to the end. Revelation is not quite so simple. There is an introduction, a middle section and a conclusion, but within that there are repetitions, visions within visions and themes which seem to disappear, only to re-emerge later.

John gives the same events several times, expanding the detail and providing fresh viewpoints. For instance, there are three series of seven judgments: the seals (beginning in chapter 6), the trumpets (from chapter 8) and the bowls (chapter 16). At first sight these are successive events, but on closer examination they turn out to be different perspectives on the same thing, since all end at the last judgment. The overall effect is not so much of a road that passes through various points *en route*, as of a net of interconnected symbols and events with layers of meaning.

A second feature of the book's structure is due to a fact that today's readers easily forget: it was written first and foremost to be listened to, not simply read. Those who did read it in detail would be repaid by the depth of meaning mentioned above. Most hearers, though, would need signals to help keep them on track. For this reason, John uses numbers (and multiples of them) with special significance: seven means completeness, four refers to creation, two is the number of witness, and twelve is the people of God. These numbers would have been well known, and are drawn from the Bible and Jewish tradition. John uses repeated phrases (always with a slight variation) to tie together related passages. For instance, the peoples of the earth are described in variants of 'every tribe and tongue and people and nation', which would act as a reminder to those who heard the book read out.

Sometimes John links passages together by beginning the second section before he has ended the first one, rather like the hooks on a model train. A good example of this is at the beginning of chapter 8, where the angels with seven trumpets are introduced in verse 2, and then the preceding vision of seven seals is finished off in verses 3–5 before the sequence of trumpets continues.

Another trick is to insert one series of visions inside another. The vision of heaven in chapters 4—5 is followed by the seven seals in 6:1—8:3, but the vision of the seals is broken by chapter 7, which returns us to the world of the saints and a vision of worship before we come back to the judgments on earth. In this way, John holds together his message about the judgment of the world and his vision of the role of the Church.

One section that is not tied to any other is chapter 12, where John makes a new start. In fact, the theme of the chapter picks up from chapter 11. In order to explain chapter 11 more fully, he goes further back in time, effectively beginning his story over again, and so signals that with an abrupt change.

The book as a whole is written as a single letter to the seven churches. Like all letters of the period, it has a certain type of greeting and conclusion that frame the book as a whole.

The book has one very important structural feature. Chapters 10 to 11 form the centrepiece of the work, around which the rest is constructed. The first nine chapters lead up to it, and the last ten chapters explain it and draw out its consequences. It is in these two chapters that the (literally) central message of the book is found.

Brief outline of Revelation

The complex structure of the book makes it possible to pick out various patterns which may be mistaken for the one and only pattern of the whole composition. It is better simply to sketch an outline of the major sections and then pick up themes as they appear.

1:1–8	Introduction
1:9–20	Introductory vision of the risen Lord
2:1—3:22	Jesus' messages to the seven churches
4:1—5:14	Introductory vision of heaven leading to:
6:1—8:1; 8:3–5	Seven seals
(7:1–17	The role of God's people)
8:2; 8:6—11:19	Seven trumpets
(10:1—11:14	The role of God's people—and the central message of the book)
12:1—14:20; 15:2–4	The battle between the people of God and the forces of evil
15:1; 15:5—16:21	Seven bowls
17:1—19:10	God's victory over Babylon
19:11—20:15	Judgment of the world and the victory of the saints
21:1—22:5	The new creation and the city of God
22:6–21	Conclusion and final greetings

Further reading

A lot has been written on the book of Revelation, much of it useful, but a fair bit of it very misleading. Readers who are familiar with the literature will be able to tell what I have read (and more embarrassingly, what I have not!) This commentary is intended as an introduction to the book, and if you want to read more, the following few titles will be useful.

The books that have most helped me to form my own views are both by Richard Bauckham:

The Theology of the Book of Revelation, New Testament Theology Series (Cambridge University Press, 1993) is a short but comprehensive guide to the thought and message of the book.

The Climax of Prophecy, Studies on the Book of Revelation (T. & T. Clark, 1993) is an academic work dealing in depth with some of the issues of the first book. Very heavy stuff, best suited to the reader who knows Greek. Some Hebrew is helpful too.

John Sweet, *Revelation* (SCM Press, 1979) is a very good classic commentary and readable with it.

G.B. Caird, *The Revelation of St John the Divine*, Black's New Testament Commentary Series (A. & C. Black, second edn., 1984) is a beautifully written commentary, full of theological and devotional sensitivity.

Robert W. Wall, *Revelation*, New International Biblical Commentary (Hendrickson, 1991) attempts to relate the message of Revelation to scripture as a whole.

More accessible commentaries include the following:

Michael Wilcock, *I Saw Heaven Opened*, The Bible Speaks Today Series (IVP, 1975) is a straightforward attempt to explain the relevance of the book to modern Christians.

Murray Robertson, *The Future of Humanity* (Albatross Books/BRF, 1993, out of print) is a pocket-sized commentary which applies John's message of spiritual warfare to the structures and concerns of today. Unfortunately, it does not deal with the first three chapters, as these were assigned to a companion volume.

In the last few years, three huge commentaries have appeared, each one weighing in at around 1000 pages, and weightily academic. Knowledge of Greek is helpful in reading these, but not vital:

David E. Aune, *Revelation*, Word Biblical Commentary Volumes 52a, 52b, 52c (Thomas Nelson, 1997, 1998, 1999) is a detailed examination of just about every aspect of the book and its interpretation through history. Aune argues that it was composed in varying stages, drawing on existing Jewish and Christian sources.

G.K. Beale, *The Book of Revelation,* The New International Greek Testament Commentary (Eerdmans/Paternoster, 1999) is similarly detailed. Beale takes a rather calvinistic approach which majors on the fixed fate of both the redeemed and the damned.

Grant R. Osborne, *Revelation,* Baker Exegetical Commentary on the New Testament (Baker Academic, 2002) takes a broadly evangelical approach, while acknowledging the possibility of a breadth of interpretations.

For those who are interested in John's use of scripture, there is a useful short chapter in Steve Moyise, *The Old Testament in the New: An Introduction*, Continuum Biblical Studies Series (Continuum, 2001). On the Internet, the place to begin is the Revelation section of *The New Testament Gateway*: www.ntgateway.com.

From these sources, anyone who gets addicted to studying Revelation will be able to locate hundreds of other titles.

A brief personal note

I have gained great pleasure, a good deal of benefit, and some frustration in the writing of the present book. For all this, I would like to thank the series editors for asking me to write it, and the authors of all the books and articles I have read, who cannot be listed here. There are bound to be mistakes and misunderstandings in what I have written. Where these have not been borrowed from other writers, they are entirely my own!

Thanks, too, to Brian Lipscombe and Jason Boyd for commenting on parts of my original manuscript. Sometimes I even took their advice.

Thanks to my editor, Naomi Starkey, for asking me to revise the book, and for being exceptionally patient when it took longer than I had optimistically anticipated. Thanks, too, for her rigorous and challenging editing.

Finally, thanks to my family, Sarah, James, Laurence and Polly, for their encouragement and patience. The finished product is dedicated to them.

BLESSED READERS

John begins his book by explaining what sort of work his readers are to expect. The first sentence, which, as in most books from the ancient world, also acts as the title, declares it to be a 'revelation' or apocalypse which has come not simply from John himself but from Jesus Christ, the risen Lord of the Church, who in turn is conveying God's message. The Greek could also mean that the revelation is about Jesus, which is also true.

To the first readers or, in most cases, hearers of the book, this would explain what type of literature to expect. Firstly, it would be an apocalypse, dealing with the events of earth and heaven and the last days; and secondly, it would be a prophecy (v. 3)—a message from the risen Lord to his Church.

While apocalypses took many forms, John's original audience would not be surprised, and might well expect, to find the message conveyed in rich and wonderful symbols, which they would recognize from their knowledge of scripture and their experience of similar kinds of writing. However, they would most certainly expect to find a message of relevance to them, for this was also a prophecy.

To today's readers, prophecy tends to mean a foretelling of the future, and there is some of that in Revelation. But that is too narrow a view of prophecy. The biblical prophets, and the prophets of the early church, intended their message to speak to the situation of those who first heard it. They were not fortune tellers, but bringers of God's word to God's world. So Revelation claims to be a message from Jesus to the Christians of the seven churches in Asia Minor to whom it is addressed.

Witnesses

These opening verses also signal the main theme of the book—witness. John is a witness who bears testimony to what he has seen and heard, and he received it via an angel (whom we do not meet until chapter 10) from Christ, who in turn bears witness to the truth of God. Indeed, in verse 5 Christ is described as the 'faithful witness'.

The great calling of the Church is to be a witness: to proclaim in word and deed the message of the gospel; to tell out to the world what God has done. In being witnesses, Christians both tell of their own experience and also pass on a message that comes from God himself, is borne by Jesus to the world, and lives on in his Church.

This idea is suggested by the repeated use of the word 'servant' (v. 1). The readers of the book are God's servants, as is John, through whom the message comes. The word translated 'servant' literally means 'slave'. Some people object to this word as giving too servile a view of Christian discipleship, but that is to miss the point. In the Greek Bible with which John's readers would have been familiar, 'slave of God' translates a Hebrew phrase meaning 'servant of the Lord' which is frequently used of the prophets. It is a term of honour, denoting those servants of the king who have been brought into his confidence and share a knowledge of his plans (see, for instance, Amos 3:7: 'Surely the Lord does nothing, without revealing his secret to his servants the prophets'). The servants of God are those who know God's plans. Servants are also those who carry out their master's wishes. To hear the word of prophecy is to be galvanized into carrying it out, or proclaiming it further.

Hearers

To pass on the message, or to act on it, we need first to be hearers of it. John's opening verses include a blessing on the one who reads it out, and thus shares its message, and on those who hear and take to heart its teaching (v. 3). This is not simply a pious wish. Communicating the word brings a share in the work of God and his prophetic message. To be open to the word of God is to let him into our lives, to get to know him, and to learn how to serve him. John refers only to his own book of prophecy, but it is true of all the Bible. As we read, reflect and pray, we can expect to be blessed; blessed by a deeper knowledge, but also by a deeper experience of the God who speaks to us, fills us with his message and sends us out to speak good news to the world.

PRAYER

Father, as you speak to us through your word, give us grace to understand it, to live by it and to share it with others.

POSTMARKED HEAVEN

John now writes a second introduction because, while the book is a prophecy in the style of an apocalypse, it is also in the form of a letter. In the New Testament, letters are the common way of bringing pastoral advice, and Revelation is also intended as a pastoral letter.

These verses follow what was by now a well-established way of writing a Christian letter. Like most letters of the ancient world, it begins by stating from whom and to whom it is written. Pagan writers would often include a brief blessing or prayer to a god. Christians tended to extend this section into a lengthy thanksgiving or a hymn of praise to God (compare the way Paul begins his letters).

This letter wishes grace (God's free giving of his love and salvation) and the peace it brings (v. 4), both with God and in the inner self. This wish is rooted in the nature and work of the eternal and unchanging God, the Lord of past, present and future. It comes from the Holy Spirit, here called the 'seven spirits who are before his throne'. Some commentators argue that these spirits are angels—the seven who stood close to the divine throne. It is unlikely, though, that John would place angels together with God and Jesus, and in the New Testament 'spirit' usually refers to the Holy Spirit unless it is qualified in some way (as, for instance, 'evil spirits'). The number seven signifies perfection, but it also ties in with the seven churches: the Holy Spirit is the presence of God with the churches. Grace and peace come also from Jesus Christ, who, being faithful to God, has been raised from the dead as the forerunner of all who will share in his resurrection, and who is now the true ruler of the world.

Three in one

We often hear that the doctrine of the Trinity is not found in the Bible. In the sense of the philosophical statements that later theologians loved, this is true. Here, and often in Revelation, however, we see the close connection of Father, Son and Spirit, which is the foundation of the later trinitarian doctrines. We will see in 5:6 that the seven spirits are agents of the Son as well as the Father, showing the close co-operation of Father, Son and Spirit. If the Trinity is not clearly formulated in the New Testament, it is nevertheless the most biblical way of speaking of God.

Glory of the Church, glory of Christ

Although Revelation has much to say about heaven and future hope, it has as much, if not more, to say about the Church on earth. Christians have been called to be God's people here and now. We have the task of approaching God in worship and bringing others into his presence. Or, as John puts it in his deliberately 'biblical' language, drawing on Exodus 19:6 and Christian tradition (compare 1 Peter 2:9), we are God's kingdom and his priests (v. 6), because of what Jesus has done for us as the expression of love. Revelation does not mention the love of God all that often. In fact, many commentators condemn it as falling far short of the true Christian ideal of love, so don't forget that here at the outset we are told that all the work of Christ flows from love, and that love was such that it led Jesus to die for us. The rest of the book is an exploration of how to have a priestly ministry in the midst of a hostile world for which Jesus died.

This Jesus who died will, in the end, rule all things in glory. If his reign is hidden now, seen only by those who put their faith in him, there will be a time when it will be clear to all, and those who killed him (that is, all whose sins led him to the cross) will wail or mourn over him (v. 7, combining Daniel 7:13 and Zechariah 12:10).

There are two ways of taking this statement. It could mean that they will wail in terror at judgment, but it could also mean that they will mourn in repentance for their sins, as they recognize the enormity of their error and turn again to God. Probably John is being deliberately ambiguous here, for, as we shall see, both possibilities remain open. Judgment is ultimately the response to God's love, which human beings can accept or reject.

God, who is the beginning and end of all things (v. 8: alpha and omega are the first and last letters of the Greek alphabet), desires nothing more than to draw all people back to himself, the one who has created the world, sustains it in being and is the final purpose and goal of the universe. In him, creation will find its true joy and purpose.

PRAYER

Father, Son and Holy Spirit, help us to serve you, to worship you and love you with all our hearts.

3

REVELATION 1:9–20

OVERWHELMING VISION

John received his vision on the island of Patmos, about 65 miles from Ephesus. He was there, he says, on account of God's word and the testimony of Jesus. Probably, then, he was in exile for his public proclamation of the gospel. Such a punishment was generally reserved for highly placed citizens who were likely to cause embarrassment, and it is possible that John was a prominent person in his home town, though we cannot be sure of this.

Neither can we be sure whether John was still on the island when he wrote his letter/book, since his mention of Patmos (v. 9) is in the past tense. What is certain is that Revelation is not simply a verbatim account of a vision or series of visions. It is shot through with careful and clever references to scripture (though it never merely quotes word for word) and other religious writings of the day; it has a very careful though complex structure, and is obviously the result of deep reflection. Yet we need not doubt that a visionary experience underlay it—a vision or visions received while John was 'in the spirit' (v. 10), which probably suggests a trance. Nor need we doubt that it was a vision, or series of visions, of enough power and importance to convince John that he had the basis for a much-needed message to his churches.

Bible pictures

John's vision came to him on the Lord's day, which probably means Sunday, the day on which Christians worshipped in celebration of the day of Jesus' resurrection. And it was Jesus that he saw.

This was no vision of the carpenter from Nazareth; neither was it the Christ of the resurrection appearances, displaying the wounds of the cross. This is a figure of awe, and almost terror. The description, like most of the visions of Revelation, is not a literal picture of what, if anything, John really saw. In fact, as the history of art shows us, it is almost impossible to make an accurate drawing of many of John's visions. They are literary 'images' depending on the force of the words and the meanings conjured up by their references to the Bible.

John sees one like a 'Son of Man' (v. 13), a reference to the figure in Daniel 7:13 who represents the people of Israel. This Son of Man,

26

though, has white hair and clothes, like Daniel's 'Ancient of Days'—God himself (Daniel 7:9). Also like God himself, he can be described as the first and the last (v. 17; see 1:8, where God is called Alpha and Omega). He wears the girdle of a high priest and from his mouth comes a sword, which can only be the word of God (see Hebrews 4:12). His face shines like that of Moses after meeting with God (Exodus 34:29).

We can see how John weaves together various biblical images to give a picture of the power of the ascended Christ. Jesus, says John, stands as the representative of God's people, interceding for them and offering sacrifice like the Jewish high priest, but with greater effectiveness, for he shares the nature of God, and the sacrifice he offers is himself. Like Moses, he speaks God's word, which is his weapon against falsehood and evil, and he shines with the glory of God.

It is not surprising that John should fall down at the feet of this apparition (v. 17), but Jesus comes to bring not fear, but hope, and victory over death. His power is not to stun John, but to encourage him; not to overawe him but to take away fear—even the fear of death.

This awesome image is not all that John has to tell us about Jesus, but it is enough for now. The One whose thunderous voice speaks through John to the churches is a figure of power, and he offers both hope and challenge. Yet he is not, for all his awesomeness, a distant figure. The stars in his hand and the lampstands among which he walks represent the seven churches. In Zechariah 4, seven lampstands represent the eyes of God, ranging through the world, so it is likely that the light of the lamps is the presence of God (the sevenfold Holy Spirit) in the churches. The Church is empowered by the Spirit for its priestly and prophetic work of service and proclamation.

In their turn, these seven churches represent all churches, for seven is the number of completion and fullness. Jesus has the Church in his hand, and stands among his people. He may sometimes have harsh words to say, but in the end he is on their side, and his power is exercised on their behalf and is available to them.

PRAYER

Lord, give us a vision of your glory, that we may draw on your strength for the tasks you give us to do.

The HOLDER *of* ETERNAL LIFE

Like a play within a play, John gives us seven letters within his letter. Perhaps they are better called 'messages', since they lack some of the normal signs of a formal letter. They are addressed to seven churches in the Roman province of Asia, roughly what we would now call Turkey. We know that there were more than seven churches in the province (Colossae, for example, was not far away), and it may be that John is writing only to the Christian communities where he was well known, or where there were particular problems to be dealt with.

On the other hand, we have already seen that seven is a symbolic number, suggesting a message for all the Church, and perhaps for all the churches in Asia, with a special address to certain problem communities.

The order in which the churches are named follows the route a messenger would take in a roughly circular journey from Ephesus along the roads of the day. Presumably each church would receive its own copy, which was expected to be read aloud to the congregation (1:3) at its meeting for worship. Such a setting would reinforce the impact of the book, with its interludes of praise and adoration.

The fact that it was to be read aloud also helps us to understand the structure of Revelation, with repeated variations on a particular phrase, three series of seven visions, and so on. These act as markers to the listeners, keeping their attention and helping them to make sense of a letter that would take over an hour to read.

Spiritual realities

Each message is addressed to 'the angel' of each church. A lot of debate has focused on the identity of these angels. Are they the guardian angels of each church? If so, why should John write to them? And in what sense could a letter be addressed to an actual angel? Or are they simply human representatives of each church, for the word literally means 'messengers'? If so, why should Christ address only them when the whole Church is expected to listen? Perhaps the best explanation is that they are symbolic, representing the churches' spiritual nature.

A church is not just a physical thing, either a building or even a collection of worshippers, but is a spiritual reality, a community of those with a shared faith, a shared experience of God and a share in the Holy Spirit. That community has a life of its own, with its particular ethos, gifts, vision and mission. John is told to write to the churches as spiritual entities, whose spiritual life is in fact in danger, whether their outward appearance is healthy or not.

So Jesus appears in John's first vision both standing among the lampstands that represent the churches, and holding in his hand the seven stars that are their spiritual life. Ultimately, it is this spiritual life that matters, for it is that which lasts for eternity.

The use of lampstands as images for the church points to a key theme in Revelation: witness. The churches are there to shed the light of the gospel, so that the world may see the love and grace of God. The spiritual life of the church is not an abstraction but a matter of concrete service. A sure sign of its spiritual health is the degree to which it is involved with the world in word and deed.

Stars

The fact that stars are used to represent the eternal life of the church is probably a dig at the role astrology played in the ancient world, both as a means of telling the future and in pagan religious symbolism. For many in the ancient world, life was governed by an inescapable fate. The sensible person simply accepted what came. For Christians, however, both future and spiritual security are found in Jesus. God alone rules our destiny, and with that knowledge we do not need to know what is to come, save to be sure that he will be there waiting for us.

Another reason for rejecting astrology (and a thousand and one other forms of divination), apart from its lack of effectiveness, is a moral one. The logical consequence of the idea of a fixed future is that human actions do not matter: the future is fixed by the stars. Christians believe that the future depends on their actions, their faith and their response to God's love. Part of Revelation's message is that the future very much depends on the ministry of the royal priesthood which is the Church.

PRAYER

Lord Jesus, in you alone are we secure,
and in you alone we put our trust.

5 REVELATION 2:2–7

EPHESUS: LOVE & DOCTRINE

Ephesus was one of the major cities of the Roman province of Asia, along with Smyrna and the capital, Pergamum. The town was a prosperous port and trading centre, dominated by the great temple of Artemis, which was known as one of the wonders of the ancient world. Paul had evangelized there, and fallen foul of both local religion and trade interests (Acts 19:23–41). In the midst of such a city, and in the light of the mingling of religious ideas that was common in Asia Minor, it would be easy for Christians to be led astray. To their credit, the Ephesian Christians had stood firm.

True doctrine

Indeed, it would seem that they had become very zealous in their defence of right doctrine. They had carefully evaluated visiting Christian teachers and rejected their claim to be apostles. They opposed the activities of the Nicolaitans, a group that we will consider in more detail later. In the face of pressure to give up on their faith, they showed patience and endurance. All this is commendable.

In fact, a high regard for doctrine is vital to the life of the church. Without it, there can be no test of conformity with basic Christian teaching, and no check on what actually constitutes Christianity itself. Indeed, false teaching that would pervert the true gospel was an expected sign of the end times (Matthew 24:24; 1 John 2:18ff).

Yet the Ephesians' regard for sound teaching carried with it its own danger, and one into which the church had fallen. They had lost love (v. 4), and so fallen foul of one of the other expected signs of the end (Matthew 24:12).

Had they become judgmental and unyielding? Quite possibly.

Any community that feels itself under threat tends to tighten its rules and become less tolerant of dissent, and the Church is no exception. In our own time, we can see trends which look to touchstones of orthodoxy (as defined by each differing group) and which lead to condemnation of those who differ. There is a fine line to tread between holding to the faith and accepting those of different opinion, but if there is a choice to be made, it is better to err on the side of love.

The church of Ephesus has fallen and is called to repent. Perhaps their description as 'fallen' (v. 5) carries a reminder of Isaiah 14:12: 'How you are fallen from heaven, O Day Star, Son of Dawn!' The star that is the church of Ephesus has plunged into the depths of love-lessness and must return to its former love or die. The verse from Isaiah was seen as a reference to the fall of the devil, and, like Satan himself, the Ephesian church had lost the sign of God's grace.

Church of death

Christ's threat to come and remove their lampstand (that is, the church itself—1:20) is probably not a reference to his coming at the final judgment, though it may well include that. The threat is much more immediate: their unloving attitude will bring its own reward. Churches do die, though the universal Church is eternal, and the surest route to death is to lose love. Christ is described as the one who walks among the lampstands (2:1), the churches in their role as lights to the world. Perhaps the love in question is specifically love for outsiders, who need to hear the gospel.

For all its doctrinal uprightness—and, probably, fierce moral recti-tude, for they tend to go together—there would be little welcome extended by the Ephesian church, little concern for the needs of its neighbours, and little support for the weak within the church. None of this is a recipe for life and growth. Purity can be maintained by building barriers, but love cannot.

The task of the church, then, was to hold fast to the faith by all means, but never to lose sight of the greatest of the commandments, to love. Love, after all, is the clearest sign of living faith.

PRAYER

Father, give us grace to discern your truth and perseverance to hold
to it, but above all, give us love for you, for our sisters and brothers
in Christ, and for the world in which we are called to serve you.

SMYRNA: POVERTY & RICHES

Smyrna (the modern town of Izmir) lay 35 miles north of Ephesus and vied with it for pre-eminence in trade and political influence. After its destruction in war, it had been rebuilt in 290BC as a model city and was famed for the beauty and grandeur of its buildings. It was an important centre for the worship of the emperor, and housed a large Jewish community.

In contrast, the Christian community was poor and persecuted. It is worth noting that only two of the seven churches receive unqualified praise from the risen Christ (the other is Philadelphia), and both of them are noted for their poverty. The spiritual danger of material wealth, which is all too easily mistaken for divine blessing, was a reality then as now.

The poverty of the Smyrnan Christians is more than offset by their spiritual wealth, however. In the Bible, while poverty is never seen as a virtue in itself, it is frequently connected with God's blessing, for the poor have nowhere to turn but to God, and so become a byword for simple trust.

Witnesses

The Christians of Smyrna are facing persecution by their more prosperous Jewish neighbours, probably in the form of denunciation to the Roman authorities as members of an anti-imperial cult. Some will be imprisoned for a short time ('ten days' merely indicates a short time) as a prelude, probably, to death. They must hold firm to their faith and be prepared to witness to the reality of Jesus by their deaths.

The Greek word for witness, *martys*, gives us the term 'martyr': one whose witness has been taken to its ultimate conclusion. Revelation comes close to using the word in its modern sense, for all Christians, says John, must be prepared to die for their faith if that is what is demanded of them.

The result of faithful witness is eternal life, which is the crown of victory given to the conquering faithful, so this message comes to Smyrna from the one who himself 'was dead and came to life' (v. 8). The way of discipleship follows the path of Jesus to the cross, and beyond it to deathless life.

Most of the readers of this commentary do not expect to face any real danger for their faith, so it is difficult for us to remember that martyrdom is demanded of many of our brothers and sisters in Christ. It has been said that the 20th century saw more Christians martyred than in all the rest of the Church's history. It is a salutary reminder that, for Christians, the worst that can happen is not death but the loss of eternal life.

Satan's synagogue

John's description of the Jews of Smyrna as the 'synagogue of Satan' (v. 9) is one that sits uneasily with our properly sensitive consciences. We have seen too much of the results of anti-Semitism to be easy with such terms, yet for John the situation was different. Christianity and Judaism, each developing from their common roots, were beginning to go their separate ways. Jews were increasingly seeing their Christian neighbours as members of a new religion or as unacceptable heretics, rather than as people following one of many legitimate forms of Judaism. They were seen as blasphemously offering worship to a human being, and one who had died as a condemned criminal, under God's own curse (Galatians 3:13). Jewish converts were beginning to be expelled from the Jewish community. For many Jewish Christians it was a loss of friends, family and identity. It was also a loss of protection, for Jews alone were exempt from the demands of Roman civil religion, with its demands of worship offered to the gods of Rome and to the emperor himself.

For Jews to denounce those who, like themselves, shared a fierce loyalty to the one God of the Hebrew scriptures seemed to Christians a most un-Jewish behaviour. Surely these were not true Jews, but had fallen prey to the devil himself!

The Smyrnan Christians are therefore probably undergoing local persecution instigated by their Jewish neighbours. Some may die, but if they hold fast they will share in the victory of Christ, conquering even death itself.

PRAYER

Lord Jesus, when we must speak for you, give us courage.

PERGAMUM: *the* DEVIL'S CAPITAL

By now, it is fairly clear that the description of Christ that begins each of the messages to the seven churches is taken from John's first vision in 1:12–20. Each aspect of that vision ties in with some aspect of the situation of the seven churches. So far, we have seen the fallen star of Ephesus and the resurrection promise to Smyrna. Pergamum, the provincial capital, is addressed by the one who 'has the sharp two-edged sword' (v. 12). Roman provincial governors had the power of summary execution—the *ius gladii*, the right to use the sword—but the true ruler of the world is Jesus, whose word cuts not the body but the soul and the binding power of sin.

Each of the seven messages begins with a connection to the first chapter of Revelation in its description of Jesus, and ends with a promise to 'whoever conquers', which looks forward to the end of the book (chs. 21—22). The Christian's conquest is the endurance of persecution and suffering as a faithful witness to Jesus, and is the theme of the book as a whole. The reward of that victory is eternal life, symbolized by the tree of life, freedom from the second death, and the other images of victory that colour the final chapters of Revelation.

This means that the seven messages cannot be dealt with fairly if they are taken out of their context as part of the whole book. At one time many scholars tried to do this, suggesting that they were earlier epistles which had been stuck into the book to give it greater relevance. Very few experts believe this now, but preachers still fall into the trap. We should avoid sermon series on the seven letters that do not refer to the rest of the book.

Heart of evil

Pergamum is not only the capital of Asia; it is Satan's home. There are many reasons why this was an apt description. The city was the site of a great temple to Zeus (whose magnificent altar, with a frieze showing the battle of the Greek gods against the earth giants, can be seen in the Pergamon Museum in Berlin). It was also the centre of worship of the healing god, Asklepios, 'god of Pergamum'. To Christians, the worship of these deities was not simply ignorance or folly, but was worship offered to demons (1 Corinthians 10:20).

The best reason for the title, however, was that Pergamum was the prime centre of the emperor cult. It housed a temple dedicated in his lifetime to the emperor Augustus, and to Roma, the goddess who was the personification of Rome. Technically, the emperor was not worshipped; prayer was offered to his 'genius', or guiding spirit, though in the Eastern empire the distinction was rarely made, as there was already a tradition of divine kingship in Eastern thought. For that matter, many emperors disliked the practice, but few discouraged it and some revelled in the honour. Certainly, Domitian, emperor at the time of John's writing, liked to be addressed as 'Lord and God'. This was a title that Christians could not in conscience use.

Quite possibly that is how Antipas met his end (v. 13). We are told nothing of this martyr, save that his death was part of a time of intense pressure on the church, a pressure that the church had successfully resisted.

Resisting the devil

Whether it was the lure of a pure church leading away from love in Ephesus, the persecution of the church by those who should know better in Smyrna, or the pressure of paganism at Pergamum, the church was under threat. In each case, that threat is seen as being the devil's work, and is something to be identified and resisted.

In our sophisticated age, belief in the devil seems old-fashioned, and indeed such a belief is not an article of the creeds. (The force of evil can readily be seen embedded in unjust laws, human institutions and the like.) All the same, it is vital to realize that the church still faces active opposition in many places today for which the term 'demonic' seems fitting. At Pergamum and throughout Revelation, that opposition is mainly from a state that demands more of its subjects than is its due. We today need to identify the opposing power and be aware of the need to resist.

PRAYER

Open our eyes, Lord, to that which opposes you,
and help us to resist.

8

GOOD NEIGHBOURS *or* WITNESSES?

The church of Pergamum has so far stood firm against the direct attacks of Satan's city, yet there is another danger that is not so obvious, for it comes from within.

There are some members of the church who are described as holding the 'teaching of Balaam' (v. 14). In the Old Testament, Balaam is a rather ambiguous character, a non-Israelite prophet who was hired by Balak, the king of Moab, to curse the invading Israelites. Under God's influence, he was able only to pronounce blessings (Numbers 22—24). He was later credited with leading the Israelites astray so that they joined in the fertility cults of Moab, committing adultery with Moabites and worshipping their gods (Numbers 31:16). As a result, he became a byword for those who would lead Israel astray.

Linked with the 'Balaamites' is another group, the Nicolaitans, presumably followers of someone called Nicolaus, of whom we know nothing. Both groups seem to have had much the same sort of ideas, but what were those ideas?

Living in the pagan world

Since Balaam was said to have incited the Israelites to join in with the pagan practices they discovered in Moab, it seems reasonable to assume that something of the sort was going on in Pergamum. We know from elsewhere in the New Testament that some Christians felt that their Spirit-filled lives gave them immunity from the consequences of sin. The Corinthians argued that sexual promiscuity was irrelevant both to their lives and to Christ, and could be indulged in without harm (1 Corinthians 6:12–20). Similarly in Corinth there were those who said that meat which had been used in pagan sacrifices was harmless for Christian consumption—a view with which Paul agreed, but which other Christians could not accept (1 Corinthians 8—10). Food sacrificed to idols had been forbidden by the church in Jerusalem in its decree to Gentile converts (Acts 15:20–29).

Some later forms of 'gnostic' Christianity (which saw salvation as the possession of spiritual *gnosis*, or special knowledge) took a view similar to the Corinthians', and pursued it to extremes. It seems likely that in Pergamum, and indeed other churches in Asia, a similar situation had arisen.

For Christians, avoiding contact with paganism could be tantamount to social ostracism. Social, political and business life centred on the worship of pagan gods. Meals were eaten in their temples, trade guilds had patron deities, and over all was the cult of the emperor, a binding force of political conformity. Christians could lose social prestige, friendship and wealth. Why not, then, make an outward show of conformity? Christ was the one true Lord, there was only one true God, so what harm was there in making a show for form's sake?

Fitting in

We can sympathize with a view like that, for although being a Christian carries lesser dangers in today's Western world, few Christians like to be seen as odd or unsociable. We are also aware of how easy it is to stand merely for conservatism or tradition rather than genuine Christian virtues, yet we face a real twofold danger.

Firstly, conformity with the world can, if we are not careful, lead to a habit of acquiescence in things that really do matter.

Secondly, and more importantly, such deadly conformity robs the Church of effective witness. An outward show of pagan worship would simply send the message that Christ is but one of the teeming multitude of deities, with no greater claim than any other. Such a message is a far cry from the gospel that the Church is called to proclaim.

For us, perhaps the danger is of suggesting that Christianity is merely one lifestyle or philosophy among many. It is 'all right for those who like that sort of thing'. In first-century Pergamum or in any of our cities today, such a message is a denial of Jesus and his claims.

REFLECT

*Where do we compromise the gospel by fitting in
too readily with our culture?*

A NEW NAME

If we are right in seeing the false teaching at Pergamum as conformity with the world, verse 16 is rather worrying. The Pergamene Christians are called to repent. To many readers today, their stance may not seem all that sinful, yet this is one of the main themes of Revelation. The world in which Christians are called to live out their discipleship is not a neutral territory. It is one pervaded by attitudes, social and political systems, that add up to hostility towards God.

The church at Pergamum is so far holding fast, and showing courage in doing so. From within, however, comes a teaching that may soften resolve and kill the church more effectively than any persecution. And of course, the fornication mentioned in 2:14 could well be literal. Some of the Pergamenes, like the Corinthians before them, could well have been much more enthusiastic partakers in certain aspects of pagan worship than a mere show of conformity required.

The whole church is therefore called to repent. Accepting some who differ in opinion may well be commendable tolerance, but failure to show up the dangers of their arguments and practices is another matter. Christ threatens to use the sword of his mouth (v. 16): compromise may have helped them avoid the Roman sword, but the judgment of God is unavoidable.

The Spirit of prophecy

Like each one of the messages to the seven churches, this is a prophecy for all the churches. The problem may be at its most severe in Pergamum (and Thyatira, as we shall see) but it is a perennial danger.

The message comes from the Spirit of God, whose task is to communicate God's will to his church. The task of the church, in its turn, is to listen to what God is saying. All too often, the church pursues its own apparently reasonable agenda, but that does not mean that it is obeying God.

In Revelation, John uses two terms to stress the role of the Spirit. The description of the Holy Spirit as the seven spirits before God's throne (1:4; 5:6) points to the Spirit as the indwelling power of God for the seven (and all) churches. Elsewhere John uses the more usual 'Spirit of God', the Old Testament term for the one who inspires the prophets. The Holy Spirit is both indwelling life and the bringer of God's word.

There is an unavoidable tension between the call to steadfastness and the call to be receptive to the Spirit of prophecy. When the Spirit reveals something new to the Church, in worship or mission or theology, it is easy to ignore it as a dangerous innovation. On the other hand, not all that is new is inspired by God. Hence the Church often seems to progress through debate and dissent (and Revelation itself is an obvious part of that process). As long as the overriding spirit is of love, the process will indeed be progress.

Jesus people

Once again, Christ's message ends with a promise to those who conquer. They will receive the 'hidden manna' (v. 17). According to Jewish tradition, in the end times God would again feed his people on manna in the age of the Messiah. For Christians this has already come true in the giving of Jesus, the bread for the life of the world (John 6:31–35, 58), and is celebrated in the eucharist. Ultimately, that spiritual sustenance will be theirs for all eternity.

They will also be given a new name, inscribed on a white stone. Both of these images are obscure, and several interpretations have been suggested. White stones were used as admission tickets to banquets and as signs of acquittal at trials. The name is probably that of God or Christ, as with the church of Philadelphia (3:12). In 19:12, Christ himself has a new name known only to himself. This denotes a new identity, since in John's day people's names were held to encapsulate their personalities, their 'true selves'.

Victorious Christians will find their true selves in their relationship with Jesus, and will be acquitted at the last judgment, gaining entrance to the marriage feast of their Lord, of which the present eucharist is but a foretaste.

PRAYER

Lord, as we feed on you now, make us hungry for your word,
hungry to do your will, and hungry for you.

The GROWING CHURCH

Thyatira was the least important of the seven cities politically, but its church receives the longest letter. Its central place in the seven messages may well suggest that its problems were well known. Certainly 2:23 suggests that Christ's response to the church will be a lesson for all the churches.

Despite the stern warning Jesus has for the Thyatiran Christians, their church has much in its favour. Its life is developing, and the signs of the Spirit's work (see Galatians 5:22–23) are abundant.

We tend to think of spiritual growth as being something that applies only to individuals. The seven messages to the Asian churches remind us that growth is necessary for churches as well. The Ephesian church grew in zeal for doctrine, but theirs was a lop-sided growth that needed to be balanced by a growth in love. At Thyatira, there seems to be more balanced development (v. 19). There has been an increase in love, and also in faith. In Revelation, faith tends to mean faithfulness. Christian faith is not just about believing a set of doctrines, but about having trust in another person—God. For Christians, virtues are not philosophical abstractions, but principles that guide one's way of life. Love is no mere sentiment, but shows itself in service. We are not told whether this is service to God or to fellow Christians, but it is unlikely that John would make that distinction. To serve Christ is to serve others.

It would be nice to think that a community which was visibly growing in love and service would gain the respect of its neighbours, but the world is rarely so fair. Patient endurance is another necessary virtue. We are not explicitly told what problems the Thyatirans faced, but on the evidence of Smyrna and Pergamum it seems likely that some sort of persecution was taking place, although not so violent as to need special mention. Quite possibly it took the form of social ostracism, or at least avoidance of Christians by their pagan neighbours.

They need no more correction or teaching, and their Lord does not lay on them any further burden (2:24).

Jezebel

The phrase 'any other burden' recalls the language of the apostolic decree of Acts 15:28, which forbade, among other things, the eating of food offered to idols. Eating such food is one of the things encouraged by 'Jezebel' (v. 20), who is the fly in the ointment at Thyatira. The name is obviously John's nickname for this prophet who is leading the flock astray (elsewhere in Revelation, the word translated 'beguiling' is used only of Satan and his minions). Eating the food of idols is probably John's shorthand for a teaching of compromise with paganism, along the lines of the Nicolaitans.

Jezebel, the pagan wife of King Ahab of Israel, was legendary as a perverter of the faith of Israel. The daughter of the king of Damascus, she was a keen promoter of her own faith in the fertility god Baal. She was accused of 'many whoredoms and sorceries' (2 Kings 9:22), a reference more to the fertility rites of Baal than to her own behaviour, though this did not stop short of arranging murder (1 Kings 21:1–16).

Prophet v. prophet

Jezebel 'calls herself a prophet' and was no doubt accepted as such in the church of Thyatira. This was the problem. What do we do when two prophets disagree? Both claim the inspiration of the Holy Spirit, and both may offer words that sound, on the face of it, quite reasonable. Yet to the prophet John, Jezebel is a deceiver who is virtually in league with the devil.

It was an old problem with no easy solution, save that of 'wait and see', as in the confrontation between the prophets Jeremiah and Hananiah (Jeremiah 28). John in fact takes a similar line: Jezebel and her followers will not last long (2:22–23). The future will decide.

Sadly, it seems that the Thyatiran church did not last long either. There appears to be no record of it after the end of the second century. Did it disappear through persecution, bearing faithful witness to the last? Did it perhaps become so compromised that it became indistinguishable from the pagans around it? We cannot know. When John wrote, the Thyatiran Christians had no more knowledge of their future than we have of ours.

PRAYER

Lord give grace to your Church to grow in love, faith, service and endurance; and discernment to recognize your voice out of all the clamour of the world.

11 REVELATION 2:20–29 (I)

TRUSTING *in* GOD

The prophet Jezebel is leading astray some of the Thyatiran Christians, but into what? Thyatira was an active centre of commerce, dominated by its merchants and the trade guilds to which they belonged. (Lydia, the seller of purple cloth in Acts 16 was a Thyatiran.) So numerous and influential were these guilds that the archaeology of Thyatira provides us with most of our information on such guilds for this period.

The guilds were dedicated to various pagan gods, who functioned much like patron saints. Guild business and social life would be centred on the appropriate temple. In practice, this may have meant little more to many guild members than dinner in a favourite restaurant would to business people today. To others, it would undoubtedly have been a deeply religious event. Whatever view the participants had, the fact remained that guilds were run under the auspices of what to Christians were idolatrous cults. Their meals were the results of pagan sacrifices, and their business agreements were in the name of false gods. Could Christians take part in such things?

Refusal to do so could mean ruin and ostracism. Compliance could be seen as denial of Christ. Since Jezebel encouraged the eating of food offered to idols (v. 20), it seems likely that she, like the Balaamites of Pergamum and the Nicolaitans, saw no harm in Christian involvement in such bland worship. She could probably cite Paul, who agreed that food offered to idols was mainly a matter of individual conscience (1 Corinthians 8:4ff), yet Paul knew there were spiritual dangers involved (1 Corinthians 10:14ff). We do not know whether Jezebel had similar concerns.

Deep dangers

If this were all, then John's strong attack may be understandable as one who disagreed, but we may well feel more sympathetic with his target. There are hints that there is more going on, however. The reference to the 'deep things' and to the promised star (vv. 24, 28) suggest that gnosticism and astrology are in view. This may be all the more likely when we remember the original Jezebel's 'sorceries'.

Gnosticism (from *gnosis*, the Greek for 'knowledge') was a religious tradition which claimed that salvation came from secret knowledge given by God to those who were worthy of it. Gnostics claimed to know the 'deep things of God'. Such knowledge set them free from the ordinary world and gave them spiritual protection, so that they could encounter evil without succumbing to it. This teaching found a fertile ground in Christianity, with its apparently similar stress on spiritual freedom and the teaching of Jesus. The great difference was that Christianity presented an open call to receive God's grace in Christ, whereas gnosticism presented a secret knowledge.

For John, this is a denial of the gospel, and the 'deep things' are deep things of Satan. They create a sense of superiority, a religious élite to whom the doctrine (and possibly morals) of the common herd do not apply. They create a religion of merit, as well. Instead of receiving God's freely offered gift of salvation, the gnostic achieves it through study, power of intellect and initiation in the mysteries of the cult.

Exploring evil

On the other hand, Jezebel herself may have argued that Christians are empowered to enter into things that others would see as wicked. For some gnostics, their spiritual protection enabled them to indulge in immorality and idolatry with impunity. While Jezebel's 'fornication' is a standard metaphor for idolatry and false teaching, it could also be literal, as it was for some Corinthians (1 Corinthians 6:12–20). Perhaps some of Jezebel's followers plunged into sinful activities (quite easy at some guild banquets, which could become pretty wild affairs), believing themselves to be spiritually protected.

A similar attitude may have been held towards the astrology that was so much a part of the ancient world, and which would be consulted by prudent traders. For Christians, though, the future is held in God's hands, and he alone controls it. Reliance on the stars is a denial of trust in the true Lord of the future.

PRAYER

Thank you, Father, that your gift of salvation is open to all,
regardless of wisdom, intellect or talent.

12 REVELATION 2:20–29 (II)

JUDGMENT & VICTORY

The risen Christ has given Jezebel time to repent. We are not told how, but it may well be that John has had a brush with her before, and she has continued in her teaching. If so, this may indicate that the problem at Thyatira is long-standing.

Now the time of reckoning is approaching. Those who have committed adultery with her will suffer 'great distress' (v. 22) and her children (that is, her followers) will be struck dead (literally, 'will be killed with pestilence', v. 23). Probably we should see two groups here: those who have flirted with her teaching but are not fully committed, and a distinct group in the church of Thyatira that is committed to Jezebel's leadership. Jezebel herself will be thrown on a bed—in illness and distress.

In a book as full of symbolism as Revelation, we need not take these threats too literally (but see 1 Corinthians 11:30). Whatever John envisages, the time is short for the false teachers of Thyatira.

Together with all the other churches, Thyatira must be prepared for persecution, and in that time only a strong and distinct Christian faith will survive. Compromise will be no protection, and a faith that has been watered down will lack the strength necessary for survival. Now is the time to repent and to learn to trust in God alone.

Holding fast

Thus the task of the Church is to cling to what it knows to be true, the teaching passed on to it by the apostles, and to the growth in faith and love that that teaching has brought. Above all, what they have is Christ, and he is worth all that they may gain by compromise with the world, and more. The path to final victory is faithfulness to Christ.

This church too receives a promise, to share in the final rule of Jesus over the nations (vv. 26–27). The word translated 'rule' (v. 27) literally means to 'shepherd', and there is a double meaning here. The promise quotes Psalm 2:9, prepared for by the description of Jesus as 'Son of God' in 2:18 (the only time in Revelation), which is a reference to verse 7 of this messianic psalm. In the psalm, the iron rod or sceptre is the instrument of judgment and conquest, shattering the pride of the world like clay pots, yet it can also be the shepherd's staff of protection and guidance. Then the clay pots are broken that they might be remoulded, as in Jeremiah 18:1–11. As in Revelation 1:7, the coming judgment of Christ may be salvation or doom. Either way, the Church must be firm in its witness and uncompromising in its devotion to Jesus. Indeed, it is only through such witness that there is hope of salvation for the nations. If Christ's own people are seen not to bother too much about loyalty to him, how can those who do not believe be expected to turn to him? If the Church is not seen to repent of its sins, how can it call the world to repentance?

In this sense, authority over the nations does not wait for the end of time. By faithfulness to Christ, moral uprightness and loyal witness, the Church is called to exercise moral authority here and now. Its very existence should be a statement of an alternative and greater authority. The question for today is still one of compromise. Is there anything in the Church and in Christian living that truly distinguishes it from the world? John's call to hear what the Spirit is saying to the churches is still pertinent.

Star of glory

The morning star, Venus, brightest of the stars, was associated with victory and rulership. For those who abandoned their trust in the stars, the true ruler and victor would be theirs—Jesus himself, the brightest star in heaven (22:16).

Again, the message to the local church looks forward to the end of the book. Indeed, there have been hints throughout the letter to Thyatira of what is coming. Jezebel is described in terms reminiscent of the whore who is Rome/Babylon (ch. 17), while harlots and sorcerers are excluded from the new Jerusalem in 21:8. While she perhaps sees herself as reasonable and avoiding extremism, she is identifying with all that represents enmity to God.

PRAYER \

Lord, how often we lose our grip on the truth and follow the star of the world! Restore us and hold us fast.

CHURCH *of the* LIVING DEAD

The city of Sardis had once been the capital of Croesus, king of Lydia, fabled for his wealth. Now its fortunes were in decline. Its mighty fortress was impregnable—except that it was now deserted, and had fallen twice to enemies who had crept up on it secretly. In John's day, Sardis boasted a temple to the mother goddess Cybele, and a powerful Jewish community. Either of these interest groups might have been expected to oppose the Christian church in their city, yet there is not the slightest hint of persecution or opposition in this fifth message. The reason is that the church is effectively dead.

It has not been wiped out, nor has it died from lack of interest. To outside eyes this is a lively and vibrant church, with a reputation. Yet from God's point of view, death reigns in Sardis. The reason for this death is that Christ has not found their works 'perfect' (v. 2). This does not mean flawless, but literally 'completed' or 'fulfilled'. In complete contrast to Thyatira, whose works have grown to maturity, the start made at Sardis has come to nothing. To be sure, there is still a church there, but it does nothing. There has been no opposition to Christianity in Sardis because Christianity is not being proclaimed. There is nothing but a harmless outer show.

Hollow church

We are not told exactly what was going on at Sardis, but we can make a good guess, for we have modern analogies. It is easy for a church to put on a show. Its services may be lively and enjoyable, they may be beautiful and apparently reverent, but the substance of the church's witness and spirituality can all the same be hollow. The church may be a fun place to visit, but it will offer no challenge to lives and morals, no call to repentance and no threat to anyone else. It will not face persecution, but it will not gain eternal life either.

This is the threat to the church at Sardis. The one who holds the spiritual life of the churches, the seven stars, and who gives the life-giving Holy Spirit (the seven spirits) is only too well aware of the lack of life there. He stands ready with the Spirit's resources for witness, but they are not called upon.

Like the city itself in times past, the church is unprepared for the surprise visit of its Lord (Matthew 24:42–51). Once again, this may refer to the second coming, but also to much sooner judgment, as the church eventually withers away.

Hope

Yet there is still hope, even though the church is described as dead. The Lord who calls to them can raise the dead and heal the sickly. An ember of their first faith still glows, which may yet be rekindled. They are still aware of the teaching they first received. Some of the Christians have made a stand and tried to follow Christ wholeheartedly. If the church follows their example, being true to the call it received in baptism, it may yet live. The clothes that many have soiled (v. 4) are probably a reminder of the white robes worn by the newly baptized. They can still become an eternal sign of righteousness and new life, the uniform of victory. In 7:14, white robes are the sign of the martyrs' triumph through suffering. Those who are faithful to the baptismal call to witness, Jesus will proudly proclaim to God the Father (Matthew 10:32–33). The call is to be alert and watchful, active in witness and service.

The signs, though, are not good. As the situation stands, the church of Sardis will be blotted out of the book of life (v. 5). To Greek citizens, this would suggest being struck off the register of citizens of the new Jerusalem. To Jews it would mean being removed from the list of those favoured by God. Either way, the message is stark: repent or be doomed.

PRAYER

Lord, keep us awake and watchful. Keep us faithful and active. Do not let us fool ourselves with outward show, but enrich and nourish our inner lives, our witness and our service.

FAITHFUL CHURCH

The next message is a far happier one. Like that to Smyrna, this letter carries no condemnation. Also like Smyrna, the church in Philadelphia is weak in the eyes of the world, yet the 'little power' it has is bolstered by the love of God (v. 9), and it has been faithful to Jesus in the face of persecution by the local synagogue.

This message, then, comes from the one who is himself utterly trustworthy, the holy and true one (v. 7). 'True' in Greek thinking meant 'real', while in Hebrew it carried the idea of trustworthiness. Both senses apply here. The trustworthy reality on which the church relies is found in Christ, who carries the authority of God himself, the Holy One of Israel who has shown himself to be real and trustworthy throughout the history of his people.

Jesus, the trustworthy one, holds the future of the church, for he has the 'key of David'. This is a reference to Isaiah 22:15–25, in which the ambitious royal steward, Shebna, is replaced by the trustworthy Eliakim. In the same way, Jesus replaces all that his followers have previously relied upon, and becomes the basis of their security. There is also a reference back to 1:18, for the risen Christ holds the keys of Death and Hades. The one who has conquered death through the resurrection has the power to overcome death and unlock the realm of the dead for his followers.

Christians therefore need not fear even death itself, for to them it becomes the doorway to eternal life. That doorway stands open to the church at Philadelphia and their eternal destiny is secure, as long as they stand firm.

So far, they have indeed stood firm, loyal to the word of the gospel that they accepted. For them it has become a 'word of patient endurance' in the face of the 'synagogue of Satan' (vv. 9, 10). Like the Smyrnan Christians, the church of Philadelphia has no doubt found itself exposed to Roman law by being expelled from the protection offered by belonging to Judaism.

Trouble ahead

Their trouble is by no means a thing of the past. The church has been tested by its enemies, but now a time of trial faces the whole world as the judgment of God draws near. Jesus is coming, and his coming will be heralded by a time of tribulation.

The Jews had long held that the coming of the Messiah would bring a time of testing to the world, and Christians shared that view. Jesus promises his faithful followers that they will be preserved in this time.

In some circles, this is interpreted as a promise that God will miraculously keep Christians safe from the afflictions that will strike unbelievers. Some even believe that God will remove Christians physically from the world so that they will not bear the full brunt of the time of trial. This view (the 'secret rapture') is based on 1 Thessalonians 4:17, where Paul is reassuring his converts that those who are still alive on the day of resurrection will not miss out on heaven. Paul certainly does not mean that they will miss out on tribulation, and there is no hint of such a view elsewhere in Revelation.

The best way to take verse 10 is as a promise that Jesus will keep his followers firm in their faith and hope in the troubles that lie ahead. By holding firm, they are certain of their heavenly crown (v. 11).

Endurance

Indeed, far from being assured of freedom from trials and suffering, the Church is assured of them. The victory is promised to those who conquer, or overcome, and as we shall see, that conquest consists in the endurance of suffering for the sake of the gospel. In verse 10 the Philadelphians are commended for keeping Jesus' 'word of patient endurance', which could either mean obeying his call to endurance or telling others about their Lord's own endurance. Either way, it places the ability to endure at the heart of Christian witness.

PRAYER

*Lord Jesus, hold us firm when we are tempted
to let you down in the face of persecution,
mockery or lack of earthly support in our faith.*

15 REVELATION 3:7–13 (II)

PILLARS *of the* FAITH

The time of trouble that John foresees may on the face of it appear daunting. It will be a time of unrest and suffering for the world, and it will be a time of increased persecution of Christians, as we shall see later in the book. It is also a sign of hope, however. It means that Jesus is close, and that the final vindication of the Church is drawing near.

In the end, those who have persecuted the Church will bow down and admit that their victims were right after all. The image of persecutors (here the Jews of Philadelphia are most clearly in view) bowing down is basically one of victory for the Church, yet it is more than a triumphant 'I told you so!' In the Old Testament, Israel is seen as finally being victorious over the nations, who will acknowledge both their defeat and the worthiness of the God of Israel. Israel will then become the nation that leads others to worship the true God (Isaiah 45:14; 60:14; Ezekiel 36:23). The promise of the salvation of the Gentiles is now coming true through the Church's recognition of Jesus as Messiah. This enables John to reverse the Old Testament prophecy: the unbelieving Jews who have rejected the Messiah will be able to recognize him in the faith of the mainly Gentile Church. Paul uses a similar argument in Romans 9—11. The final judgment remains open, with the possibility of either salvation or condemnation for those who currently reject Christ.

Window of opportunity?

With this possibility in mind, there may well be a secondary meaning to the 'open door' that Jesus has set before the church (v. 8). The New Testament writers use this term to represent opportunity for preaching the gospel (1 Corinthians 16:9; 2 Corinthians 2:12; Colossians 4:3; Acts 14:27). It is possible that John also has in mind the opportunity that lies before the Church to proclaim the word of Christ, and so to bring even their opponents to repentance. The main meaning, though, is of the Church's certain entry into the kingdom of God.

Even if there is no explicit reference to the Church's witness in verse 8, it is vital to remember that this is one of the major tasks of the Church. Indeed, in Revelation it is *the* task of the Church. Wherever opportunity presents itself, the Church is called to bear witness to Jesus, and to make opportunities to do so as well.

Final destination

The concluding promise to the Philadelphian church is one that would have struck chords of recognition with Revelation's original audience. The church that is victorious will become a pillar in the temple of God. This takes up a common Christian theme, that the dwelling place of God is not a building but his people, who are themselves his temple (1 Peter 2:5). Pillars (v. 12) are of course a symbol of strength and stability, often left standing when all else has fallen. This sight may well have been seen in Philadelphia a generation earlier, when the city was rocked by an earthquake.

The city was rebuilt with imperial aid and given the additional name, Neocaesarea, in honour of the emperor. Christ's promise to give the name of new Jerusalem to his Church is a pertinent reminder that God is the one who rebuilds what is broken and upholds what is steadfast. The Church will also bear the name of God and of Jesus, marked for ever as his.

The temple in which Philadelphia will be a pillar is partly a reference to the coming city of God, which will be his dwelling (21:2–3), containing no temple because it effectively is itself a temple. The reference is also partly a statement of their present role. Those who remain steadfast in adversity are a support and strength to the whole people of God, giving encouragement by their example.

God of the poor

We have already seen that the two churches receiving unqualified praise are also notable for their poverty or powerlessness. Revelation is true to a major strand of biblical teaching, which sees God as on the side of the poor and defenceless. If he is biased to the poor, then the Church should be also. Too often, we are swayed by the world's idea of power and success, rather than by the very different viewpoint of God.

PRAYER

Father, thank you that you are biased. Thank you that you lean to mercy rather than judgment, and to the defenceless rather than the powerful.

SUCCESSFUL CHRISTIANS?

The city of Laodicea was as fabled for its wealth as Sardis once had been. It was a banking centre specializing in currency exchange, it had a thriving clothing industry fed by the glossy black wool of the local sheep, and it housed a hospital and medical school well known for its eye treatments. At nearby Hieropolis were hot springs with reputed medicinal properties. All these facts provide the images for this, the most tragic of the seven messages to the churches. Even in the dead church of Sardis, there were some who followed Christ faithfully. Of Laodicea, Christ has nothing positive to say.

Lord of creation

The message comes from the one who is the Amen (v. 14), another divine title applied to Jesus. In Isaiah 65:16, blessings and oaths are made literally in the name of the 'God of Amen'. The liturgical term 'amen' means 'so be it', and so NRSV translates Isaiah's phrase as 'God of faithfulness'. John can apply this title to Jesus because he is the 'faithful and true witness' who embodies God's steadfastness and trustworthiness (in stark contrast to the Laodicean church). All that we need to know of God's love, saving power and promises to his people can be seen in Christ.

More even than this, Christ is the origin of creation, the one from and through whom all things come to be. The idea is expressed more fully in John 1:1–5, but the phrase used here is reminiscent of Colossians 1:15–20, a letter that was intended not only for Colossae but also for Laodicea (Colossians 4:16), and would have been well known to the church there.

Speaking of Christ as the origin of creation is a way of saying that God's purposes of salvation are not a last-ditch attempt to put things right, but are part of a plan that spans the whole of time. It is also a reminder that the world in which we live is God's, and as such is the place where God is served. There is a perennial temptation for Christians to see their faith and worship as being about some 'spiritual' realm that has little or nothing to do with everyday life. If God is the creator, then creation is his area of activity, the object of his love and the place where he is served. It is particularly important to keep this in mind when reading Revelation, for, with its repeated visions of heaven and the future, we may be tempted to forget that the purpose of the book is to inspire us to witness here and now.

Sickening church

The Laodiceans are neither hot nor cold (v. 15). This is often taken to suggest that Jesus would prefer them to be either spiritually zealous (hot) or even to be against him (cold). In fact, though, both hot and cold refer to something positive. The church here is like neither the healing hot springs of neighbouring Hierapolis, nor the refreshing cold streams of nearby Colossae. It provides neither spiritual healing nor refreshment for the soul. It fails to challenge Laodicea's material- ism and idolatry, and offers no alternative to the values of the society around it. It is like Laodicea's own water supply from the cliffs of Hierapolis—tepid and laced with unpalatable minerals. The church is useless, and Jesus will spit it out. (The older translation, 'spew', gives the force of the term.)

The poor showing of the church is grounded in complacency. The Laodicean Christians share the wealth and prosperity of their city, and it is easy for them to see their church as successful. Perhaps they even see their well-being as a sign of God's blessing. Certainly there is a misguided strand of thought among some Christians today that mis- takes material wealth for spiritual riches, and proclaims a 'gospel' that promises material success. Both the Laodiceans and their current counterparts are about as wrong as you can get. In reality, they are pitiful in their spiritual poverty and blindness, and lie naked to the judgment of God.

Of course, they can point to a strong strand of Old Testament teaching that promises just such material blessing, but they may still miss two important factors. Firstly, much of the Old Testament sees this world as all there is: blessing is tied to the land and its prosper- ity because there is no life to come. Secondly, such blessing is linked to keeping God's commandments, and in Revelation that command is to be steadfast in witness and patient in suffering.

REFLECT

What values of our culture run against the gospel? Have we absorbed them into our church, or do we challenge them?

LOVE & GLORY

The Laodicean church is content to be a sharer in the riches of its native town. The sources of those riches have their spiritual counterparts, though, and in these the Laodiceans are completely lacking. So the message of the risen Lord comes to them: seek out a spiritual wealth that will resist the fire of judgment (see 1 Corinthians 3:13), righteousness that will cover their spiritual nakedness, and healing for spiritual blindness.

The image of gold refined by fire (v. 18) is another pointer to the necessity of tribulation, which burns away the dross of compromise and idolatry. If the Laodiceans recover their mission and vision, they will face suffering and opposition, but they will also gain the gold of salvation, the promise of victory. So far, they have shown nothing of the works that Christ demands of his Church. Where is their witness to the truth of the gospel? Where is their challenge to the sins of the world? By silence and complacency they testify to the irrelevance and pointlessness of their faith.

Loving judge

The thoroughgoing condemnation of this church is delivered not in vindictiveness but in love. There is still time to repent and to become what they are called to be. If there were no hope, there would be no message. The message of condemnation is itself a sign of God's love, and of the distress they are causing to their Lord.

Indeed, it is to this, the least worthy of the seven churches, that one of the most famous statements of God's love is delivered. Jesus stands at their door and knocks (v. 20), waiting for them to hear and admit him. The one who has opened the door to heaven for the church of Sardis has now come to his church at Laodicea and finds the door shut in his face.

It will not always be this way. The one who knocks is the Lord of the church, and he will gain admission. The question is whether he will then invite his servants to join him for supper. The image of Jesus at the door recalls Jesus' parables of the bridegroom. In Luke 12:35–38 the master returns from the wedding banquet and invites those servants who are still alert to join him in his own extension of the feast. In Matthew 25:1–13 the unready bridesmaids find the door locked against them. The bridegroom has arrived, and they have missed the wedding supper. The Laodiceans have at present locked out Christ, but will discover that in truth they have locked themselves out of the kingdom of God.

Another allusion is to Song of Songs 5:2: 'I slept, but my heart was awake. Listen! my beloved is knocking.' For Jews of John's time, this was interpreted allegorically as the searching of God for Israel. For the Laodiceans there is hope here. The bride is asleep, but her heart is awake. She can rouse from her slumber to meet the bridegroom. She must awaken before it is too late, and rediscover her love for God.

All these images that cling to the picture of Christ at the door reinforce the true motive of his condemnation. It is not the sentence of a legalistic judge but the desperate plea of the rejected lover.

Final promise

Just as the greatest declaration of love is reserved for the most disappointing church, so the greatest promise is offered to it. The one who is victorious will share in the reign of Christ (v. 21), seated with him on the throne. (Just which throne this is, and how Christ got there, are the subject of the next two chapters of Revelation.)

It is a mistake to ask over whom the victorious Christians will reign. The point is that the promise to this church (and all the churches, v. 22) is that they will share in the life and glory of Christ himself. Salvation is about more than living for ever in heaven. It is about the transformation of human existence in the presence of God. More than that we cannot really say, for 'what we will be has not yet been revealed. What we do know is this: when he is revealed we will be like him, for we will see him as he is' (1 John 3:2).

PRAYER

Father, we do not know what you will finally make us in Christ,
save that it will be the outworking of your love. Keep us firm in
that love till then, that we may never lock you out,
and may not be excluded ourselves.

GOD HIMSELF

After the initial greetings and challenges to the seven churches, the main body of John's book begins with an invitation from the risen Christ (the voice he had first heard, v. 1; compare 1:10–13) to enter heaven itself. Revelation's understanding of heaven is not quite what we mean by the term. To us, heaven is the dwelling place of God and the final destination of his people. In Revelation, it is where God is to be found, but it is itself a place where conflict occurs and good and evil both exist for a time.

Perhaps the best way of expressing it is to say that heaven is seen as the realm of spiritual reality that underlies the world we see. Events in that realm affect what goes on on earth, and, more surprisingly, heaven is affected by earthly events. In the final vision of God's triumph, both heaven and earth will be remade and evil banished from both the physical and spiritual dimensions of creation.

By presenting this view of the spiritual realm, John reminds us that there are no actions without their spiritual consequences, and no spiritual experiences or beliefs that do not affect everyday life. John's vision of heaven is not a mystical flight from reality but a reminder of the hidden depths to everyday life and discipleship.

Indescribable God

The centre of heaven is a throne room, which will turn out also to be a temple. Several writers have pointed out that the description of the throne room reflects that of the Roman emperor. This does not mean that John sees God as simply a greater version of an earthly ruler. It is rather that he sees the pomp of earthly power as a vain attempt to mimic and usurp the rule of the true King. Compared to God's rule, though, the greatest king of earth is an insignificant pretender.

At the centre of heaven is the throne of God (Isaiah 6:1; Ezekiel 1:26). There is no real attempt to describe God. Instead, John writes in terms of precious stones, and stones whose very colour was highly variable. It is a vision of brilliance and richness, but beyond that words cannot go. While owing much to Ezekiel 1, which also speaks in terms of precious stones, John stops short of Ezekiel's vision of a human form (Ezekiel 1:26).

There are two reasons for John's reticence. Firstly, any attempt to describe God would fall short of reality and come close to idolatry, for it would limit the power and majesty of the reality. Secondly, God is not a physical being, and John is aware of that fact. What he sees on the throne is no human or animal shape but a presence that cannot be limited to physical terms. John is going out of his way to avoid the trap of anthropomorphism, for trying to describe him in human terms limits the limitless reality of God.

Some writers object that John still thinks of God in human terms, for the one on the throne holds a scroll in his hand in 5:1 and elsewhere speaks out loud, but this misses the point. In speaking of God at all, we have to use imagery; and human imagery, while inadequate, is still better than any other. What we must never lose sight of is the fact that it is imagery, and John sets this squarely in front of us at the outset.

Let God be God

If imagery is unavoidable, it may seem pointless to bother about what kind we use. However, our images govern the way we think. A religion that pictures its god as a giant warrior will have a different view of the divine from one that sees him in a crucified carpenter. The Bible, of course, uses both images—as well as a host of others. Part of John's message in Revelation is that the crucified one is the key to understanding all the others.

For that matter, how often have we heard the phrase, 'I like to think of God as…?' The very phrase says that we want to be comfortable and unchallenged by our view of God. The point of remembering his indescribable nature is that it stops us from fitting God into our own comfortable categories. Our task is not to confine God to the scope of our imaginations or desires, but to be open to what he wants to tell us about himself, about his will for us and about ourselves. We need to let God set the agenda, and that is easier if we have no neat boxes into which we think we can fit him; or at least if we let the boxes of our images be as flexible as possible.

PRAYER

Father, keep me from the temptation of hearing only
those words of yours that confirm my prejudices.
Instead, transform me by your word.

HEAVEN & EARTH

The throne of God is surrounded by a jewelled rainbow. On the face of it, this is just one more trapping of magnificence, but the rainbow was the sign of God's covenant with Noah (Genesis 9:13–17), his promise never again to destroy the inhabitants of the earth. As such, it was the symbol of the mercy of God. John emphasizes this by using the Greek word for the rainbow (*iris*) rather than the word for the warrior's or hunter's bow that is found in Genesis. We see God seated on a throne set against the backdrop not of his power, or his wrath, or his judgment, but his mercy.

In all that follows, with the accounts of the dreadful judgment of God, we must keep this symbol in our minds. God is acting not out of a desire for vengeance or a delight in destruction, but in mercy. Exactly how judgment and mercy intermingle will be explained as the book unfolds.

Kingdom of priests

God's throne is not the only one. Twenty-four elders sit on their own thrones before God (v. 4). Many commentators see these as angelic beings, the council of God (see, for example, Job 2:1; Isaiah 6:2) but 'elders' is an unusual term for angels, so they are much more likely to be human beings.

There were 24 priestly families (1 Chronicles 24:4–6), and this leads some commentators to see the elders as the Old Testament saints. While this offers a clue to their purpose, elsewhere in Revelation there is no particular interest in distinguishing the Old Testament people of God from the New. For John, there is one people of God, characterized by their faithful witness (see ch. 12). The number 24 is also reminiscent of the twelve patriarchs plus the twelve apostles, a combination that is later seen written on the walls of the new Jerusalem, which stands for the people of God (21:12–14). The elders stand for the whole of God's people. They offer worship, which ties in with their priestly role, while they also wear the crown of kingship. John has already described the Church as a kingdom of priests (1:6; compare Exodus 19:6; 1 Peter 2:9) and the crowned elders fit that idea. 'Kingdom' in biblical thought means not just a realm but a kingly rule, so to be a kingdom can also mean a sharing in the rule of the kingdom. Here the representatives of God's people have become a part of his heavenly council. Those who are charged with preaching the gospel are involved in the plans of God himself (Ephesians 1:8–10).

Once again, as with the angels of the seven churches, John is reminding us that the reality of God's people is different from its earthly manifestation. On earth, both the Old and New Testament people may seem weak, sinful, persecuted or prone to failure. From the spiritual perspective, they are crowned servants of God. You could say that the elders represent both how God counts his people and the destiny that awaits them. The present reality is different, as Jesus' witnesses await their vindication and final salvation (6:9–11).

The task of the Church is always to seek to make real in its present life something of the destiny that awaits—to become what we are. In that sense, the criticisms and commendations of the seven churches are based on the extent to which each church made manifest the kingdom of God in its own life. The same standard is, of course, that by which the Church of today is judged.

God of Sinai

The thunder and lightning (v. 5) are typical biblical trappings of God's presence, as at Mount Sinai (Exodus 19:16). They provide a further reminder that the God of Christians is also the God of the Old Testament, and reflect the Exodus symbolism that is so important to John. In popular thought, especially among non-Christians, there is a divide between the God of the Old Testament and the God of the New. The Old Testament God is seen as a vengeful judge, hurling thunderbolts and plagues, while the God revealed in Jesus is the God of love and forgiveness. That view cannot survive an actual reading of the Bible. John knows full well that the God of Sinai is the God whose love brings freedom out of slavery—and that judgment is the real consequence of rejecting the salvation that Jesus brings.

PRAYER

Father, give grace to your people, that in our life and witness
we may model the kingdom you have promised us,
and so draw others into your rule.

SPIRIT *of* CREATION

The spirits we have already encountered are a symbol of the Holy Spirit (1:4). John's source for this image is Zechariah 4:2 and 10, where seven lamps on a lampstand represent the 'eyes of God which range through the world'. The God who is at the centre of John's vision, and of his book, is the giver of the Spirit.

In Revelation, Zechariah's lampstand has become the seven stands that represent the seven churches (1:20). The lamps for the stands are the seven spirits. John reminds us that the light, the vitality of the church, comes from the Holy Spirit who is God's gift to his people. Light is also a symbol for the message of the gospel: the Spirit is the one who equips and enables the Church for its task of witness.

Creator God

At the same time, we need to remember that Zechariah's seven torches, the Spirit of God, range through the whole earth. God is the creator, and his Spirit is the Spirit of creation, not just the possession of the Church. The Spirit stands before a crystal sea, which represents (among other things) the primal chaos out of which creation came and over which the Spirit of God hovered (Genesis 1:2).

Christians often need to be reminded that God is not active in the Church alone. To imagine otherwise is to limit the work of God and to foster an unbiblical division between the works of creation and redemption. The whole earth is the Lord's and he is at work in it. Often the task of the Church is to spot where God is at work in the world, and to take its cue from that.

Some Christians would argue, for instance, that joining forces with non-Christians who have a similar goal (such as social reform, or environmental awareness) is a betrayal of God. In fact, it is quite the opposite. It is an acknowledgment that he is to be served in all of his creation, and a recognition of the breadth of the Spirit's work. What is not acceptable, of course, is a watering down of the specifically Christian content of the Church's task and beliefs. That is the primary temptation that Revelation is written to counteract.

Sea of troubles

Part of the magnificence of the divine throne room is a crystal sea, another glittering jewel of heaven, but it would also have evoked a range of images in the minds of John's hearers. It would have reminded them of the Red Sea through which God brought his people to safety (Exodus 14:21–29). It was seen as a metaphor for baptism (1 Corinthians 10:2), through which he still brings his people to safety. It could be patterned on the model sea in Solomon's temple (1 Kings 7:23–26), which was used for ritual washings (2 Chronicles 4:6).

Most of all, though, in the Bible the sea is generally an image of destruction and of chaos. The crystal sea stands for the abyss from which evil comes, and over which God will triumph, for in the end there will be no more sea (Revelation 21:1).

That there should be a symbol of chaos and evil in heaven may at first seem strange, but we should remember that heaven is the realm of spiritual reality, not the place of eternal blessedness. The crystal sea is part of the richness of John's picture of the spiritual realm, and reflects the New Testament conviction of spiritual as well as earthly evils (Ephesians 6:12). At the same time, it is a symbol of God's deliverance of his people. The sea stands before God's throne because he is Lord over even the forces of destruction, and can bring good even out of the machinations of evil. Overall, then, we are presented with a picture of the merciful God who saves from the forces of chaos.

As the book develops, we shall see in greater detail how spiritual evils translate into earthly, historic terms. What is becoming apparent even at this stage, however, is that in his visions of heaven John is deeply concerned with the everyday life of the Church in the world. Day by day, it is difficult to see the good within much that happens in God's world. John calls us to trust the Lord of creation and hold firm to the promise that he is indeed in control, and that victory is assured.

PRAYER

Open our eyes, Lord, to the work of your Spirit in the world
around us, that we may know where and how to serve you.

The SONG of CREATION

Completing the vision of the heavenly throne room and temple are four fantastic creatures. They are patterned on the cherubim of Ezekiel's vision, which John follows fairly closely, while remodelling the details. In Ezekiel, the cherubim who support, and form the wheels of, God's chariot-throne have four faces (Ezekiel 1:6, 10, 20). In Revelation, those faces have become four separate creatures, which in Jewish thought represented the greatest of God's creatures: the lion, lord of wild beasts; the ox, strongest domestic animal; the eagle, most powerful bird; and the human being, made in the image of God. So here the four living creatures stand for all created beings.

They are full of eyes, which we have seen to be associated with God's Spirit, and so represent God's watchful awareness of his creation. The creator is intimately involved with his world. In the Bible, creation is not simply God's initial act of making, but his continued preservation and sustaining of all that exists. Together the creatures sing something very similar to the song of the seraphim in Isaiah's vision of God (Isaiah 6:3).

This is the purpose of creation, to give glory to God by its very existence and to sing his praise (v. 11).

The coming one

God is described as the one 'who was' (v. 8), for he predates all things, and everything has its being through him. He is the one 'who is', for despite his hiddenness from sinful human sight, and despite many appearances to the contrary, God is still there to be known, served and worshipped. And God is the one who 'is to come' in final victory, bringing judgment and salvation. Perhaps there is a hint here of the mysterious longing of creation for its redemption and renewal that Paul mentions in Romans 8:19–25. Creation will find its consummation in union with its maker.

In this chapter the emphasis is on God as creator, but, true to the biblical tradition, John cannot be satisfied simply with creation. There are hints throughout of God's redeeming work, such as the presence of the 24 elders, the sea of destruction and redemption. In the rest of the Bible, creation is almost always linked with the need for redemption (Genesis 1 and Psalm 8 are the main exceptions).

In our time there is a renewed emphasis on the spirituality of creation, both within Christianity and in various strands of New Age thought. Modern-day paganism and witchcraft, and Christian creation spirituality, as well as less coherent forms of mysticism, all stress the unity of creation and of the place of human beings within it. This ties in with a proper concern for the environment and eco-logical awareness. We are a part of creation, and to stand apart from it, seeing it merely as a resource or plaything, is ultimately suicidal. For there to be true hope, however, we must be aware of the need for redemption both of sinful humanity and of the world in which we live. The Christian hope is for a new creation, encompassing all that God has made.

Eternal worship

The people of God, the elders, join their voices with the song of creation (vv. 9–10), and praise their creator. In court ceremonial, they offer their crowns as kingly subjects of their high king.

This is one of the bases of Christian worship. It combines praise and self-offering to the one whose very presence is both glorious and infinitely desirable. God is seen this way because he has made us to function, to find our true selves, in a relationship with him. Just as most lovers will say that they feel most fully themselves in the pres-ence of their beloved, so human beings (and indeed all things) are most authentically themselves when they acknowledge their creator and give him praise.

All worshippers have surely at some time gained the sense that their worship is joining in with the praises of heaven and the whole of creation. Those brief flashes of exalted experience are in fact windows into the reality that John reminds us is the actual truth. Worship is the business of heaven and earth, and whether we feel it or not, our worship, from the grandest cathedral to the humblest prayer group, is part of that perpetual praise and service.

PRAYER

Holy, holy, holy, Lord God our creator, give us such a glimpse of your glory that we too may join in the song of all creation.

The GREAT REVERSAL

Having set the scene of heaven's worship of its creator, John continues to follow the pattern of Ezekiel's vision, for he now sees a scroll in the hand of God (Ezekiel 2:9–10). Like Ezekiel's scroll, it is written on the front and back, which indicates the great amount of its contents.

Scholars have argued for years as to what exactly the scroll signifies. The seven seals have been taken to indicate a legal document, such as a will, which often had multiple seals. In that case, it is the testament of God's inheritance, to be opened by a human being who is worthy. Others have seen it as the book of life, containing the list of all the redeemed (perhaps the book mentioned in Daniel 12:4, which was sealed till the end of time). Others see it as the original of the Jewish law given to Moses, and yet others as the forecast of events to come. The fact is that we are not told here what its contents are. All we can be sure of at this stage is that it is a book of immense importance: the seven seals tell of its universal scope. Eventually we shall find that it contains God's plan for the final triumph of his kingdom.

A mighty angel (v. 2) calls for one who is worthy to open it. This is no ordinary book, and it will need an extraordinary person to break the seals.

Tears in heaven

No one comes forward, and John weeps at the loss (v. 4). Can it be that God's plans are to be thwarted? Is there no one who can bring into the light the mysteries of salvation? It is a moment of purely human relief in the drama of heaven. Amid the awesome events of God's court, a human being sheds tears. It is also an affirmation that God has room in his designs for human weakness and human feelings.

Conquering lion

John is not left desolate for long. One of the elders, who act throughout the book as a kind of chorus, as in Greek drama, commenting on and explaining the action, tells him that the Lion of Judah, the Root of David, has conquered and can open the book (v. 5).

Both of these descriptions are titles of the Messiah. In Genesis

49:9, as Jacob blesses his sons, Judah is described as a lion's whelp. So the Messiah, who was to come from the tribe of Judah, became the Lion of Judah, a term that occurs, among other places, in the Dead Sea scrolls (the library of a Jewish sect from Qumran, by the Dead Sea).

An even more popular messianic passage was Isaiah 11:1–10, where a new king of the house of David is foretold. He will spring up like a new shoot from the root of Jesse and bring a time of peace and well-being.

Sacrificial lamb

Images of conquest and power are what John hears, but what he sees is different: a Lamb bearing the marks of sacrifice (v. 6a). To be sure, it is a Lamb with power, for its seven horns are a symbol of perfect strength. Indeed, the word translated as 'Lamb' could be used in John's time for a full-grown sheep. The key to understanding it, however, is the fact that it has been slaughtered. The strength of this Lamb lies in its passage through death to new life.

It is, of course, Jesus. The images of conquest and power are correct, but John is telling us that the victory comes about through the self-sacrificing love that took Jesus to the cross. Real victory comes only to the one who lays down his life. To John's readers, the Lamb speaks of the passover sacrifice that marks the coming of freedom, and the Servant of Isaiah 53 who is sacrificed like a lamb.

This is the prime example of the principle that runs through the teaching of Jesus: that love and forgiveness, sacrifice and service are the true values of the kingdom of God. The way of Christ turns the values of the world upside down. It is through these new values, lived out to the point of death, that Jesus is worthy to reveal the destiny of the world, which is made possible through his death and resurrection. It is on the response to Jesus that salvation and judgment hinge.

PRAYER

Father, help us not to be seduced by the world's definitions of success, but to seek the love and service that mark those who share in the rule of heaven.

The LAMB ENTHRONED

The final characteristic of the Lamb is its seven eyes, which are the seven spirits. Jesus is the giver of the Holy Spirit. In Zechariah 4:10 the seven eyes of God range throughout the world. So we are being told that the Spirit who ranges the world, and who is the motivating force of the Church, is the Spirit of Jesus. It is through the Spirit that the presence of Jesus is made real to his people.

The Spirit is therefore intimately connected both with God and with Christ, a further hint at the threefold nature of the divine which was to become the doctrine of the Trinity.

The king takes his throne

Chapter 5 is widely recognized as being based on an eastern enthronement ceremony, in which the new king is presented along with his credentials and then enthroned. In 3:21 the risen Christ declares himself to be on a throne; here we see how he got there.

John's vision of the Lamb of power who is also the conquering Lion of Judah is the presentation of Christ as the king. Yet this king has conquered by self-sacrifice, through which he becomes the giver of the Spirit of life. He approaches the throne of God (v. 7; see Daniel 7:13) and takes the scroll that only he is worthy to open. We should suppose that he also takes his place on the throne with God, for in Revelation 7:17 the Lamb is 'at the centre of the throne'.

Once he has taken his place, the heavenly court fall down before him and offer a new song (v. 9). In the Old Testament, the call to 'sing a new song' to the Lord marks particular acts of deliverance and victory by God (see, for example, Psalm 98:1; Isaiah 42:10). In this case, the victory is the supreme triumph of the cross. John is presenting in this passage the spiritual reality that lies behind Calvary. The death of the Messiah, and his resurrection and ascension, are his enthronement over all creation.

It is significant that the elders hold censers (v. 8), which represent the prayers of the saints. The risen Christ is now, with God, the recipient of the prayers of the Church. Prayer brings us into the presence of God, right in front of the throne—and there we find that we pray to Christ as well, as he shares the Father's rule.

Christ our passover

The sacrificial Lamb calls to mind the lamb of Passover, the festival of deliverance from Egyptian slavery. This connection is made clear in the song of the court. He has ransomed his people, as if from slavery, and made them a kingdom and priests (vv. 9–10; compare Exodus 19:6).

What is more, he has ransomed them from all the peoples of the earth. Here for the first time we meet the strong emphasis of Revelation that salvation is not intended for one particular race or nation, but for all. The first exodus resulted in the choosing of Israel. The final exodus is open to all.

According to NRSV, the redeemed 'will reign' on earth (v. 10). However, there is a variant reading in some ancient manuscripts, which has the present tense: 'they reign on earth'. At first sight, this is more difficult to understand, and so is to be preferred as the correct reading (because a scribe would be less likely to 'correct' an easy reading, but might amend a difficult one). Also, in 1:6 the Church is described as being, here and now, a kingdom composed of priests.

If this reading is correct, it sounds a note of encouragement for a beleaguered Church. What to the world may seem weak, outmoded and powerless already has a share in the kingship of Christ. Those who suffer for their faith, who are called to witness in their poor and stumbling way to the gospel of Jesus, are already royal priests, mediating the love of their king to the world.

This is more than a word of spiritual comfort. It sets up the Church as an alternative to the power systems of the world. The Church can rule, not by the methods of the world, but by providing for its members an alternative concept of community, based on love, equality and forgiveness. To those outside that community, its presence should be a witness to the possibility of a fellowship based on love and service. The Church is called to be living proof of a different authority.

PRAYER

Lord Jesus Christ, as you have done so much for us, and so gained a crown, may we reflect your love and sacrifice to those around us.

CRESCENDO

The heavenly worship builds to a crescendo as countless angels add their voices to the song of the elders and the four creatures. You may have had the experience of hearing a piece of music build to a glorious conclusion and wishing that somehow that moment of triumphant exultation could last for ever. Here in heaven it does. That seems to be the effect that John is aiming for.

The hymn to the Lamb is more than verbal fireworks, though. It follows closely the pattern of the hymn to God in 4:11. God is worthy because he created; the Lamb is worthy because he was slaughtered. Both hymns are based on a recognition of what the one who is worshipped has done.

It is often said that the sheer vision of God is the basis of the purest worship, and the goal of mystics, both Jewish and Christian, has been to seek such a vision. Certainly the 'Holy, holy, holy…' of 4:8 is the response of the heavenly court to the presence of God. The longer and more substantial hymns recount the deeds of God and the Lamb.

Worship is rooted more in thankful response to God's acts than in anything else, because it is when the people of God recognize the extent of his love through his acts of creation and redemption that worship follows. This is not a lesser sort of worship, as though there were something wrongly selfish about responding to God's gift. He is not bribing us to worship. God is not a passive object of reverence but an actor in his own drama. His true character can be appreciated only in his actions, which are those of a giver. We are created to receive God's love. He is not a narcissist who needs to be admired by his fans, but an artist who pours himself into his creation and a parent who gives himself to his children. Worship is the response to such boundless giving that it pours out beyond the limitless confines of God's own being and takes shape in creation and in creation's redemption.

Giving to God

This makes sense of what at first seems a contradiction. In both 4:11 and 5:12, God and the Lamb are worthy to receive glory, honour, power, wealth and so on. (It is characteristic of John's style that he never repeats a phrase exactly, though the sense and structure remain recognizably the same.) We may ask how God can receive more of these qualities than he already has by nature. In an absolute sense, of course, he cannot. In the language of worship, however, he can. It is in the human response to God that these attributes are recognized and shown to be fitting for God's character. He is not only almighty and all-knowing; he has also shown himself through his acts to be worthy of such power and might. In a real sense, by offering himself as our object of worship, God stands under human judgment. The worship of his people is their discernment that he is worthy to receive such praise.

Of course, such judgment is two-edged. Those who fail to recognize the absolute fact of God's worthiness in the end judge themselves, for they have failed to recognize the eternal truth that undergirds creation.

Holy Trinity

Finally, the chorus of praise spreads out beyond the limits of heaven to embrace all that exists, as every creature sings praise to God and to the Lamb (v. 13).

The same praise is offered to the Lamb as to God. When we add to this the close relation of the seven spirits who are the Holy Spirit to God and to Christ, we are as close to the doctrine of the Trinity as we can get without using the word. In Revelation there are those who receive worship: God, Christ and the Spirit. And there are those who worship: the elders, the four creatures, the angels and all creation (compare 19:9–10). That is to say, the holy Trinity is worshipped by all that is made—and for which he has poured himself out in self-giving.

PRAYER

You are worthy, O Three in One, for your love brought us into being, shared our life and death, and established a new creation, where we will know and love you for ever.

The SEVEN SEALS

Revelation was definitely written so that it would yield much to careful study. At the same time, we need to remember that its main audience would have been those who listened as it was read aloud. This helps to explain its structure. John uses recurring patterns of phrases, numbers and symbols that would stick in the minds of his hearers and help them to understand his message.

One of these patterns is a set of three series of seven judgments (seven seals: 6:1—8:5; seven trumpets: 8:2—11:19; and seven bowls: 15:1—16:21). These 'seven-series' are linked together: each consists of a set of four judgments followed by a set of three, suggesting disasters on earth and judgments from heaven. The first two seven-series also contain interludes showing the role of the saints in the events described. Once again, the number seven is significant. These are events and judgments of universal scope. John is dealing with the fate of the whole world.

For those who see Revelation as a detailed prophecy of events still to come, the seven-series foretell a future of increasing disaster on earth, as God lets loose his judgment prior to the final coming of Christ. This is unlikely, for, as we shall see, each of the seven-series ends with the final judgment (6:12–17; 11:15–19; 16:17–21).

The series of judgments each tell the history of the world from different perspectives, and with different emphases. John has written several accounts that complement each other, rather than trying to fit everything into one simple narrative. Revelation keeps going over the same ground, but each time adds a new dimension, showing new ways of interpreting the world's story, the Church's situation and the hope of humankind.

Words of Jesus

In Mark 13, with its parallels in Matthew 24 and Luke 21, Jesus spoke of the end time, and the signs of its coming: wars, earthquakes, famine, persecution and the shaking of the heavens (Mark 13:7ff, 24ff). John probably knew, if not the actual Gospels, the story that lay behind the Gospel accounts. His narrative does not include the bits about the fall of Jerusalem (Mark 13:14–19), which in his day was already in the past. It also leaves out the warning against false prophets (Mark 13:21–23), for that is dealt with elsewhere.

For both Jesus and John, these are not a catalogue of signs that will one day come to pass, but a description of the way the world is, and a key to understanding world events in the light of God's coming kingdom. In the years since the resurrection of Jesus, the Church and the empire had seen the earthquakes of AD60 in Asia Minor, Nero's persecution in AD64, the eruption of Vesuvius with the destruction of Pompei and Herculaneum in AD79, and the great grain famine of AD92. None of these events had heralded the immediate return of Jesus. Nonetheless, we are told, the current age is the last days. Since the coming of Jesus, all the world's history has been the history of the last days. This is not because his coming is imminent in time, for no one knows the time in history of his coming (Mark 13:32–33), but because all life must now be lived in the light of that coming.

Living in hope

John has adapted the words of Jesus to help his readers understand their own situation. This is the continuing task of God's people—to take the message of Jesus and apply it to their own day.

As we look at the events of our world, we are called to interpret them in the light of Christ. Wars and violence must still be met with a message of reconciliation and a warning of judgment. Environmental disaster and exploitation call for a reminder of humanity's responsibility to its creator. Economic exploitation demands a message of concern for the poor and powerless. Persecution calls for faithful and courageous witness. Tears in the fabric of society tell of judgment on materialism and individualism, and ask for a message of community that should be modelled by the people of God.

Once again, we see no promise of safety for God's people. They live in the world and share the world's woes, which for them are a call to faith and perseverance; to the rest they are a call to repentance.

PRAYER

*Father, enable us to take the gospel message
and speak it boldly to the suffering world.*

VIOLENCE

As the Lamb opens each of the first four seals of the scroll, one of the four living creatures who represent creation calls, 'Come!' Some see the invitation as not to the rider, but to Christ, whose coming is sign-posted by the turmoil on earth. This is not likely, except indirectly: the horsemen who appear are ultimately harbingers of Christ's return, but the call is directly to them.

The inspiration for the four riders is Zechariah 1:8–10 and 6:1–8, where coloured horses pull chariots that patrol the earth and bring God's judgment to the nations. Unlike those of Zechariah, the colour of the horses in John's vision is significant.

Conquest

The first horse is white (v. 2), and represents conquest. Some commentators see this as the triumphant progress of the gospel (Mark 13:10), or of Christ, because of its colour and the crown of its rider (see 19:11–16). White, for John, is not the colour of heaven or of the saints, however, but simply the sign of victory. There are earthly victories brought about by the power of armies, but they are victories only of fear. John's readers would have known of the defeat of the Roman armies by the mounted archers of Parthia in AD62. This empire, built on the ruins of Persia, remained a threat to Rome and a source of fear to the Eastern empire for centuries.

The conquering hero on a white horse, the symbol of victory, looks at first sight to be an image of the judgment of God (albeit a strange one), yet this conquest is achieved only by the pain and suffering of others. The much-vaunted Roman peace, the *pax Romana* that Roman propaganda held up as one of the great benefits of the empire, was based on the grim reality of the legions and the iron grip of Roman rule. The white-robed conqueror is a deceiver, offering glory but delivering only pain—or worse. Not only is earthly conquest hollow, but it seduces its worshippers away from the one who alone can give conquest over death and evil. And that conquest is available only to those who are willing to suffer in the service of love.

War

The glamorous image of the conqueror is, in reality, based on the red of carnage (v. 4), though propaganda then as now denies this. The empire was not, in John's day, much at war, yet many would have remembered the 'year of four emperors', a time of civil strife that followed Nero's suicide in AD68. For Jewish Christians, the rebellion of Judea, culminating in the fall of Jerusalem in AD70, was a recent reminder of the reality of Roman 'peace'.

Nearly two thousand years later, war is still the mainstay of human activity. The greatest conflicts of human history are a living memory, and since 1945 more lives have been lost to warfare than in the two World Wars combined. The Middle East, Central Asia, the Balkans and Iraq have become bywords for conflict. At the time of writing the present book, terrorism looms large as another variation on the historic theme of conflict. All these, says John, are the judgment of God and the herald of the new age.

Judgment of the nations

Are we seriously to say that God sends wars to punish humanity? It seems far from the actions of a loving God. Such a question misses the point.

Firstly, it is not so much that God sends them as that they are the natural consequences of human sin. God's judgment lies in his acceptance of those consequences. In Romans, Paul wrote that God had 'given up' sinful humanity to the consequences of sin (Romans 1:24, 26, 28). The judgment of God consists in having to lie in the bed we have made.

Secondly, though, there is hope. The consequences of estrangement from God are grim: a world given over to greed, self-interest and strife. Those very consequences may just make us look for some other way, a way that lies open to the eye of faith and is found in Jesus Christ. That hope is not great if all we can see is the judgment itself—a point John makes clearly (Revelation 9:20). But as we shall discover, judgment goes hand in hand with the call to repentance.

PRAYER

Lord, help us to hear, above the turmoil of war, your call to peace.

FAMINE & DEATH

War brings with it other horrors: famine and disease. The shortage signified by the third rider is survivable, but harsh (v. 6). The staple diet of grain sells at over ten times its proper price. The slightly more luxurious commodities of oil and wine are still available, though. For those with money, life goes on, but the poor, as always, can barely survive. The extent of the famine is actually governed by a voice from the midst of the four creatures—presumably the voice of God or Christ. It is John's way of telling us that amid the seeming turmoil of the world, God is working, bringing hope and judgment.

Hidden in the picture of the judgment of God is also a call for justice. Part of the condemnation of the sinful world is that in times of shortage the poor suffer as much as they do. Just as the harshest words for the churches were reserved for the wealthy, so here John betrays his sympathy for the poor. The Bible frequently ascribes a similar sympathy to God. Part of John's purpose in detailing injustice is to motivate his readers to seek to redress the balance of the world, by witnessing to the justice of God.

Pale horse coming

The fourth rider sums up and includes the first three. The Greek word translated as 'pale' literally means green, here the colour of a corpse (v. 8). There is a wordplay which is hidden from us, for in Greek 'death' can also mean pestilence, in the wake of which comes Hades, the Lord of the dead, gathering the victims of battlefield, famine and disease (see Ezekiel 14:21). The reference to death by wild animals conjures up the terrible fate of some of the wounded in war. It also forms a link with the next seal, and the vision of Christian martyrs, some of whom would have met their end in the arena as fuel for the insatiable bloodlust of the Roman mob.

For all its horror, this vision, and that of the preceding three riders, brings only a limited judgment (a quarter of the earth is affected). It presages the final judgment, but does not yet bring it. This gives us another indication that we are looking at a picture of the present state of the world, seen as the end times (as are all times since the resurrection). At this stage, judgment is still limited, for there is yet time for repentance, if only these events are seen for what they are—God's warning shot across the bows of the world.

Delight in death?

Bloodlust is a charge that is often enough levelled against the book of Revelation itself. We have seen that John interprets the strife of the world as God's judgment and call to repentance. Does he also delight in the same vision as the crowd in the amphitheatre, although reserving that fate for enemies of the Church?

It is obviously possible to read the book this way, but it is not a very satisfactory approach, for it ignores the repeated calls for repentance and the open-ended nature of the final judgment. John presents the terrible fate of so many of the world's inhabitants as a call to see that fate as less terrible than it could be. For Christians, death is not the worst that can happen. It is instead the gateway to eternal life, and is far less dreadful than denial of their Lord. The very fact that death is seen as the ultimate fate is a sign of the lack of hope in a world without God. Thus, for those without faith, the world's woes are both a judgment and a call to repentance. For those with faith, they are a means of growing in grace and an opportunity to share the love of God and the hopeful message of his coming kingdom.

The real question John poses is about where we turn for hope in the face of invasion and civil war, famine, disease and persecution. In an age of terrorism, AIDS, global warming and international injustice, where is there hope for the world?

The immediate passage does not answer the question, which is asked directly at 6:17, but to ask the question is to prepare the way for the answer. Or rather, we should say, the Answer, for he is coming, and the turmoil of the world prepares his way and calls us to be ready for him.

PRAYER

Lord, may our vision include eternity, against which death is not to be feared, as long as we do not lose you.

CALL *for* JUSTICE

The opening of the fifth seal introduces another aspect of judgment. John sees the souls of the martyrs under the altar (v. 9). This is the altar in God's heavenly throne-room temple, and may also be his throne. While the temple in Jerusalem had separate altars for incense and blood sacrifices, the heavenly altar seems to do both jobs. In the earthly temple, the blood of sacrifices was poured out at the base of the altar. Here, the lives of the faithful witnesses (the meaning of the Greek word *martys*) are presented as sacrifices offered to God.

The idea of martyrs as sacrifices had become common in Jewish thought, where their death was seen as an atonement for the sins of Israel (4 Maccabees 17:22). For Christians, atonement is the work of Christ alone, but the image of sacrifice is still applied (compare Philippians 2:7–8; 2 Timothy 4:6). The faithful witness of those who have died for their faith is the ultimate act of self-offering to God. John sees those who have made the supreme sacrifice kept safely under the watchful care of God.

This is part of the answer to the objection that Revelation is full of death. It is, in fact, full of the promise of eternal life, which is held up as the alternative to death for all who have faith. The saints under the altar symbolize not only those faithful witnesses who die, but all who bear testimony to Jesus.

How long?

The martyred souls cry out for vengeance (v. 10), which is a far cry from Jesus's own call for forgiveness. And so it may be. The desire for payback is a human trait, and even the righteous can be prone to such frailty. God's reply suggests that the real thought should be of vindication. How long will it be before the inhabitants of the earth are seen to be wrong, and the witness of the saints justified?

From the world's perspective, the death of martyrs is their defeat. It takes the eye of faith to see the reality—that they are clothed in the white of victory. In the end, the judgment of the world will be reversed by the judgment of God, and the martyrs who have been declared guilty will be shown to be right.

Until then, they must wait, for they have a role in God's plan. It is a common theme in apocalyptic writing that the vindication of the martyrs must wait until God's purposes are fulfilled (compare Daniel 12:5–7 and, outside the Bible, the apocalypse known as 1 Enoch 47). At the moment, the role of the martyrs is still unclear, though all will be explained (11:3–13). Until then, it is enough to know that martyrdom will continue, and that God sees it as necessary.

Justice for the innocent

A second meaning of the martyrs' call is a demand for justice. They call out to the God who is 'holy and true'—that is, the one who embodies justice and uprightness. Not only must the martyrs be seen to have been right, but justice must be done. They have been falsely condemned and the cause of justice has been betrayed. Like the blood of Abel (Genesis 4:10), the shed blood of the innocent calls for a reckoning.

In that sense we can see the martyrs as standing not only for God's cause, but for all who are falsely accused and done to death. Today as much as at any time, the innocent suffer for the sake of expediency and ideology. Whether it is the silenced voices of political dissent, eliminated street children, the conveniently ignored deaths of farmers who stand in the way of 'development', or those whose very humanity is cloaked under terms like 'collateral damage', blood still cries for justice.

Part of the witness that the people of God are called to give is to his justice. The followers of one who was himself the innocent victim of political cynicism are surely called to bear testimony to justice in this world; to be themselves a foretaste of the coming justice of God.

Once again, we see that what seems to be an other-worldly, mystical vision of heaven has a call to those who live out their lives in the here and now. The vision of God's coming kingdom is an incentive to live in the light of that kingdom and to call the world to embrace its values and outlook.

PRAYER

Father, open the eyes of your people to the injustice of the world, and their mouths to proclaim your judgment.

STANDING *before* GOD

The opening of each seal on the scroll of God is accompanied by a vision of God's judgment. None of these is the content of the scroll, for until all have been opened, the scroll itself cannot be read. They are preparations for the reading of the scroll, which will put in motion the events it contains.

Now we approach the climax of the breaking of the seals. The end of creation as we know it has arrived and all that remains is the final judgment. The prayer of the martyrs for vindication is granted as the present age draws to an end. In a great cataclysm, all that seem most stable—stars, mountains and islands—are shifted out of place (vv. 13–14). This is language drawing on the standard apocalyptic vocabulary of the day and making use of the imagery of the Old Testament (Joel 2:10, 30–31; Isaiah 13:9ff; 2:10ff; 34:4; Ezekiel 32:7–8; 38:19; Hosea 10:8; Amos 8:8).

When all that seems most steadfast in the world is stripped away, there is nothing to come between human beings and the vision of God. Then they must face him and the consequences of their deeds. The Old Testament sources for John's imagery are often predictions of judgment on idolatry, which is far more than false religion. It is the primary sin of putting trust in what is created rather than in the creator. Whatever human beings may hide behind, be it self-deceit, ideology or even religion, must in the end disappear, and reality will stare us in the face.

Here the result is fear and mourning (vv. 15–17). The vision of God does not provoke worship, but only a desire to hide.

Love and wrath

This is perhaps the best image of the judgment of God. It is not the image of a law court, where God tries the case of each, and pronounces salvation or damnation. It is the response of those who have held God at a distance throughout their lives and find that they can do so no longer. In their lives they have fostered an attitude, an approach to life, that carries with it nothing of the world to come, and so there is nothing left that is compatible with the vision of God. In the end we must respond to God, perceiving either his love or his wrath. For those who have, however imperfectly, sought to engage with God, to serve and to love him, the final vision is of a long-lost home. For those who have made themselves strangers to him, he is too terrible to contemplate.

As the awful result of sin is revealed, people of every station in life find themselves in the same situation. Wealth and power are ultimately no shield, and all ask the same question: 'Who is able to stand' in the face of God and his Messiah? In fact, there are those who are able to stand—those who stand before the throne of God—and we shall meet them in 7:9. They are those who have put their faith in Christ, and so have been raised up with him.

For now, though, the focus is on the judgment that falls on unbelievers, of whom the powerful and rich are mentioned in particular, since they are the prime movers in the sinful structures of a world that tries to exist without God. They have placed their trust in wealth and influence, buying or manipulating their way to all they need or desire. But at the end of life and time, they discover that they have stored up treasure in altogether the wrong account.

It is a bleak vision, but is it the only one? We noted that the response of people to the coming of Christ in 1:7 could be taken in two ways, as despair or repentance. Does the present passage leave only the possibility of despair? As things stand, yes, it does, but this is only one perspective on the world's history and the coming of the kingdom of God. Human sinfulness has resulted in injustice, the destruction of people's lives and the death of the saints of God. The culmination of such a path is irrevocable destruction. There are other perspectives, however, and these also need to be explored.

For the present, we can note that 21:24 envisages the kings of the earth, who now cower before the coming God, entering the city of God with tributes of worship. How these two possibilities can be held together will unfold as John shares his vision with us.

✓ PRAYER

Heavenly Father, the time will come when we meet you face to face and see in Christ the vision of your love. May that meeting be the crown of a life lived in your love and service.

BELONGING *to* GOD

Before the final seal is opened, there is an interlude in which the powers of destruction are held back until the servants of God are marked with the seal of God. Once again, John couches his vision in the imagery of Ezekiel, where executioners pass through Jerusalem, slaying all who have not been marked on the forehead with the sign of loyalty to God (Ezekiel 9:4–6). The winds are more bringers of judgment like the four horsemen (compare Zechariah 6:5).

To call the present passage an interlude, therefore, is slightly misleading. It switches our attention away from judgment to the activities of the people of God. What are they doing while the seals are being broken? Chapter 7 is part of a series of visions that runs parallel to the visions of judgment. ('After this I saw' in verse 1, and also throughout the book, refers to the sequence of visions but does not necessarily mean that this is what John wants us to understand to have happened next.) Chapters 4 and 5 showed the heavenly reality that lies behind the events of earthly history, and in which the events on earth are rooted. Chapter 7 now looks at the status of the people of God amid the judgments on earth. In the second seven-series, beginning at 8:2 and 6, there comes the third alternative vision, in which the people of God are seen to be the bringers of hope to those who suffer God's judgment. There is a sequence of judgment that alternates with a sequence of salvation.

Chapter 7 also ties together the seals of the scroll and the trumpets that follow. Connecting with the seals series, it answers the despairing question of those who cannot hide from the wrath of the Lamb, 'Who is able to stand?' (6:17). Those who are marked with the seal of God, and who are before his throne (7:9), are able to stand.

Property of God

The image of the seal suggests ownership: the servants of God bear his stamp (more literally, his slaves are branded!) and are marked as belonging to him. The seal is his name, or the name of Christ (14:1; compare the mark of the beast, 14:9–11). They will be brought safely through the great ordeal (7:14) that marks the coming of God's victory. This does not mean that they will be protected from physical harm. Both experience and the words of Jesus suggest otherwise (Mark 13:9–13). Christians are a part of the world, and are not immune from the disasters brought by the four riders of 6:1–8. What they do have is hope, and the ability to see the disasters as part of God's activity and opportunities for his service. Where the world sees only destruction and hardship, the Church is told to proclaim repentance and trust in God. This is not easy. It brings persecution, and there are times when the horrors of the world can shake faith in God, but it is then that God holds his people firm.

The seal is a sign of its bearers' immunity from judgment and a protection against the spiritual dangers that follow in the wake of the warnings of God. This is where the interlude connects with the coming seven trumpets. The winds held back by the four angels suggest a new spate of judgments and, in fact, tie in well with the environmental disasters of 8:6–12 rather than the human violence of the first four seals.

The vision of the seven seals has dealt only with physical hardships but, as the seven trumpets will make clear, those hardships carry spiritual consequences. There is the possibility that they will bring about repentance, an awareness of human limitations and the need for meaning and hope from beyond the confines of human life. But they may lead to the rejection of God and the placing of hope in that which is other than the almighty creator.

Faced with human mortality, we search not for the hope of eternal life but for ways of extending human life for a few more years, at whatever cost. Faced with events beyond our control, we are tempted to seek means of controlling the world through our own strength, or we turn to superstitions, seeking out clairvoyants, astrologers and other false sources of comfort.

Those sealed with the seal of God have a hope that looks beyond the confines of this life and, in so doing, enriches the present life. It is no shame to admit that life is often beyond our control; it is terrible to have no faith in the God who is himself in control.

PRAYER

Father, when I am tempted to forget you or to place my trust in
that which is less than you, remind me that I belong to you,
and that you hold me safe.

READY *for* BATTLE

It is tempting to wonder whether the sealing of God's servants does not have a wider reference. In the New Testament, 'seal' is used to describe God's gift of the Holy Spirit (Ephesians 4:30) and is Paul's description of circumcision (Romans 4:11), to which baptism is closely connected (Colossians 2:11–12). Since the gift of the Spirit and baptism are closely linked (for example, 1 Corinthians 12:13), it may well be that John intends a reminder of the permanent nature of baptism, both as a sign of God's steadfastness and a call to his service. This would fit well with the fact that the sealing is a protection from the final judgment of 6:17, but not from all the dangers and tribulations of bearing witness in the fallen world.

The call to service is certainly in view in these verses, where John hears the number of the sealed as 144,000, drawn from the twelve tribes of Israel. In fact, the list of tribes is rather strange. Although the Old Testament is not wholly consistent in its list of the tribes, there is none that corresponds with this list in Revelation 7. Here Judah comes first, rather than Reuben, the firstborn son of Jacob, presumably because the Messiah is of the tribe of Judah. But Dan is not mentioned, and is replaced by Manasseh, one of the sons of Joseph (though the other half-tribe of Ephraim, Joseph's other son, is missing). This may be because Dan was seen as the rebellious tribe (Genesis 49:17), but it is just as likely that the list was included from memory, since the actual tribes were only of historic interest and do not matter to John.

The people of God

What does matter is the symbolism: 144,000 is the square of the number of the tribes of Israel, multiplied by 1000 to give a suitably large number. Once we realize that the number is symbolic, many interpretations of the list of those sealed cease to carry much weight. John is not speaking of literal Jews as, for instance, a remnant of faithful Israel. Neither is he speaking of a select number of Christians, such as the martyrs or those who will come to faith during the final days of judgment. Nor does the number refer, as the Jehovah's Witnesses would have us believe, to a specially blessed band of the redeemed who are destined for a more glorious eternity than the rest of God's people. In fact, those sealed must represent all Christians, or we would be left with the strange notion that some believers are sealed by God to protect them from the time of trial, while others are not. And if we are right in seeing an allusion to baptism, then those sealed are certainly all the faithful.

This becomes clear in verse 9, where John sees a great multitude before the throne of God. He is using the same contrast between what is heard and what is seen as we met in 5:5–6. There he heard of the triumph of the Lion of Judah, but saw a Lamb; yet the Lion and the Lamb were the same. Here he hears of the sealing of 144,000, but sees a numberless host, which turns out to be in fact the same people. Those sealed are all Christians, described in terms of Israel, for the followers of Jesus now stand as the people of God (Romans 9:6–8).

The army of the Lord

Why, then, does John speak of the people of God as a selection from the tribes of Israel? The clue is found in the Old Testament, where a census of tribes, and a levy from them, is sanctioned by God only for times of war, when men over the age of 20 are counted. The likely model for John's picture is the census of Numbers 1. The people of God are characterized as God's army, called to his service and to fight for his holy cause.

There is an interesting contrast here with one of the Dead Sea Scrolls, known as the War Scroll, which describes the coming final conflict between the 'sons of light' and the 'sons of darkness', the pagan nations. This is expected to be a literal war, and the members of the Qumran community are given detailed explanations of troop placements, tactics and the way the war is expected to go.

John too sees the people of God as an army, but his image of the final war is different. Just as he transformed the Jewish nationalism of the Lion of Judah into the universal sacrifice of the Lamb that was slaughtered, so he transforms the final conflict from one of literal warfare to one of sacrificial witness.

PRAYER

Father, as you call us to be yours, so keep us as your
faithful soldiers and servants.

The COMPANY of HEAVEN

After hearing the number of those sealed, John sees a great multitude which seems to contrast in every way with the 144,000. Whereas the number sealed referred to the Church on earth (7:1–3), the multitude stands before the throne of God in heaven—thus answering the cry of the unrighteous in 6:17, 'Who is able to stand?' Those who respond to the Lamb's sacrifice are counted worthy to stand in his presence. Unlike the carefully counted army of the Lord, those in heaven are uncountable. The numbered saints are depicted as drawn from the tribes of Israel, whereas the multitude is from every nation, tribe, people and language (see 5:9). Nonetheless, they are the same people of God.

The 144,000 are the Church on earth, called to fight for God against those who oppose him. That is the present significance of God's people, his servants who carry out his mission in the world of conflict between God and evil. The present vision takes us forward to the final destiny of the followers of Jesus. They have endured the great ordeal which is the current experience of the Church, and which pre-figures the final victory of God (7:14). Now they join in the eternal hymn of praise to God, becoming in reality what is presently symbol-ized by the 24 elders—part of the worshipping company of heaven. In the language of later theology, the 144,000 represent the 'church militant' and the multitude stand for the 'church triumphant'.

The palm branches they hold are reminiscent of the Jewish feast of Tabernacles, the most joyful of the annual festivals. Tabernacles com-bined harvest thanksgiving and thanks for God's gift of the land with celebration of the rededication of the temple by the Maccabees. These are those who have entered into the heavenly promised land, as the harvest of God's salvation, and who now worship in the heavenly temple.

Their song praises God for the salvation he has achieved, and praises the Lamb through whom he has brought about that salvation. It provides heaven's reply to the cry of 'Hosanna' ('save us') on the lips of those who waved palm branches at Jesus' entry into Jerusalem (John 12:13). The presence of the multitude in heaven calls forth further worship from the heavenly court, for this is the final proof of God's victory and the victory of his people. They have gained the promises held out in the seven messages to the churches to 'everyone who conquers'. In them, drawn from all the peoples of the earth to be God's own people, the promise to the patriarchs of Israel that their descendants would be innumerable (Genesis 13:16) has been fulfilled.

Family of God

It is one of the great tragedies of the Church's history that Christians have failed to live up to this vision. Those who have, by God's grace, been grafted on to the stock of his chosen people (Romans 11:17ff) and included in the promises to Abraham (Galatians 3:29) have been the greatest persecutors of God's people, the Jews. Those who are destined to be a countless multitude drawn from all races and nationalities have fostered nationalism and racism, and continue to do so.

Catholic and Protestant in Northern Ireland, Orthodox and Catholic in Serbia and Bosnia, have taken Christian tags and used them to identify warring parties. The terrible tribal genocide in Rwanda in 1994 saw Christians divided by tribe rather than united by a common faith. 'Tribal blood is thicker than the water of baptism,' said one bishop.

At the same time, the vision provides hope to many. Those who are tempted to see themselves as part of a small, struggling congregation, or a faith that in much of the Western world seems to have been left behind by secular societies, may look again at John's vision and see the reality behind the illusion of the present moment.

In those very places that are examples of Christian failure, church communities still struggle to bring about reconciliation and healing. Northern Ireland has seen new experiments in ecumenical community, and the Rwandan churches have been active in promoting the task of national reconciliation and forgiveness. Salvation, which means 'wholeness, health and well-being', and in Hebrew means also 'victory', belong to our God, and to those who see the vision and, in it, triumph over failure and temptation.

PRAYER

Father, give to your divided and warring people a renewed vision of the diversity and unity of the company of heaven.

33 REVELATION 7:13–14

STRANGE CONQUEST

The people of God have conquered, but how? John does not imagine a literal battle, but is using the same contrast as at 5:5–6. The victory of the Lion of Judah turned out to be the death of the Lamb of God, and the victory of God's army is the death of his martyrs.

This multitude, explains one of the elders, is made up of those who have come out of the great ordeal (an image rooted in Daniel 12:1), by washing their robes in the blood of the Lamb. Although this sanguinary washing is often taken (especially by hymn writers) as a reference to Christ's sacrifice, which cleanses believers from sin, it is more likely to be a reference to the effect of the believers' own martyrdom. The shedding of their blood in faithful witness to Christ joins them with his death. It allows them to share in his sacrifice and hence in his victory.

This may seem a strange idea to readers brought up on the doctrine of the total sufficiency of the death of Christ. However, the death of the martyrs has no saving power in itself: it draws its significance from the death and victory of the Lamb. In a similar way, Paul saw his suffering as sharing, indeed completing, the sufferings of Jesus (Colossians 1:24). It becomes clear that John is referring to martyrdom when we look at 12:11, where the saints defeat Satan 'by the blood of the Lamb and by the word of their testimony, for they did not cling to life even in the face of death'. Here John uses the Hebrew poetic technique of parallel statements, which express the same idea in different and complementary ways—a style we are familiar with from the Psalms. In 12:11 the 'word of their testimony', even to the point of death, qualifies and explains 'the blood of the Lamb'.

The white robes, then, are the victory garments of those who have conquered by dying as faithful witnesses to Jesus. In this way, John turns the imagery of holy war on its head. True victory is not found in earthly conquest or Hollywood heroics, but in steadfast refusal to compromise with the enemies of God, even to the point of death. There are some Christians who, claiming a 'literal' interpretation of Revelation, look to a time of military conflict in which the faithful will do physical battle with the forces of the antichrist (there's a whole series of novels about this). Ironically, it misses the very point that

John is making. Those who are marked with the seal of God, and numbered as his army, are marked out for martyrdom.

If this seems a strange way of keeping God's people safe, we need to remember that the sealing of the servants of God is to protect them not from physical danger but from spiritual peril—from losing their faith in God. After all, the victory of Christ comes through the cross. Should his followers expect less (John 15:18–20)?

Loyal witnesses

If those sealed and the great crowd in heaven are the whole people of God, and are the martyrs, does this mean that John expects the whole Church to suffer death for its faith? Or does he count as true Christians only those who die for their faith? The answer is neither. In the symbolic world of Revelation, the Church is defined as those who die for Christ, but in reality John knows that not all will do so, either in his own time or (probably) in the distant future. Yet if all Christians were wiped out in some great persecution, this would not be a defeat but the final victory. It would be a victory for the martyrs who pass in the final exodus to heaven, and, we will find later, it would be a victory for God's plan of salvation.

At this stage of his book, John is making two points. In the persecution he sees looming over his own churches, and in the life of the Church at large, Christians are called to be faithful witnesses to Jesus, no matter what may come. And if the worst comes (in earthly terms), it is no less than the triumphant completion of salvation. For that matter, John is not simply directing his readers' attention to the distant future. The time of tribulation, like the whole of the end times, is here and now. Those who are tempted to compromise with the world and adopt its values, and those who suffer for rejecting that temptation, are undergoing their own part of the great ordeal and becoming part of the white-robed army of martyrs.

John's picture of universal martyrdom is deliberately exaggerated, but it is worth pondering the often-quoted statistic that the 20th century saw more Christian martyrs than all the rest of the Church's history.

PRAYER

Father, thank you for the example of the many who have remained faithful to you in the face of death. Deepen our trust and strengthen our witness, that we too may stay faithful.

RETURN *of the* EXILES

The multitude of the redeemed stand before the throne of God because they have shared in the sacrifice of Christ. This does not mean that their witness and martyrdom have earned them a place in heaven. Their place is the gift of God through Christ's death. They can come into the presence of the Holy One because the price for their sins has been paid and the barrier between God and humanity broken down by his loving self-sacrifice. They have reached the promised goal because they have clung to faith, and have not given in to the temptation to deny Christ and, with him, their salvation.

John does not teach a salvation by works. What he does insist on is the responsibility that is the consequence of salvation. God's grace is free, but it comes as a call to service, and in Revelation that service is to bear witness to Jesus.

Service continues in heaven. The word translated by NRSV as 'worship' (v. 15) can also mean 'service', with the connotation of carrying out religious duties. There is work to be done even in heaven: the joyful work of worship. Therefore, as the priests of the earthly temple could enter into the holy place to offer sacrifice, so the royal priesthood of the new creation offers itself in the presence of God.

The worship they offer is directed to the occupants of the throne, God and with him the Lamb, who is seated 'at the centre of the throne' (v. 17). Christ receives worship as one who shares the throne of God—indeed, as one who therefore shares in the being of God himself.

Promise

In this vision, John is allowed to look ahead to the final day of victory. The references to the water of life and God's wiping away of tears look ahead to 21:4 and 22:1. The triumph of the heavenly Church will come, but it is not yet here, and in the middle of verse 15 the tense of the verb changes from the present of immediate vision to the future of promised blessing. The time will come when God will 'stretch his tent over them' (the more literal meaning of 'shelter') but for now worship is a faint foretaste of the worship of heaven, and the witness of the saints is carried out in the midst of an often-hostile world.

At the same time, the vision of the future explains what the Church already is. In God's eyes, it is already a royal priesthood, a holy kingdom. The final destination will make actual what is present in potential, realizing the promise that the saints of God carry with them.

The mention of the tent, or tabernacle, continues the Tabernacles theme of the heavenly worship and evokes memories of the guiding presence of God in the wilderness (Exodus 13:21) and of the *shekinah*, the cloud of God's glory that dwelt in the Tent of God (Exodus 40:34–38). It is also related to the word used in John 1:14 to describe the dwelling of God incarnate among his people.

Strangers in the world

Verses 16–17 echo Isaiah 49:10. There the prophet offers hope to the Israelites in exile in Babylon. God will lead his people home to their own land, and along the way 'they shall not hunger or thirst, neither scorching wind nor sun shall strike them down, for he who has pity on them shall lead them, and by springs of water will guide them'.

In this world, then, Christians are exiles whose true homeland is in heaven and who hold their first loyalty to the kingdom of God. This is a common theme in the New Testament. For Paul, the Christian's home city is heaven (Philippians 3:20), while in John's Gospel Jesus tells his disciples that they are not entirely part of the world in which they live (John 15:19), and Peter addresses his Christian readers as exiles of the 'Dispersion', a term used for Jews dwelling outside the promised land (1 Peter 1:1).

None of this is to suggest that Christians do not play a full part in the life of God's creation and of the societies in which they live. It does say that they must be critical of the world and live by the values that characterize the coming kingdom. The role of the Church is to bear witness to God, and one of the ways it should do so is by holding the world up to the judgment of the kingdom of God.

From the world's point of view, the values of the kingdom are topsy-turvy. It is a kingdom in which love triumphs by self-sacrifice, in which the weak are valued and leadership is reckoned by service. It is a strange world in which a Lamb can be the shepherd.

PRAYER

Father, help us not to see the world as it sees itself,
but as you see it—far from you, but deeply loved.

PRAYER & FIRE

After the sealing of the saints and the vision of their final destiny, John returns us to the opening of the seals on the scroll of God. At first sight, the opening of the seventh seal is an anti-climax. The sixth seal heralded the final judgment; now, all that seems to happen is silence (v. 1).

This is because John has overlapped the end of the seal visions with the beginning of the next seven-series, the judgments introduced by seven trumpets. In this way, he shows the intimate connection between the visions of judgment. These cannot be three different sequences following on from each other, but are different ways of looking at the same thing. By introducing the trumpets before the seals end, he includes the trumpets within the seals. You might say that the seven-series fit within each other like Russian dolls.

A better image would be that of a microscope. As John increases the magnification, he sees that within the seventh seal there is more detail to be revealed: the seven trumpets. And they in turn will focus down into the seven bowls (15:1—16:21).

So as silence falls in heaven with the opening of the last seal, John sees the seven angels who will sound the call for the next series of judgments. These are the seven angels who, in popular Jewish thought, stood ready by God's throne as his special messengers (for example, in Tobit 12:15).

Silence in heaven

The meaning of the silence has caused much debate, but it becomes clearer when we realize that the introduction of the seven angels is best thought of as being in brackets, with verses 3–5 following straight on from verse 1. There was a tradition in Jewish writing that the praises of the angels in heaven stopped from time to time to allow the prayers of earth to be heard. Now, in the silence, an angel presents the prayers of the saints to God as an offering of incense on the heavenly altar (vv. 3–4). Since incense is often associated with sacrifice, it may well be that these particular prayers are specifically linked to the self-offering of the suffering Church.

The main point, though, is that prayer does not go unnoticed by God. It strikes straight to the heart of heaven, and all the activity of heaven ceases, to make way for it. This is a powerful image of the meaning and effectiveness of prayer. Prayer is the means by which the relationship of God and his people is cemented. It is the conversation of the people of God with their divine lover, and, like any lover, he stops what he is doing to listen to it.

Answers on earth

Prayer does not go unanswered. In verse 5, the incense vessel that brought the prayers to God is now filled with the fire of heaven and sent crashing down to earth (compare Ezekiel 10:1–7). The prayers of the saints for justice and vindication are answered by God's fire of judgment. The End, which was tottering on the brink at the opening of the sixth seal, now comes in thunder, lightning and earthquake.

These are the traditional trappings of the appearance of God, as at Mount Sinai (Exodus 19:16, 18). God comes in judgment to answer the prayers of his people.

The Bible is consistently clear that God acts in response to prayer —not always, to be sure, in the way that those who pray might wish, but always as a response to the pleas of the faithful.

The deepest truth about prayer is that it aligns the one who prays with the will of God—that it is about learning his will and not imposing ours. The end result of a life of prayer is actually to make us want what God wants. At the same time, we should give weight to the clear biblical theme of God's response to prayer: prayer causes things to happen that otherwise would not. This is not to say that prayer is a kind of magic, forcing God's hand, but to affirm that he takes account of the prayers of the faithful in the way he acts in the world. Prayer acts both on the pray-er and by evoking an answer from God.

PRAYER

Lord, sometimes in silence I strain to hear your voice.
How amazing that you are straining to hear me.
Let me never be silent when I have prayers to offer,
or noisy when you have words to speak.

The EARTH RECOILS

Now the trumpets sound and the judgments begin (compare Matthew 24:31). The first four seals corresponded closely to Jesus' words in Mark 13:7–8, and now the first four trumpets remind us of Mark 13:19–20, 24–25. John also calls to mind the plagues of Egypt from Exodus 7—11. Like the Egyptian plagues, the trumpets aim to make the people of the earth acknowledge God, and signal the deliverance of God's people—and the judgment of those who reject him.

As with the seal judgments, the disasters heralded by the trumpets are limited in their scope but more intense than those of the seals. Generally, they affect a third of the earth, rather than a quarter. John is building a picture of gradually increasing suffering, which nonetheless allows time for a change of heart in those who are afflicted. We should not think in terms of a historical sequence of increasingly severe judgments, but of an artistic progression. The intensifying of the plagues is John's way of saying that God will do what is necessary in order to bring about repentance.

It is certainly a fact of Christian experience that human self-sufficiency needs to be set aside, often painfully, before people will acknowledge God. When they do, they find, like Paul (2 Corinthians 1:8–10) that God is the one who can see them through.

Eco-shock

Whereas the first four seal judgments were the result of human violence and injustice, the first four trumpets bring about disasters in the natural world. These in turn are, of course, God's response to human sin.

They are also appropriate to our own age. If we can see the four horsemen abroad in our own time, so we can see the effects of human sinfulness on the environment. Poor land use has devastated the centre of Russia, drying up the Caspian Sea and changing weather patterns over north and central Asia. Deforestation brings regular disastrous flooding to Bangladesh. The Sahara desert continues to move south, swallowing once-fertile lands into a sea of sand. Pollution has destroyed large portions of the protective ozone layer, and the incidence of skin cancer increases. Weather patterns over Europe continue to change, so that it seems likely that formerly temperate regions will become hotter and drier, playing havoc with agriculture and changing beyond recognition much of the famous English countryside. Meanwhile the even greater threat of melting ice caps threatens huge areas of the world with inundation.

None of this, of course, is specifically prophesied by Revelation. John knows nothing of the greenhouse effect and CFCs, but the principle of God's judgment holds firm. Those who fail to recognize the creator make free with creation in ways that it cannot sustain. This is not to suggest that technology is evil in itself. It is a good and useful tool, and the Bible does not encourage any romantic notion of 'living close to nature'. However, the use of technology needs to take into account the nature of the world, and to recognize that those who use it cannot stand apart from the whole world to which they belong. What we do to creation, we do to ourselves, who are a part of it.

Supernatural plagues

The message of the plagues is that those who worship something other than God, be it false gods or human self-reliance, must live with the consequences. Once again, God gives up those who reject him to the results of that rejection.

The plagues (v. 11) are seen as having supernatural sources (the star Wormwood probably prefigures the fall of Satan in 12:7–9: demonic evil is loose in the world). This is John's way of saying that human actions, which may seem merely physical, have spiritual significance. Ambitious irrigation plans may seem devoid of religious significance, but the attitude that assumes a human right to tamper with a little-understood creation is spiritual pride of an immense degree. The supernatural origin of the plagues also continues to stress the element of divine judgment in what, to human eyes, may seem mere physical misfortune.

Once again, the distinction between the judgment of God and mere chance is one of perspective. It is as the Church calls for a recognition of God as creator that the consequences of misusing the world become a call to repentance.

PRAYER

Father, give us wisdom to use properly the resources you have given us, and to recognize our responsibility to you for the world you have made, and of which we are a part.

SWARM *of* TORMENT

The final three trumpets are heralded by an eagle, or (an alternative translation) a vulture. Flying high in the sky, hovering over its victims as a portent of doom (compare Luke 17:37; Matthew 24:28), it announces the three final woes, which bring human history to a close. The first four trumpets have not brought repentance, so now the judgment intensifies.

The first woe, at the sounding of the fifth trumpet, is a plague of locusts, but they are no ordinary insects. Echoing 8:10, a star, an angelic power, falls to earth and is allowed to open the bottomless pit (9:1). Like Wormwood, the star is an aspect of Satan's power, come to set destruction loose in the world. The fact that the key to the pit has been given to him (that is, by God) is in fact a sign of hope. For all that evil may seem irresistible, it is allowed by God as part of his plan of redemption.

The 'bottomless pit' translates the Greek term *abyss*, the deep place under the earth that joins with the waters of the sea. It is the same word as the one used in the Greek version of the Old Testament for the formless void out of which God brought creation (Genesis 1:2). As such, it symbolizes chaos and lawlessness, and is the earthly counterpart of the crystal sea of heaven. It is out of this reservoir of disorder and meaninglessness that the locusts come.

John borrows this image from Joel 2, which likens a locust swarm to God's army of judgment. Behind both Joel and John stands the locust plague of Exodus 10. Once again, the plague is intended to turn rebellious hearts to repentance.

The returns of wrong

The description of the locusts (9:7–10) heightens the sense of horror. These locusts are demonic, and attack humans while sparing the plants (9:4). We should not see any great conflict between the death of the grass in 8:7 and its sparing from the locust horde: this is the language of symbolism, not literal description.

The plague of hellish insects brings pain but not death, though its victims would rather die (9:5–6). That is, they would rather flee from God into death itself than repent and be saved. This suggests that the torment they feel may be psychological rather than physical. Aware of the need to repent, desiring salvation, yet fearful of change and clinging stubbornly to pride, the people of the earth embrace death rather than life.

This is why the locusts only harm those who are not marked with the seal of God, and it is the key to understanding a vision of horror that would suit any late-night film show. The seal of God protects his people not from physical harm but from spiritual damage. Evil is torturing only those who already worship it.

It is the very nature of evil to recoil upon its perpetrators. Those who destroy the lives and hopes of others destroy their own humanity in the process. Those who deny the life of the spirit become immune to spirituality and cannot see the hope that God holds out to them. Those who claim that only the material exists or matters live out their material lives with hope of nothing greater or better.

On this level, the abyss is the cumulative power of human evil, in which all to some extent participate and by which all are to some degree harmed. No sin is committed in a vacuum, and each wrong has its consequences both for humanity as a whole and for sinners themselves.

Lord of destruction

Finally, John reminds us that no one is truly a free agent. Whether we recognize it or not, we choose sides, serving either God or the devil. Thus the locusts of evil have a king (9:11), unlike natural locusts (Proverbs 30:27), and it is destruction, for evil in the last analysis makes nothing but only destroys what is good. Abaddon, the Hebrew for 'destruction', and Apollyon, the Greek for 'destroyer', are fitting titles for evil. Apollyon may also be a mockery of the Greek god Apollo, and with him emperors such as Nero and Domitian who aped the attributes of the god. Attractive though the trappings of popular paganism were, and tempting though it might have been for John's readers to have an assured place in society, the price of conformity with the world is too high. Even token worship of these powers is worship of the powers of darkness.

PRAYER

Father, make us aware of the consequences of our sins and, above all, of the forgiveness and freedom that are found in you.

The WAGES of SIN

The sixth trumpet releases the second woe (vv. 13–15), a demonic army of uncountable size. John hears the number, but could hardly carry out a head count! No earthly power could muster the number of troops John records (v. 16). This is an unstoppable force, rolling over all opposition. The surprising thing is that the army kills only a third of the population (v. 18). Once again, though, the real purpose is to call for repentance, not to destroy for its own sake.

The locust plague has probably inspired this vision, for in the Greek version of Amos 7:1 (though not the Hebrew), a locust horde is said to be commanded by the mythical Gog of Ezekiel 38:1–3. The army is led by four avenging angels from across the Euphrates, the eastern border of the Roman empire and the boundary of the land promised to Abram (Genesis 15:18), though never in fact occupied by Israel. Perhaps the angels represent the four winds of 7:1, which are now released.

Although these verses play on Old Testament memories of invasion (Assyria and Babylon lay beyond the Euphrates) and on Roman paranoia about Parthia, this is no human army. Death is dealt not by the riders with their colourful breastplates but by their monstrous steeds, which in fact resemble horses only in that they are ridden.

The appointed time

It was a common motif of apocalyptic that God had an appointed time for every event. This plague comes at the precise time ordained by God, for all that happens is under his control.

To us this seems a disquieting idea. Is everything truly fixed? Does the history of the world and the eternal fate of its inhabitants really run along the undeviating tramlines of predestination? And if so, what is the point of the call to repentance?

John at this point seems to share the predetermined scheme of most apocalyptic. As his book unfolds, however, we shall see that things are not quite as cut and dried as they may appear. The future in fact remains open, and the fate of the world hangs in the balance. For now, the insistence on God's appointed hour is meant as consolation. Sin may seem supreme, the persecutors may appear in control, but the true Lord of human history is God, and he will not be gainsaid.

Answered prayer

Like the judgment of the seventh seal, this woe (the sixth trumpet) comes in answer to prayer. A voice speaks from the horned altar, where incense is offered (v. 13). Incense so far has represented the prayers of the saints, so perhaps the voice belongs to the angel with the censer (8:3). In any case, the mention of the altar tells us that prayer has been offered. Presumably this is once again the prayer for vindication of God's people. Those who have suffered persecution and rejection are shown to be in the right by the coming of God's judgment on the world.

The people of God are spared from the effects of this judgment, for 9:20 shows that 'humankind' here means those who are opposed to God. The sparing of the saints is not a promise of freedom from earthly pain for the Church, for, like the locusts, the 200,000,000 cavalry represent the effects of sin run rampant rather than a literal military force. Interpreters who try to see in the fire, sulphur and smoke a prophecy of modern weaponry have missed the point. Fire-breathing monsters were common symbolic figures (see the description of Leviathan in Job 41:19–20). Here they represent the ultimate result of sin.

Sin repaid

We have seen that sin leads to destruction. The locusts represent the suffering to which wrongdoing leads. The demonic army is the final statement: sin leads to death. For the faithful martyrs, death is the gateway to eternal life and the preparation for God's pronouncement of acquittal. For those who reject God's call to repentance, it is the rejection of the source of all life and hope, and in their absence there is nothing: existence itself is at an end.

PRAYER

Lord, in our darkest times, and in the depths of the world's tragedies, you are there—working to bring good out of evil and light out of darkness. Give me eyes to see you at work and hands to work with you.

The FAILURE *of* JUDGMENT

At last the point of the horrors that John has unfolded in the opening of the seals and the sounding of the trumpets becomes explicit. They are intended to bring repentance. The fact that final judgment is preceded by a series of limited judgments has pointed to this conclusion, but here it is finally stated.

The judgments have been a call to turn away from the worship of that which is not God, and to give him the honour that is his alone. The primary sin is the worship of demons and idols. This is not to say that the gods represented by idols have any real existence, as Paul and the Christians of Corinth agreed (1 Corinthians 8:4–6; 10:19). When worship is offered to that which is not God, however, be it a non-existent deity or some material possession, or human ambition, or political or philosophical ideology, then demons are worshipped.

The demonic comes into being when spirituality is misdirected. Human beings are made for a commitment to God, and when their primary commitment is to something else, then it is opposed to God: that is, it is demonic.

In this sense, idolatry is the original sin and the basis of all others. When Adam and Eve listened to the serpent (Genesis 3), they gave obedience to that which was not God: they committed idolatry. When they sought to be like God through the power of knowledge (Genesis 3:5–6), they worshipped human achievement alone, and committed idolatry.

Catalogue of wrong

It is this exaltation of human desire and achievement above all else that lies behind the other sins mentioned by John in verse 21. Murder and sorcery are both attempts to enforce human will on others by control of God's creation without reference to him, and by removing human obstacles to personal power and gain. Fornication and theft are both about getting without paying—in personal commitment and love, and in fair trade. It is not surprising to find, then, that these sins are particularly associated with idolatry in the Old Testament.

The threat of compromise with the world, which John sees looming over his churches, is more than simply the danger of blunting the churches' witness, though that is bad enough. It carries with it the danger of accepting a sexual morality based on dishonesty and lack of love; of espousing violence as an acceptable tool of politics and trade; and of business based on exploitation and manipulation.

Shocking conclusion

With the seventh trumpet about to sound, and the total condemnation of sinful humanity waiting in the wings, do people think again and repent? No.

With a realistic assessment of human nature, John declares that those who survive carry on doing the very things that are destroying them. Like an alcoholic in search of a bottle, like a smoker ignoring the health warning, sin goes on and reaps its reward.

Or to put it another way, God has failed.

The series of judgments were meant to bring repentance, but the simple fact is that whatever woes befall the world, they do not seem to result in a great turning of people to God. In fact, the victims are more likely to curse God, to blame him for 'not doing something' (exactly what he is meant to do is never specified). The suggestion that perhaps it would be good to refrain from doing the things that bring about disaster is dismissed.

Part of the reason for this is that sin is not just the action of individuals. It is tied up in the systems of the world. Much of the disastrous evil that besets humanity has no individual cause. Who is responsible for a war? Which sinner is responsible for cutting down rainforests? Both are the result of economic and political forces that are beyond the control of individuals. Both are demonic; they belong to a realm of wrong that controls people rather than being controlled by human beings.

Repentance, then, does not come. All that is left is for God to acknowledge that there is no hope for humanity as a whole, and to bring down the curtain. But he does not, for with God there is always hope, unimaginable as it may be.

PRAYER

God, can you really fail? Yes—because we are free to reject
your grace. Show me where I make you fail, and
help me to let you succeed in me.

TURNING POINT

As with the seven seals, the final judgment is preceded by an interlude in which we see again the heavenly reality. Here heaven comes
down to earth in the form of a great angel. The spiritual truth that
underlies the events of the world is now brought into the world's
arena.

The interlude of chapter 7 showed us the sealing of the saints for
their protection, and presented them as God's army. The second
interlude will show the battle for which they are prepared.

Pivotal passage

The next two chapters mark a turning point in the book. New
symbols appear, which will be explained more fully in the rest of the
work: the beast from the pit, the great city, the conflict between the
beast and the Church. The steady progression of judgments is sus-
pended (one more seven-series will come) and is replaced with
lengthy expositions of themes.

More importantly, the people of God now figure prominently. In
fact, as we shall see, it is here that the main message of Revelation
actually begins.

Revealing angel

In 1:1, John declared that his prophecy, in typical apocalyptic
manner, was given through an angel. So far we have not met an angel
who could be said to have given him a significant message. In verse 1
'another mighty angel' comes, establishing a link with the angel of
5:2 who called for someone worthy to open the scroll of God. The
angel here is wrapped in the signs of God's mercy, the rainbow of the
covenant with Noah (Genesis 9:13) and the cloud and pillar of fire
that led the Israelites out of slavery (Exodus 13:21). Because of these
divine trappings, some commentators see this angel as Christ himself
('angel' simply means 'messenger', and doesn't say anything about
the type of messenger). The connection to 5:2 makes this unlikely,
however; this angel is simply described as a messenger of God's
salvation.

In his hand the angel bears a scroll, which is probably none other than the scroll opened by the Lamb (8:1). This point is obscured by most translations, including NRSV, as they term it a 'little scroll' (v. 2), which at first appearance suggests a different book. The reason is that John uses the Greek word *biblaridion*, a diminutive form of the word *biblion*, which was used at 5:1 and is also used to describe this scroll at 10:8. However, in the popular Greek of John's time, diminutive forms were often used simply as alternative words for the same thing. (*Biblion* is itself a diminutive of *biblos*, the basic word for book or scroll.) If the diminutive term is significant, it more probably suggests that this is a scaled-down version of the scroll from chapter 5, appearing now in a form small enough to be eaten. The identification of the two scrolls, though, is signalled by the fact that so far, with digressions and interruptions, John has been following the story of Ezekiel's call in Ezekiel 2—3.

There Ezekiel sees a scroll in the hand of God and is instructed to eat it. John sees a scroll in the hand of God, but first it must be opened by the Lamb, for revelation is now concerned with the saving work of Christ and is mediated by the risen Lord. Once the scroll has been opened (with attendant portents and revelations), it is brought to John. It is twice stressed that the scroll lies open in the angel's hand (vv. 2, 8), again indicating that this is the book that John saw opened by the Lamb. Now John must eat it (10:9) as Ezekiel did. Moreover, so far, the content of the scroll opened by the Lamb has not been revealed. Now John is to digest the scroll and declare its contents (10:11). This is the core prophecy of the book of Revelation, and is the revelation referred to in 1:1.

Word from heaven

So the angel descends from heaven, bringing a word to the world, and straddles land and sea, showing the all-embracing scope of the message of God. God is not concerned only with a minority of believers, but sends out a call of salvation to the whole earth. Judgment may not have evoked repentance, but now comes a message of salvation for all.

PRAYER

Lord, may I hear your word and make it a part of me,
so that I may speak it boldly to others, no matter what the cost.

WORD *from* HEAVEN

As the angel comes down from heaven, John's viewpoint changes. He is no longer an observer from within the heavenly court of God, but is on earth, perhaps on Patmos, to receive his call to prophesy. Such changes should not bother us, since we already know that John is not writing a straightforward story, but is presenting a complex set of insights into spiritual truth.

One such truth is that the spiritual reality symbolized by heaven is also to be found on earth. John is not a dualist, one who divides the world into good heaven and evil earth, blessed spirit and wicked flesh. The angel's descent shows again that the plan of salvation is worked out on earth, and the battle against evil is fought in the material world. Therefore the angel's oath is in the name of the one 'who created heaven and what is in it, the earth and what is in it, and the sea and what is in it' (v. 6).

It is always a temptation for Christians to see their faith as an escape from a world that often seems confusing or intolerable. This, though, is not Christianity, which is about living out the life of heaven, as much as possible, in the present world. The incarnation itself is a statement that the world is the place to serve God; it is God's creation, destined for redemption, and there is no safe 'spiritual' haven into which we may retreat.

A better way

As the angel begins his proclamation, seven thunders sound (v. 3), giving a message that John understands but is forbidden to pass on (v. 4). Presumably this is another series of judgments like the seals and the trumpets. As they affected first a quarter and then a third of the earth, the thunders might well be supposed to affect half of creation, but they do not come to fruition. We have already seen that the series of judgments fail in their purpose of bringing repentance. There is therefore no point in yet another limited, but more intense tribulation. Instead, the angel comes to bring a better approach to the salvation of the world.

The time of salvation is indeed at hand, as the mighty angel (perhaps Gabriel, which means 'strong or mighty man of God') swears (v. 6). The angel and his oath call to mind the last vision of the book of Daniel (Daniel 10—12), in which the last days are said to come after 'a time, two times, and half a time'. This 'half week' of years is characterized by the 'shattering of the power of the holy people' (Daniel 12:7), and is very important for John's understanding of the role of the Church, which must witness under persecution. For now, it is enough to know that his message is for the Church as it lives in the end times before the coming of judgment. The message is therefore urgent, and its proclamation cannot be set aside because it is difficult or inconvenient.

All this is to happen before the seventh trumpet—a reminder that the vision of the angel and the scroll belongs with the sixth trumpet. It is a call to repentance which is meant to achieve what judgments alone cannot.

Times and seasons

At this point we need to remember again that, for John, the end times are the times in which the Church lives. The seals and trumpets are not a historical forecast, but a description of the world as it is. Only the end of each series looks to the future, with its final consummation of God's triumph (v. 7) when the plan of salvation comes to full fruition.

Even that is not entirely future. The mystery that will be fully revealed in the new creation is the gospel, which is already in play in the proclamation of the Church. Judgment comes through the preaching of the good news, and consists in the response to that preaching. Therefore, whether in the first century or the 21st, the Church lives and witnesses in the time of the sixth trumpet—the time of the final call to repentance.

Indeed, chapters 10—11 should really be seen not as an interlude, a brief respite from the judgments of the seven trumpets, but as running parallel to them. Against the backdrop of the world's woes, the faithful witness of the Church sounds out a call for the world to return to its creator.

PRAYER

Creator of all, give to us, your people, a sense of the urgency of our mission to all of your creation.

BITTERSWEET NEWS

So far, to the inhabitants of the world, God's purposes are hidden. The woes of the world have not been seen as God's call, and remain puzzling tragedies. The consequences of sin have not been a salutary lesson, but a conundrum. The coming victory of God remains a mystery, yet that mystery must be made clear. In the New Testament, the term 'mystery' means some aspect of God's plan, or indeed the whole plan, which is now made plain by the gospel. Just how God intended to bring about the salvation of the world was a mystery that became clear in Jesus Christ.

It is the job of the prophet to make the mystery clear, for as Amos had said long ago, 'God does nothing, without revealing his secret to his servants the prophets' (Amos 3:7). The revealing angel takes up Amos' saying, but changes a crucial word. 'Reveal' now becomes 'announced' (v. 7), which translates the Greek word for 'proclaiming good news', or 'the gospel' (the only use of this word in Revelation). It is in the proclamation of the gospel that God's plan is conveyed to the world, and his purposes are made clear by the prophetic witness of the people of God. From the perspective of the gospel, sense can be made of the judgment of God. Indeed, the message is seen to be far more than judgment. It is the offer of God's grace and salvation.

The gospel calls people to alter their view of the world. It offers another explanation for how things are, and challenges its hearers to test their own worldview against that offered by God. Accordingly, it often finds itself in opposition to the values of the world, and is frequently seen as a threat both to individual lifestyles and to systems of government. Any such challenge can expect to be met with opposition and persecution.

Digesting the word

John is told, presumably by the risen Jesus, to take the scroll from the angel, and the angel tells him to eat it (vv. 8–9). Like Ezekiel, he finds it sweet to taste (v. 10), for the message of the scroll is one of hope for the world. The actual contents of the scroll are found in chapter 11, where we see that it is a blueprint for the Church's witness in the time of tribulation that heralds the final victory.

When John has eaten the scroll, though, it proves bitter to his stomach, for it also carries the message of suffering for the Church, which by its faithful witness is to be the means of bringing the world to salvation. Bitterness is also a sign of the double-edged nature of the gospel message. It is good news but, in the challenge it poses to the world and to sin, it is also a bitter pill to swallow, for it brings the threat of judgment and the inevitability of persecution.

Whether bitter or sweet, the gospel must be assimilated before it can effectively be preached. The image of eating the scroll is a picture of the word of God becoming a part of the life of the prophet, who in turn shares it with the seven churches and, through them, with the world. Indeed, John stands here as a symbol of the Church itself in its prophetic task. We need constantly to remember that prophecy is not merely foretelling the future, but 'forth-telling' what we hear from God to the world around us.

If the gospel challenges unbelievers to change their viewpoint, it does no less for Christians. As the seven messages to the churches made clear, the Church stands in constant danger of being conformed to the world in which it lives (compare Romans 12:2). The surest safeguard against that is to make the word of God a part of our lives.

Herald of good tidings

John is now equipped with the message of God, and is recommissioned to speak a message ('they' who speak, in verse 11, are presumably Jesus, the voice from heaven, and the angel). John is already a prophet, and has been given a message for the churches of Asia Minor (1:11), but now that message is seen to be for the whole world. To be sure, we have seen that the seven churches stand for the universal Church, but here that is made explicit, and John makes his claim to have a message of universal significance. His prophecy is 'about many people and nations and languages and kings'. The Greek could just as easily be translated 'to' rather than 'about', but the end result is the same. The message is to go through the seven churches (that is, the Church as a whole) to the whole world.

REFLECT

What bitter edge of the gospel makes us shy away from proclaiming it? Is it the fear of rejection or ridicule, the challenge of confronting sin or the challenge to our own lives?

The DIMENSIONS of the CHURCH

Now John comes to the centre of his book. Revelation 11:1–13 is the content of the scroll he has swallowed. This is his message to the Church, explaining God's plan for the mission of his people and their role in the salvation of the world. The prophecy will be expanded and explained in detail in the rest of the book.

Preserving the saints

Ezekiel, in one of his visions, saw a man with a measuring rod (Ezekiel 40:3) who measured the city of Jerusalem, as a symbol of its restoration after the conquest by Babylon. John is now given a rod and told to measure the temple of God (v. 1). Here it is a sign of preservation rather than restoration and is an indication that God, who knows every detail of his people, down to the number of hairs on their heads (Matthew 10:30), will keep them safe in the coming tribulation.

Yet 'safe' is a relative term. John is told to measure the inner sanctuary of the temple, but not its great outer court (v. 2). The temple in Jerusalem had been destroyed in AD70 during the disastrous rebellion of Judea against Rome. Before then, it had consisted of a huge outer area, the Court of the Gentiles, which was open to all, and an inner area reserved for Jews. It is this area that is measured, comprising the Courts of Women and of Men and the Holy Place itself.

The temple, of course, is a symbol of the Church. A similar idea is found in the Dead Sea Scrolls. The community that lived at Qumran considered itself (or at least its ruling council) to be the true temple, the one in Jerusalem having been compromised by false teaching. John himself is not interested in the literal temple, partly because it was long gone and partly because a literal temple has no place in his vision of the destiny of the saints. He includes the holy city (v. 2) because it looks forward to another image of God's people, as the new Jerusalem, which will appear as the book nears its close. This is a rather startling image, for the new Jerusalem belongs to the new creation and is not yet apparent. Yet in some way, no doubt very imperfectly, it ought to be apparent in the present life of the Church, as it seeks to become a community that mirrors the coming perfect community of the kingdom of God.

What does it mean to say that the inner sanctuary will be preserved, but the outer court and holy city will be trampled by the nations? The duration of this desecration points to the answer. Forty-two months is once again Daniel's three and a half times (years) (Daniel 7:25; 12:7), during which the people of God will be overcome by God's enemies. (In 11:3, we will see it again as 1260 days, assuming a 30-day month.)

The Church is to be kept safe in its core, its inner spiritual being, but the forces of the world will ride roughshod over it in its physical manifestation, its outer being. In fact, the measuring of the temple and the trampling of the outer area is another image for the truth that was indicated by the sealing of the 144,000 and the martyrdom of the saints in chapter 7. There we saw that God will preserve the spiritual life of the Church, keeping his people safe in their relationship with him. At the same time, they will undergo persecution and suffering for his sake, and will face the martyrdom that will result in their heavenly triumph.

Claiming the victory?

Nowadays we hear a lot about the victory of the Church. There are those who tell us that we should expect success—usually couched in terms of packed pews and large offerings—if only we 'claim the victory' which is ours in Christ. In fact, if a church fails to grow, or even dies out, it is deemed a failure. John's message should warn us to be very careful in our use of such language. The trampling of the temple, based on Daniel's breaking of the power of God's people, points in another direction. A church may not always, or even often, be expected to be powerful in the worldly terms of number and riches (look at the churches of Laodicea and Sardis). The immediate result of faithful witness is not always growth and plenty. It can provoke a trampling down by the forces of the world. Yet there is a victory, and there is the certainty that nothing can separate us from the love of God (Romans 8:38–39). We must learn to see that victory in God's terms rather than ours.

√ PRAYER

Lord, let us measure our success not by the world's standards,
but by yours.

FAITHFUL WITNESSES

For the same period of time that the world is trampling down the people of God—that is, during the end times which are the history of the Church—God's two faithful witnesses will be active.

The miracles performed by these witnesses (v. 6) remind us of Elijah (1 Kings 17:1; 2 Kings 1:10) and Moses (Exodus 7:19), traditional heralds of the coming of the Messiah (compare Malachi 4:4–5). The witnesses are not those prophets literally returning, however, for each one shares the characteristics of both. Nor are they another pair of outstanding witnesses from history (for instance, Peter and Paul have been suggested). The clue to their identity is found in their description as olive trees and lampstands (v. 4).

The prophet Zechariah had seen a lampstand between two olive trees, which stood for the Spirit of God illuminating the rightful king, Zerubbabel, and the high priest, Joshua (Zechariah 3—4). These are all combined in John's two witnesses to give us figures who stand for kingship and priesthood and the light of the Spirit. We have already met this combination of images in the royal priesthood represented by lampstands, which is the Church. The two witnesses, then, are the whole Church. Instead of the seven lampstands of earlier chapters, there are now two, for this is the number of witness. (Deuteronomy 19:15 lays down that two witnesses are the minimum number for a valid testimony.) The Church's witness is inspired and empowered by the Spirit of God (Zechariah's lampstand), who gives the gifts that the Church needs for its task.

During the time of persecution, then, the world does not have everything its own way. The Church is called to active witness, and will afflict the consciences of humanity with words and testimony to Jesus that flow like fire from the mouths of its messengers. Some interpreters see the fire and plagues as literal miracles that will be performed in the last days, but it is better to see them as symbolic of the impact of the gospel's proclamation. The signs of the witnesses call for repentance and prepare the way out of slavery to sin. The word of God is a powerful force, convicting of sin, bringing judgment and repentance and challenging the ways of a sinful world. To churches that may be in danger of losing heart, John brings the reminder that all power does not lie on the world's side; God's power is different, and ultimately greater.

Heralds of the kingdom

In Jewish tradition, Elijah was expected to appear as the forerunner of the Messiah, and speculation added Moses as another witness to the coming of the kingdom of God.

Jesus applied the Elijah motif to the work of John the Baptist (Matthew 11:13–14), though according to the fourth Gospel John had denied that he was literally Elijah returned to earth (John 1:21).

It was this messianic claim about Jesus and his forerunner that the Jews found, and still find, so hard to accept. On the face of it, they have the better of the argument. After all, the Hebrew scriptures, the Christian Old Testament, are pretty clear about the signs of the Messiah. He will bring in a new kingdom in which children can play near snakes, swords will be beaten into ploughshares and the holy city of Jerusalem will be a beacon of faith to the nations. Gentiles will flock to learn of the true God, and contentment and plenty will be everyone's lot.

Christians have always held that the coming of the Messiah is a two-stage process. The incarnation, heralded by the Elijah-ministry of the Baptist, brought Jesus on to the world's stage. There the work of redemption was carried out by his death and resurrection, but the process is incomplete. The Messiah must come again to bring the messianic age to fulfilment. And once again, there must be an Elijah to prepare his way.

We, the Church, are called to be that Elijah, that new John the Baptist––often wrong and misguided, always sinful, but never quite forgetting to cry out in the wilderness of the world, 'Prepare the way of the Lord' (Luke 3:4).

PRAYER

Father, give to your people the grace they need, that by their words and their deeds they may prepare hearts and minds for the final coming of your Messiah in glory.

The SALVATION of the WORLD

Despite the fiery breath and terrible afflictions of drought that the two witnesses bring, their primary purpose is to call the world to repentance. This is signified by their dress, the sackcloth of penitence, but their testimony seems to have no greater effect than the judgments of God.

A great beast arises (v. 7), which will play a prominent part in the following chapters. Here, all we are told is that it successfully wars against the Church and destroys it. Those who stood in opposition to sin have themselves been judged guilty by the world, and their power has been declared impotent. The two witnesses lie dead and unburied in the streets of the great city, while all their opponents rejoice and even exchange gifts (vv. 9–10).

The city in which the witnesses die is a place of many meanings. It is not literally Jerusalem, for that lay ruined in John's day and he does not see its rebuilding on earth. Jerusalem next appears as the heavenly city. Yet it is Jerusalem in the sense that it is anywhere that murders the prophets of God (Matthew 23:37) and rejects his anointed. It is Egypt in that it is anywhere that imprisons the people of God, and Sodom in that it is wherever the law of God is flouted.

City of God, city of evil

The symbolism of the city is important in Revelation. Cities are where people live together, work together and grow together. They concentrate all that is best and worst in the human race. Human spirituality, creativity and community gather together and reinforce one another. Heaven itself, the very presence of God, will be seen as a city (21:2–4).

In cities today you will find the great churches and cathedrals, the art galleries, museums, theatres, cinemas and industries. You will also find the drug pushers and prostitutes, the child abusers and thieves. There you will find the poor ground into abject squalor and the rich insulated from reality by their wealth. You will find slums and shanty towns, rubbish heaps that provide food for the poor, wheelers and dealers, pimps and pickpockets. It is into the city that the wealth of the countryside flows, and from which, so often, little comes save demands for more.

It is here that the witnesses proclaimed the word of God, here that they prepared for the coming of the Lord, and here that they were defeated and died.

Resurrection power

But not for long. In a joyful parody of the time of persecution, their bodies lie for a mere three and a half days before they rise again and are transported to heaven (vv. 11–12). Then a final warning judgment falls, and the unexpected happens. The surviving majority (a startling reversal of the usual biblical idea of a small remnant) give glory to God (v. 13). In other words, they repent and are converted.

This phrase can really have no other meaning. In the Bible, to 'give glory to God' is to acknowledge him as Lord. In seeing the Church's triumph over death itself, the words of witness and the judgments of God at last have their effect. Some would argue that there is no true repentance here, merely the acknowledgment of God's power in the face of overwhelming evidence. But God's power has been displayed throughout the seals and trumpets without such an effect, and the response here is one of praise and worship.

The majority of the city's inhabitants declare their faith in the God who at last has brought about their salvation. Judgment alone cannot achieve this. The disasters of war, famine and disease, of spiritual and physical evil, should point to a reliance only on God. And so they do, but not without a proclamation of the gospel.

Even the words of the gospel itself, attractive though they are to so many, may stimulate only derision, anger and hatred. As the witnesses challenge the city of evil, they provoke persecution and enmity. Their message is seen as unworldly, idealistic, puerile, or whatever.

When those who proclaim, who declare the judgment and salvation of God, are themselves seen to triumph over death, however, then the words and the deeds of God strike home. Then there is repentance, faith and the reception of the gift of salvation itself.

✓ PRAYER

Father, may all who face persecution be strengthened by your promise of resurrection.

RESURRECTION HOPE

If 11:1–13 is the main message of the book of Revelation, to which the first ten chapters lead, and which much of the rest of the book elaborates, it may well be a good idea to take stock of the story so far.

John has written his book to the seven churches of Asia Minor, and through them to the whole Church everywhere. The message is that a time of persecution is approaching, and that this time is not to be seen as exceptional but as the normal experience of the Church. Indeed, John assumes that persecution is a sign of the Church's effective witness and its refusal to compromise with the sinful world.

The Church, by definition, lives in the end times, for the coming of Christ signals the final phase of God's plan of salvation for his rebellious creation. It does not matter whether that final phase of history is only a few months or many millennia in duration. It is not the length of the end times that signals their urgency, but the fact of the coming of Christ. Since the incarnation, God has been the coming one, whose victory is at hand.

In the light of that coming, the troubles of the world, be they natural disaster or the direct result of human sin, are a call to humanity to place its reliance on God the creator and saviour, and not only on human ability or achievement. It is this search for human self-sufficiency that is the root of human sinfulness and the basic meaning of idolatry—the worship of that which is not God.

The possibility of redemption has been opened to the world by the death and resurrection of Jesus, the Lamb who was slaughtered and who now shares the worship of God himself. Human destiny now depends on Christ and on the response of the world to him.

The suffering Church

The followers of Jesus have a key role in the world's response, for it is through their witness that redemption is offered. Their witness is the testimony of the Church, which interprets the travail of the world as the call to repentance, and which offers hope though faith in Christ. Such a testimony will find itself in opposition to the systems of the world, for they are founded on the human quest for self-reliance and the denial of God. As a result, the Church will find itself caught up in a conflict with those systems, and will suffer persecution and martrydom.

John, in fact, presents us with a picture of a Church composed entirely of martyrs. To be the Church is to suffer the fate of the Church's Lord, and to lie dead in the streets of the city that slew the Lamb. Does this mean that John really expects all Christians to be martyrs? Surely not. The language he uses is a vivid metaphor for the dedication to Christ that he does expect of the Church. There are to be no half measures about being a Christian. The Church is called to whole-hearted commitment to its Lord, and to bold proclamation of the gospel. Anything less earns the condemnation aimed at Laodicea and the other churches that were tempted to compromise the gospel.

In the same way, John probably does not expect a mass conversion to follow on a literal, visible resurrection of martyrs, but the Church's attitude of hope in the face of death itself is its most powerful witness. The overcoming of the fear of death, the denial of death's power to remove hope, is its greatest weapon. So too is the perpetual resurgence of the Church. In various times and places the Christian faith has apparently been stamped out, only to resurface. Resurrection is the cornerstone of Christian faith, and its continuing experience and testimony.

The hope of salvation for the world is the new message that the scroll brings when it is eaten by the prophet, and it is the centre of Revelation's message. Hope, not judgment, lies at the heart of the book.

John does not offer a detailed blueprint for the Church's witness, though he will hint at what issues that witness must address. In each time and place in which the Church finds itself, it must discover appropriate methods of mission and evangelism. Whatever they may be, loyalty to Jesus is the necessary presupposition of its mission. That mission will bear the hallmark of sacrifice and service which should be the characteristic of all who follow the Lamb.

REFLECT

What are the hallmarks of our culture and times?
What form should our witness take today?

GOD TAKES CHARGE

With the announcement of the three woes (8:13), John introduced a sense of deepening disaster, yet this disaster was overturned at the second woe, the sixth trumpet. To be sure, it brought torment to the earth, but it also introduced the scroll of prophecy, the testimony of the Church and the repentance of the inhabitants of the great city. The force of the woes began to fade. Now the final trumpet and third woe comes, and all that John records is the victory song of heaven (v. 15).

In this way he draws out the two sides of the triumph of God. It is disaster for all that opposes him: sin reaps its own reward, and, being allowed to run its full course, destroys itself. But this is not enough. Left to themselves, the forces of evil would be self-defeating, but they would also destroy the humanity that God seeks to save. The other side of the coin is the call to repentance, which, through the witness of the Church, negates the results of sin and throws open the gates of heaven.

That is what the seventh trumpet denotes (v. 15). God has won his victory, and for the forces of destruction it is the final woe, as the destroyers of the earth are destroyed. For the redeemed, however, it is the victory of God's mercy. The woe is not described in detail, for the emphasis has now shifted to the triumph of salvation, although we are not yet given any picture of that either. John saves his final vision of redemption for the end of the book. Before then, he still has much to say about the Church's conflict and the nature of evil's defeat. Instead, the end is interpreted to us through the loud voices (presumably of the four creatures before the throne) that hymn the victory.

Triumph song

The final victory is the moment when the kingdom of God swallows up all other reigns. Jesus announced the coming of the kingdom, and that kingdom was present wherever he was. It was found in his works and preaching and in the lives of those who chose to follow him. Despite this, it was never fully present. For Paul and the early Christians, the kingdom was mainly found in the future. It was the goal towards which they strove, and the inheritance promised to the children of God. Now the angelic council proclaims its arrival. There is no longer a conflict of different sovereignties, for God is acknowledged by all as the one and only King.

Since the message of Revelation is that God is in charge anyway, it may seem a bit strange that his ultimate triumph is described as the coming of his kingdom, or rule. There is a great difference, though, between a rule that is joyfully recognized by its subjects and one that is resisted and contested.

This kingdom is ruled by God and his Messiah, the two who are inseparable, who receive worship together and who reign together. Once again we see John's implicit recognition of the divinity of Christ. The one through whom God brought about salvation is seen in the end to be God himself. This is a strong corrective to the tendency, found both in the early church and in some spirituality today, to see God as a judge who has to be placated by the sacrifice of Jesus. Critics of Christianity often, and with some justification, lampoon this as a picture of God's delighting in the torture and death of his Son. Nothing could be further from the biblical vision of the God who takes the pain and sin of the world on himself. Jesus is God's Messiah, and the fact that both rule together reminds us that salvation is, from start to finish, the work of God, who was 'in Christ… reconciling the world to himself' (2 Corinthians 5:19).

In the same way, Revelation reminds us that the judgment of God is also the wrath of the Lamb (6:16), for judgment and salvation are inseparably linked. If we see the six trumpets and the events of 11:1–13 as paralleling each other, then we see the collision of God's judgment and his salvation, out of which salvation emerges triumphant. The worlds of heaven and earth merge, and out of them comes the new creation, a new heaven and earth, in which the kingdom of God takes up and transforms the sinful world of today.

In the light of this hope, the Church, while it lives in the reality of the time of judgment and persecution, the time of the six trumpets and the trampling of the holy city, nonetheless lives also by the light of the kingdom to come, the time of the seventh trumpet.

REFLECT

God's rule will swallow up all our systems of power and politics.
We need always to be aware that they are temporary and to strive
to live in the light of the coming kingdom.

The END of the FUTURE

Like the seven seals, the seven trumpets encapsulate all of history, and as the 24 elders add their voices to the praise of God, the worship of heaven builds to a crescendo.

It is a climax that signals the end of history. God is hailed as the one who was and who is, but no longer as the one who is to come (v. 16). The future to which the history of the world was moving has arrived, and has met its consummation in the presence of God. He has taken power and reigns, the forces of the world have had their day, and now all things have been brought together in the joyful acknowledgment of his rule. God is no longer the goal to which his people aspire but the continual presence in which they are to live.

Faithful servants

The judgment arrives, and it is first and foremost the time for rewarding the servants of God. As we might expect, these are the 'prophets' and the 'saints' (v. 18), the usual term for the people of God. They are also all who fear his name—in other words, those who repented at the fall of the city and the resurrection of the two witnesses. These are the people who had gloated over the destruction of the Church and sided with the beast from the pit of chaos in its war against the saints. Now, though, like the labourers in the vineyard (Matthew 20:1–16), they come late to receive the same reward as those who toiled all day.

Interpreters who see Revelation as a book that gloats over the downfall of the wicked (or who wish to gloat so themselves) tend to miss this point. The real triumph of God is not that evil is destroyed, for evil is self-destructive. His victory lies in the rescue of so many, for this chapter visualizes the salvation of most of humanity.

Answered prayer

At the breaking of the seventh seal, there was silence in heaven as the prayers of the saints were heard. Those prayers were answered in judgment. At the seventh trumpet, we see the same event from a different perspective, and hear the song of heaven. This too is a response to the prayers of the saints, to the daily prayer of all Christians: 'your kingdom come, your will be done...' (Matthew 6:10).

The difference between the result of the seals and the outcome of the sounding of the trumpets is found in the faithful witness of the Church. You could say that John provides alternative views of the progress of history. In the first series of seven judgments, we see the course of a sinful world that ignores all warnings. In the second, we see the outcome of a world that contains the leaven of the disciples of Jesus.

Destruction destroyed

Once the salvation of the many has been celebrated, the destroyers of the earth are themselves said to be destroyed (v. 18). The elders' song echoes the themes of Psalm 2, in which the king of Israel, God's anointed, triumphs over the nations. These nations will include those who do not repent, but the meaning is wider than merely a reference to sinful human beings.

The nature of the destroyers of the earth will become clearer as the book progresses, but we have already been given hints as to their identity. The forces of destruction, the beast, the riders unleashed by the first four seals, the wicked city—everything, in fact, that works against the intended destiny of creation—are the true enemy over which God triumphs and against which his followers are called to fight. These are the 'powers and principalities' (Ephesians 3:10), which include, but are greater than, the sins of individual people. With these opponents gone, nothing hides the presence of God from his creation, so the inner sanctuary of the heavenly temple is revealed to human sight. In the earthly temple of Old Testament times, the unapproachable nature of God was symbolized by the ark of the covenant. This was hidden in the central sanctuary, the holy of holies, and was seen only once a year by the high priest. Now the reality for which it stood is revealed for all eternity.

✗ PRAYER

Father, thank you that nothing can come between you and your people, for we have access to your presence through Jesus Christ.

49 REVELATION 12:1–6

COSMIC CONFLICT

The beginning of chapter 12 comes as a surprise; there is no obvious link with the previous chapter. The writer has twice taken us up to the end of history, and twice he has drawn back from describing it. In the first series of judgments (the seven seals), the Church was assured of spiritual security and ultimate triumph. In the second series (the trumpets), the Church was revealed as the means of bringing salvation to those who would otherwise perish. Now John backpedals again, to restart the story of the conflict between the forces of destruction and the people of God. Chapters 12—22 are effectively the first half of the book repeated in detail in the light of God's plan, which has now been made clear in chapter 11. Indeed, 12:1—14:5 is a detailed explanation of chapter 11, the contents of the Lamb's scroll.

To achieve this explanation, John uses images that were well known to the world in which he lived, including stock pictures from apocalyptic literature and a myth which was widespread in ancient times.

The mother and the serpent

In Greek legend, the great serpent (Greek: *drakon*) Python sought to destroy the goddess Leto because it was foretold that her son would be the slayer of the serpent. Leto was rescued by Poseidon, god of the sea, and gave birth to Apollo, who duly killed Python.

In the Babylonian myth of creation, the sea monster Tiamat was killed by Marduk, the god of light and son of Damkina. The links with the sea are seen in Revelation's dragon, who breathes out a flood of water (12:15), calls a great beast out of the sea (13:1) and, like Tiamat, knocks a third of the stars from the sky (12:4).

From ancient Persia came the story of the dragon Azhi Dahaka, who was fought by Fire, son of Ahura, the god of light. In Egypt, Isis was pursued by the dragon Typhon, slayer of her husband, Osiris. In time, Isis gave birth to Horus, who destroyed the dragon.

John's readers would have been familiar with at least some of the variations on this ancient pagan myth, and with the Old Testament passages (see below) that also make use of it. The point is that the hope of salvation from evil and chaos, which such stories embodied, has now become reality—a reality known to the Church and shared through its witness with the whole world.

Baptizing the pagan

Some Christians are disturbed at finding echoes of pagan thought in the Bible. This attitude even leads fringe groups such as the Jehovah's Witnesses to ignore Christmas (once a pagan winter festival) and forbid the pagan practice of birthday celebrations.

The biblical writers are wiser. In the God of Israel they see the fulfilment of the hopes of the world, the reality to which the myths of old were shadows and pointers. Genesis takes the story of the flood, with its affinities to ancient Babylonian tales, and uses it as the vehicle for a lesson on sin and redemption. Isaiah can use the story of the woman in labour and the defeat of the serpent (Isaiah 26:17—27:1) as a picture of God's victory over evil. John can use images that struck chords in the minds and hearts of his readers and, through them, state the purpose of the people of God.

The point is that the hopes and aspirations of the world are not a threat to be avoided but a dream that finds its waking reality in Christ. We celebrate the winter festival (in the northern hemisphere) as the feast of the one who brings light to the darkness of the world, and warmth to hearts locked in the coldness of sin. We each celebrate our own birth, for life is the gift of God, and our coming into the world is a part of his work of creation, the opportunity of a life lived in his love and service.

We can read again the myths of the conflict between chaos and order, light and darkness, and know that the struggle has truly taken place. God in Christ has confronted the forces of evil and defeated them through the cross.

We can also be encouraged to seize hold of the language and the stories of the cultures in which the Church lives and serves, and to use them as vehicles for the gospel. We can be encouraged to use our imagination and creativity in the task of witnessing to the world.

PRAYER

Father, open our eyes to the desire of the world for hope, that we might share the hope that is ours in Jesus Christ.

MOTHER *of* SALVATION

If John has used a pagan myth for the shape of his story of the dragon and the woman, he has thoroughly baptized it by peopling it with biblical characters. A good analogy that has been put forward is that of a modern political cartoon. For instance, Red Riding Hood and the wolf may be drawn with the faces of politicians. The message is easily understood: one is being represented as naive and trusting, the other as a menace to his career or policies.

The glorious woman in labour is drawn from Eve, the mother of all (Genesis 3:16), whose offspring will smite the serpent's head (Genesis 3:15). She is the woman who brings forth the Messiah (Isaiah 7:14), and, more importantly, she is Zion who brings forth a son and many children (Isaiah 66:7–8). In other words, the woman represents the people of God; she is crowned (the mark of the saints) with the twelve stars of the patriarchs and apostles (v. 1), from whom comes the Messiah, who will defeat the serpent.

The woman has been seen as Mary, the mother of Jesus, and that is a fair interpretation, so long as Mary is herself representative of the people of God. She has been seen too as the Church, but that is fair only if the Church is recognized as being one with the entire story of Israel. She is, in fact, the whole historical people of God, whose pilgrimage through the centuries has resulted in the birth of the Messiah.

His story

John reminds us that neither the Church nor the individual Christian lives in a self-contained moment of time. The troubles and triumphs, temptations and virtues that we experience from day to day are part of a story that goes back to the dawn of recorded time and beyond. Through that time, God has been active in the world, bringing his people to the point where he could become one of them. And he has remained active since then, working out the consequences of the incarnation in the lives and deeds of his followers.

We are a part of that story, bound to it by faith and experience. It is our story that is being told in the symbolism of the woman and the dragon. We have been taken up into the story of God and his Christ, and have become players in the drama of salvation.

Perfectly wicked

Against the woman comes the dragon (v. 3), with seven heads and seven crowns. Seven, the number of completeness, suggests that this creature is the perfect epitome of evil, so it comes as no surprise to find that this is Satan, the devil himself (12:9). He is red, the colour of persecution and bloodshed, and, with his crowns, he claims kingship in competition with God and the saints. Like the greatest of the beasts that opposed the people of God in the book of Daniel, the serpent has ten horns, the symbols of power (Daniel 7:7, 20)—for, make no mistake, evil is powerful.

The dragon's tail knocks a third of the stars to earth (v. 4). These stars are probably other angels who follow Satan in rebellion (see 12:7). Evil is deceitful and seductive, and drags others along with it. Some interpreters suggest that the stars are those of God's people who have been led astray, both the rebellious Israelites of the Old Testament and also Christians who are tempted to go the way of the world. Certainly, anything that can drag angels out of heaven should be taken seriously as a threat! John's fear for the Church is that it may underestimate that threat, and, in speaking words of compromise, may find that it has been led away from the gospel and been caught by the sweep of the dragon's tail.

In our day, the devil is out of fashion, and evil itself is doubted. We prefer to speak of fallibility, of misdirected potential. In the face of unreasoning destructiveness, of the negation of creativity, hope and life, we are dumb. Yet the 20th century alone saw such evil as to beggar description. Call it the devil or not, it exists and it is strong.

Yet there is one who is destined to break its power, and in the end to defeat it utterly.

PRAYER

Lord, when we are confronted with the reality of evil,
keep before us the other vision—of your life and grace,
of your goodness and victory.

GOSPEL STORY

Here, the life, death, resurrection and ascension of Jesus are covered in just two verses. Despite Satan's attempt to destroy him, he evades defeat and ascends triumphantly to heaven. There is no doubt that the woman's child is Christ, for he is to rule the nations with a rod of iron (v. 5). We have already met this reference to Psalm 2:9 in the letter to Thyatira (2:27) and will see it again at 19:15 when Christ returns in triumph. John, who seems often to have the Hebrew Bible in mind, deliberately quotes the Greek translation, the Septuagint. There the word for 'rule' is literally 'shepherd'. Once again we see the ambiguity of Christ's victory. The iron rod may well be an instrument of discipline and wrath, but it can just as well be the defensive weapon of the shepherd-protector. Which it will be depends on the response of the nations, in which the Church's witness will play no small part.

Short story

Why, though, is the subject of the four Gospels condensed into two brief sentences? Firstly, John's intended readers are Christians, who know the story well. It is the foundation of their faith and the reason for their existence. They need no more extensive reminder.

Secondly, the story being told is the tale of God's people and their conflict with Satan. To be sure, the hope of victory and the meaning of their history centres on Christ, but it is their task and calling that is in view.

Defeated dragon

The story of Jesus is portrayed as an escape from the dragon, yet from an earthly perspective, there was no escape at all. The conflict with evil that began with the temptation in the wilderness ended at Calvary. From the viewpoint of heaven, the picture is vastly different. It was through his death that the forces of evil were defeated—a defeat that was made apparent by the resurrection, and leads the Church to worship Christ as the Lord of glory.

Protected people

Meanwhile the people of God remain under his protection. The woman, who disappears from the pagan myth after giving birth, remains the centre of attention here. Like ancient Israel, she is kept safe in the wilderness, the place of pilgrimage and meeting with God (v. 6). This safety is no more a physical protection than any of the other promises of God's protection that Revelation gives. The period of 1260 days is once again Daniel's three and a half times, the time of persecution and spiritual warfare. That time begins as soon as the child is snatched away to heaven, that is, from the day of Jesus' resurrection. Once again, John makes it clear that the present times are the time of tribulation, which continue throughout the Church's history. The image of the woman's nourishment in the desert is a repeat of the sealing of the 144,000 (7:3–8) and the measuring of the inner temple (11:1–2): it is in a place prepared by God. The spiritual security of the people of God is assured. They cannot be defeated in the ultimate sense, but they can and will know tribulation. This, after all, is only to be expected. Jesus' escape from the dragon was by way of the cross, and so may be that of his followers.

Desert refuge

In the Bible, the desert is an ambiguous place. It is where Israel meets God, but it is also the place of testing. There the Israelites worshipped the golden calf (Exodus 32:4) and complained about God. There God led them for 40 years until he had forged a people of faith. It was to the desert that Jesus was led by the Spirit for his own time of testing (Mark 1:13). The Church never has an option about the testing. It can be challenged by persecution or by being ignored, by complacency or by decline. The test is in the response: are we strengthened and inspired, thrown into greater reliance on God, or do we despair?

John's image for God's security is therefore not a passive one. To be kept by God is to be continually challenged and made to grow in faith and devotion. Hence the woman is not merely kept, but nourished. God's security is not stagnation but growth.

PRAYER

Lord, nourish us with your word and your body and blood,
that we might grow in faith and grace, and, in our desert
pilgrimage, be forged into your people.

The DEVIL'S DEMOTION

The account of the child's escape from the dragon is not all that John
has to tell us about the significance of the coming of the Christ-child.
Just as chapters 12—14 are an explanation of chapter 11, here verses
7–9 explain verse 5 and are in turn interpreted by verses 10–12,
before the story of the woman and the dragon resumes at verse 13.
Once again we see the complex structure of Revelation, with visions
within visions within visions, all tied into a whole to present a dazzling
message that strives to reach beyond the limits of mere words.

War in heaven

War breaks out in heaven (v. 7); the devil/dragon and his followers
are expelled by Michael, commander of the heavenly host, and come
crashing down to earth (v. 9). John's image is influenced by the
angelic battle in Daniel 10:13 and 21, where Michael struggles against
the angels of Persia and Greece, and Daniel 12:1, which looks to a
final battle between Michael and the rebel angels at the end of the
world. The victory, however, is not really that of Michael, even though,
as the guardian angel of Israel, he was the most important angel in
Jewish tradition. The acclamation of victory that follows in Revelation
12:10–12 makes this clear. Once again, what John hears explains the
significance of what he sees. It is the victory of Christ, shared with the
martyr Church, which is the defeat of Satan.

In visionary language, John is describing the consequences of the
appearance of the child. Through his death and resurrection, Jesus
has conquered Satan's power, and there is no longer any place for the
dragon in heaven.

Devil in heaven

The notion that there ever was a place for Satan in heaven strikes us
as strange, but there are two factors that help us understand the idea.

Firstly, 'heaven' is the spiritual realm, not the final destiny of the
saints and redeemed creation. It is the sphere in which the spiritual
significance of earthly events is played out, so it has its dark side. By
showing the dragon (identified with the serpent of Genesis 3, the
bringer of sin and deceit) expelled from heaven, John is making a

profound point. The coming of Christ, and above all his death and resurrection, has already scored the decisive victory against the forces of darkness. They are not yet fully defeated, but any hope they may have of eventual success has been removed. The consequences of the rebellion in the garden of Eden are being undone, and a renewed humanity is to be allowed once again into the presence of God. The serpent's head is crushed underfoot, and its power removed.

The second factor is found in the evolution of Jewish and Christian thought. 'Satan' means 'adversary', and in the first biblical appearances where he is named as such, he is part of the heavenly council of God. His job is that of prosecutor of sinners. He is the one who points out human error and demands justice for it (Job 1—2; Zechariah 3:1). In later thought, Satan became the adversary of all that was good.

With the coming of Jesus, forgiveness and mercy rule supreme. There is no longer any place in heaven for one who points up sin, whether out of a desire for justice or from a love of trouble, for the price of sin has been paid.

Just mercy

We have to be careful, though, to avoid suggesting that Christ's sacrifice somehow acts against the justice of God. The biblical term 'justice (or righteousness) of God' refers more to his faithfulness to his promises than simply to a concept of legal exactness. Salvation is the work of the one God from beginning to end, as he remains true to his promise of mercy. The one who is to come with salvation is, after all, God himself. Indeed, the work of salvation is in line with God's justice as it is presented in the Bible. God's judgment as it often appears in the Old Testament is assumed to have a bias towards forgiveness. (See Jonah 3—4 for one of the best, and most humorous, examples of this.) Mercy is always on offer to the penitent, and finds its consummation in the cross of Christ, where the incarnate God bears the burden of human sin on his creatures' behalf.

√ PRAYER

*Lord of mercy, let us never be deceived into thinking
that we are beyond the reach of your forgiveness.*

WINGS *of* EAGLES

The fall of Satan from heaven marks the arrival of salvation and the kingdom of God. This does not refer to the final victory, but to the exaltation of Jesus as Messiah. He is now enthroned in heaven, having struck the decisive blow against sin and evil on the cross. We can tell this simply by the fact that these verses obviously comment on the expulsion of the dragon from heaven by the enthronement of the woman's child in verse 5.

Nonetheless, the cry of praise in heaven (vv. 10–12) has a sense of looking forward to the final coming of God's kingdom. It has been made a reality by Jesus. By his authority the accuser has been cast down, and can no longer charge the followers of Jesus with their sins. The coming of the kingdom is about wiping away sin through the death of Jesus.

Victorious Church

The Church shares in Jesus' victory, and no longer needs to fear condemnation (Romans 8:1). Once again, though, we are reminded of the nature of the Church's victory. The people of God can overcome Satan; indeed, they already have overcome him by the blood of the Lamb. On the other hand, this overcoming is not an easy 'claiming of victory', which some would have us believe. The devil is defeated but not destroyed. He has come down to earth in vicious anger, and resisting him takes the very blood of the saints (vv. 12, 17).

It is by their faithful witness, their refusal to be daunted in the face of death, that they triumph. To conquer by the blood of the Lamb is to share his death, and so gain his resurrection (v. 11). The suffering of the saints is a sign of victory, not defeat.

Heaven, then, can rejoice; but woe to the earth, to both believer and unbeliever, for the fight goes on there until the full total of martyrs has been attained, and the full number of sinners redeemed (6:9–11; 11:13).

Continuing conflict

Evil has been emptied of ultimate significance by the cross, but its power is still real in the here and now. The dragon falls to earth and seeks to wipe out the people of God (the woman), but she is given eagle's wings to flee into the desert. Since verses 7–12 are essentially a repetition of verse 5 in greater detail, verses 13–14 repeat verse 6, stressing that the people of God are to be kept safe from the spiritual consequences of Satan's attacks during the three and a half years of persecution. The eagle draws attention again to the Exodus theme (Exodus 19:4; Deuteronomy 32:11–12), when God bore his people from Egypt on eagles' wings, and fed them with manna.

Unable to shake the true security of God's people, the dragon heads off to make war on the rest of her children—the rest, that is, in distinction from Jesus, for he is the firstborn of many children of God (Romans 8:29). Verse 17 repeats and summarizes verses 13–16 and stresses that the threat from the devil does not lie in the past, but is a present reality. It is now that he hunts around, seeking whom he may devour (1 Peter 5:8). Those other children, the Church, are described as the ones who are obedient to God and who are faithful in their proclamation of the gospel.

Redeemed humanity

Chapter 12 is dominated by the images of Eve and the serpent, and this gives us a further insight into the nature of the people of God. The woman does not represent merely the Church, nor even all of Israel. She is the symbol of the new humanity that God calls into being through the offer of salvation. The Church has a crucial role in the new humanity, by bringing to faith the many who hear and see its testimony. It can never claim, though, to be all that God will save. As the closing chapters of Revelation will reveal, that number is vastly greater than we may sometimes dare to hope.

PRAYER

'Those who wait for the Lord shall renew their strength,
they shall mount up with wings like eagles' (Isaiah 40:31).
Lord, may it be so.

The ANTICHRIST

In his war against the saints, the dragon calls forth a pair of beastly allies. They call to mind the land monster Behemoth, and the sea creature Leviathan, whom God fights in Job 40:19 and Psalm 74:14. Together with the dragon, they will form a blasphemous parody of the holy Trinity.

The first of these allies is a beast that is summoned from the sea— that is, from the waters of the bottomless pit, the place of chaos (11:7). The beast is a composite figure, drawing on the description of the four beasts in Daniel 7. Daniel's beasts represented four successive empires of increasing wickedness. The beast in Revelation combines the characteristics of Daniel's creature, having, like the dragon, seven heads and ten horns (13:1), the signs of the devil's power. It is therefore to be seen as a kind of incarnation of the dragon. It has apparently suffered death, but lives again (13:3). As the devil's parody of Jesus, it is the antichrist, the vehicle of Satan in the world. At the same time, the echoes of the Daniel passage suggest that it has imperial claims, followed by the whole earth and acclaimed for its power.

Evil empire

John's readers at this point would surely have recognized the Roman empire. Like the beast, imperial power came out of the sea, its ships, bearing officials and soldiers, rising over the western horizon. The monstrous power that held the allegiance of virtually all the known world was based in Rome. It called for unswerving allegiance, and even worship. From the Christian point of view, the beast demanded what could only be offered to God, and so it carries blasphemous names (13:1). We are not told what these names were, but they could be found in imperial inscriptions and on Roman coins: the claims of emperors to divinity, and the demand of worship offered both to the emperor and to the spirit of Rome. The emperor Domitian, it was said, demanded to be addressed as 'Lord and God'.

This does not exhaust the significance of the beast, however. In chapter 17 we shall see Rome riding the beast, for the beast is not Rome alone. By combining the four empires of Daniel into one composite creature, John signals that here is not simply a single power, but the concept of empire itself. Here is the machinery of worldly power—armies and politicians, oppression, injustice and cruelty. Here is the ambition of states when they march over the borders of weaker neighbours to bring slavery, oppression and genocide. Here is greed, hitching a ride on the coat-tails of power, looking for opportunities to loot and annexe. It is the city we met at 11:8 and will meet again in Babylon/Rome. With its apparently invincible armies, glittering wealth and universal rule, the whole known world followed the Rome-beast, besotted by its power. Yet, says John, this adulation is nothing less than the worship of the beast's master, Satan himself.

Dangerous blessing

From John's point of view, Rome was the current manifestation of antichrist, though many Christians, such as those of Sardis and Laodicea, would have disagreed with him. Rome provided prosperity (for some) and peace, at least according to the imperial propaganda machine, which extolled the benefits of the *pax Romana*, the Roman peace. John, like other perceptive writers, knew that this was not the whole story. Such peace as there was, was won at the cost of freedom and of enforced conformity. The Roman writer Tacitus gives one of his characters a telling saying: 'Rome makes a desert and calls it peace' (*Agricola* 30.5). Prosperity depended upon acknowledging Rome's supremacy and, above all, its divinely granted right to rule.

How could those who proclaimed the Lordship of Christ bow the knee to another 'divinely appointed' lord? How could those who worshipped the living God burn the official offering of incense to Caesar?

The idea that antichrist is not a single individual, located in a comfortably distant future, but a pervading spirit found in the here and now, is not unique to Revelation. Another John—the writer of 1 John 2:18, 22; 4:3 and 2 John 7—had already made the same point. These times, wherever the Church finds itself, are the end times, and the beast may be encountered here and now.

PRAYER

Father, give us the discernment, and the courage, to recognize the beast when it appears.

UNDERMINING EVIL

The beast makes great claims for itself, and so speaks blasphemy against God, the one true ruler of all (vv. 5–6). Ironically, it is God who allows it to do so. The use of the passive, 'it was allowed' (v. 5), is a typical Jewish way of speaking of God, originally used because the name of God was too holy to be spoken. It passed into Jewish and Christian writing as an accepted way of describing God's actions.

The beast is seen to be the same one that we met at 11:7, and it makes war on the Church for 42 months (v. 7; 11:2). No doubt, it and its master see this as a sign of their own power. In fact, it is part of God's plan of salvation, in which the Church, witnessing in opposition to the antichrist, suffers the martyrdom that brings conversion to the world (v. 7).

Temple of God

The beast slanders (the basic meaning of 'blaspheme') and derides the dwelling of God, which turns out to mean people who dwell in heaven (v. 6). This is, in fact, the Church on earth, whom it wars against and conquers. The image is of the people of God as his living temple (11:2; 1 Peter 2:5) within whom he dwells. They are physically on earth, and are called to serve God there, but their true homeland is in heaven (Philippians 3:20), and in Christ they have a share in that final dwelling even now. In the knowledge of that eternal destiny, they must be prepared to face with endurance and faith either captivity or martyrdom as required.

The authority of the beast is also permitted by God, and for the same reason. Satan may believe that he has imbued the beast with his own power (13:2), but in the end such power is exercised only because it fits God's purposes (compare John 19:10–11). This raises the question of why God lets such evil exist. The answer that Revelation presents (and any such answer must in the end be inadequate) is that God allows evil to run its course so that he might bring good out of it, and let the evil destroy itself. Such an answer, of course, can only make sense if, in the end, good will triumph. John affirms that the decisive battle has already taken place on the cross, and that the final consummation will follow in due course.

Eternal plan

The stark choice which is presented between the worship of the beast and of God divides the inhabitants of the world. They are either in the Lamb's book of life or they devote themselves to earthly power (v. 8). In the Greek of verse 8, the most obvious meaning is that it is the Lamb who was slaughtered from the foundation of the world, rather than that the names were in the book from the beginning. NRSV has altered the word order (which is grammatically possible) in order to bring verse 8 into line with 17:8, which does apply the phrase to the names in the book of life.

It is better to go with the more obvious meaning wherever possible, however, and we should see here a reference to the eternal nature of God's plan of salvation. The death of Jesus was not an emergency measure, but a part of God's plan from the beginning. Salvation for sinners has always been his intention.

In the light of 17:8, though, we are still left with the uneasy image of a book of the redeemed which appears to have been finalized before time began. At the same time, John is clear that repentance is open to all, for otherwise the Church would not need to witness and suffer. The names in the book of life can be removed (3:5) and in 21:24 the rebellious kings of the earth appear effectively to have been added to the book. The notion of writing in the book before the foundation of the world is not about strict predestination, any more than the Lamb was literally slain before the world began. Both verses (13:8 and 17:8) stress the same point. Salvation is part of God's eternal purpose, that Christ should die in order to offer a way for sinners to return to God.

This is not mere theory, says John; it is happening now, in the present age, so give heed (v. 9)! Persecution will result in imprisonment and death (v. 10). This is a deliberate echo of Jeremiah 15:2; but there it is a threat of punishment for rebellious Judah, while here it is the consequence of faithfulness, which must be shown in patient suffering, the essence of the martyrs' witness. NRSV takes the phrase about death by the sword to mean a banning of violence by Christians (the Greek is very obscure), but the reference to Jeremiah makes this unlikely.

PRAYER

Father, we praise you for the love that will not let us go but plans salvation from the beginning of creation.

FALSE PROPHET

As if the beast from the sea, the 'incarnation' of Satan, were not enough, another beast arises. This one comes from the earth (v. 11), which actually helped the woman against the dragon (12:15–16), and its appearance is far from fearsome. It has horns like a lamb. To a casual glance, then, it may seem helpful and benign and may even be mistaken for Christ, but its voice betrays its true nature.

False religion

By this stage, readers familiar with the sayings of Jesus might well be expecting a false prophet, for the Lord had linked the rise of such deceivers with the appearance of false messiahs (Mark 13:21–22). Indeed, the second beast is henceforth called the 'false prophet' (16:13; 19:20; 20:10). Hence, unlike the true Lamb's seven horns, it has two, the number of (false) witness. It arranges miracles and calls the world to worship the first beast (vv. 12–14).

It would have taken John's readers no time at all to recognize the apparatus of the imperial cult—the state religion with its temples to the genius of Caesar and the goddess Roma. The second beast's miracles reflect some of the gimmickry that was actually used either to impress the gullible or to lend drama to the celebrations of the cult. The statue of the beast in verse 15 reminds us of the statue in Daniel 3, and would call to mind the great statue of Domitian in Ephesus. The satanic parody of the Holy Trinity is now complete. The dragon is pretender to the throne of God. The beast which is antichrist bears the marks of death and resurrection. The false prophet mocks the work of the Holy Spirit by directing worship towards Satan and his beastly manifestation.

The second beast is a deadly threat to the lives of those who do not worship the imperial power. At the time when John was writing, persecution was probably slight and sporadic, but when it came, it was most likely focused on the emperor cult. A simple test of loyalty to the emperor was to burn a pinch of incense at his altar. Failure to do so was treasonable, but compliance was a denial of Jesus, the one true Lord.

No doubt, some of John's readers thought nothing of such acts of loyalty to the empire. They wanted to be good citizens; they could point to the divine origin of the state (Romans 13:1–7) and to the non-existence of idols (1 Corinthians 8:4). This was neither effective witness to Christ nor spiritually harmless, however, for behind the glitter of the empire lay the deadly reality of spiritual evil.

There was also a mundane economic incentive to comply with the state religion. While there was no literal ban on dealing with those who did not join in the imperial cult, failure to participate could affect one's business (v. 17). Pagan temples guaranteed trade deals, hosted merchant guilds and formed a deep-seated part of the fabric of society. Withdrawal from that part of life could affect the business interests and the social life of Christians.

There were therefore apparently good reasons for Christians to conform to social and religious expectations. They would avoid threat to their lives, they would avoid social and economic disaster, and they could justify it all with a theological argument.

John's reply is to extrapolate the present situation. What will they do if, in parody of the sealing of the saints, the beast demands that all be marked with the sign of his ownership (v. 16)? Ownership marks were not unknown. Slaves could be branded, loyal soldiers bore tattoos or brands of their legion, and some pagan devotees bore brand marks of their cult. The mark of the beast is a metaphorical one (though the economic implications were real), but is nonetheless true. To go along with imperial worship is to swear loyalty to that which opposes God. The time to stand fast is now. There can be no compromise with any power which demands the honour that is rightly due to God.

Pressure

Pressure to conform to the world's expectations has always been the Church's greatest temptation, and it has often yielded. Discerning the point at which to resist is never easy, but it is necessary (Romans 12:2). Christians must tread a fine line between adapting the gospel to a given time and place and losing sight of it altogether.

PRAYER

Lord, grant us discernment, to know your will and to distinguish it from the demands of the world.

The MARK of the BEAST

We have so far ignored one characteristic of the beast that is obviously important to John since he mentions it twice: it has received a mortal wound, but lives (13:12). Obviously, this is Satan's mocking version of the death and resurrection of Jesus, but can we say any more than that? The clue to understanding John's symbol comes in the last verse of the chapter, where the mark of the beast borne by its worshippers is said to be the number of a human being. There are many possible interpretations of this mark, but there is one that is particularly compelling.

Number games

In the ancient world, there were no special symbols for numbers, such as the Arabic system that we use. Instead, letters of the alphabet were used, so that a = 1, b = 2, j = 10, k = 20 and so on. By adding together the letters of a name, a number could be arrived at, which was held to carry a description of the character or fortune of the individual. This process of number substitution is called *gematria*. It so happens that if the Greek form of 'Nero Caesar' is written in Hebrew characters, it adds up to 666. If the Greek word for 'beast' is put into Hebrew letters, it also adds up to 666. In fact, there are various other numbers that could be derived from Nero's name, but this one has more symbolic resonance. It is one short of 777, the triple number of perfection. Thus, the number of the beast is that of an imperfect trinity.

All this may seem a bit far-fetched to us, but in John's day *gematria* was a popular way of interpreting names, finding correlations between them and making coded references to people. There is a well-known piece of graffiti at Pompeii, which reads, 'I love her whose name is 545.' The woman in question would have known who was meant, but few others would. John obviously expects his readers to recognize the number of the beast. The fact that the number is derived from a Hebrew version of a Greek word is not a problem, since we know from other sources that this sort of cross-language puzzling went on. In fact, there is a document in Aramaic that uses precisely this formula for Nero. John probably expected his readers already to be familiar with the significance of the number, even if most of them knew no Hebrew.

Fatal wound

Can we be sure it was Nero? At least one early copyist of Revelation was certain, as he replaced 666 with 616, the number of the Latin form of Nero transliterated into Hebrew. In the passage itself, the wound of the beast suggests that the identification was correct. Nero committed suicide in AD68, but his death was widely thought to be a ruse. A legend quickly grew up that he was in hiding and would eventually return, perhaps at the head of a Parthian army, to reclaim his throne or to inflict punishment on the empire that had turned against him. (The Senate had declared him an enemy of the people.) This idea was particularly widespread in Asia Minor, which had suffered little at Nero's hands, and where he had been a popular emperor.

The death of Nero seemed to have dealt a fatal blow to the empire. It led to the 'year of four emperors' (AD68–69) as civil war broke out in a struggle for the throne, yet the empire survived and carried on even stronger than before. Vespasian, fresh from putting down the Jewish revolt in Judea, brought stability and renewed prosperity. So, for John, the myth of the returning Nero becomes a symbol for the empire's ability to survive disaster and come back renewed. At the same time, Nero is a fitting symbol for all that is bad about the beast. Not only was he a tyrant whose excesses were too much for the Romans themselves, he was the first great persecutor of Christians. When rumour attributed the great fire of Rome (AD64) to him, Nero found the Christians a handy scapegoat and executed many with a savagery that drew the sympathy even of the bloodthirsty Roman mob.

The image of the antichrist, then, is one which can be summed up in a particular individual, but which is far more than one person. In the same way, we speak of Hitler and thereby encompass all the atrocities of the Nazi regime, whether they were carried out at his direct order or not.

PRAYER

Father, uphold all those of your people throughout the world who face the spirit of the beast and suffer for their faith.

NAMING *the* BEASTS

If we are right in seeing the beast of Revelation and its false prophet as a system rather than an individual, whether Nero or some other, what are we say about its identity? Was John referring only to Rome? It seems very unlikely, especially in the light of what he writes later, in chapter 17. The beast is any power system that gives itself a status due only to God. The second beast is any system of belief and worship that bolsters the claims of the first beast. It is the religious and philosophical justification of injustice, oppression and idolatry. It is the propagandist who speaks reasonable words in support of wrong.

Naming names

Throughout the Church's history, the image of the beast has been used to condemn the opponents of Revelation's interpreters. Protestants have identified the beast with the Pope or the Catholic church. Catholics portrayed Luther and Protestantism as the antichrist. Both of these should seem equally shocking to Christians today, yet similar claims continue to be made in both religion and politics. Ronald Reagan's infamous description of the USSR as an 'evil empire' drew on the same tradition, while America is described as the 'Great Satan' by Islamicist propagandists. In the 'war against terror' that has marred the start of the 21st century, similar apocalyptic language is bandied about by all concerned.

If John's dreadful warning about the beast is to be heeded, it has to be more than a handy playground insult. The main characteristic of the beast is that it claims the allegiance that only God can command. That must surely be our starting point if we are to apply it to our own age. Some candidates immediately suggest themselves. We have already mentioned the Nazis. We could speak also of Cambodia's Khmer Rouge regime, and the Stalinist rule of Russia, in each of which the state demanded total control, complete obedience. In more recent years, unquestioning self-sacrifice has marked terrorist groups, which demand complete dedication to an ideal that most religions would regard as perversion, at the very least.

These are obvious examples of the beast's modern incarnations.

They are also safely distant from the lives of most Western Christians. Surely, though, the beast's claims are at times felt much closer to home. An uncharitable newspaper once described a Christian politician as someone who would never let his faith get in the way of his politics. Whether or not it was true in his case, it points up the danger very well. There is a temptation to accept the claims of institutions close to home as reasonable and normal. They need to be subjected to close scrutiny, for quite often they are claiming too much. It is salutary to remember that the beast may seem to be slain, only to rise up again.

Seductive words

If state and society carry within them the possibility of manifesting the spirit of antichrist, so do religion and ideology. Karl Marx's main criticism of religion was that it was used to give divine sanction to an unjust *status quo*. The most disturbing thing about the second beast is that it looks like a lamb. Even the Church can become the false prophet when it preaches support for the establishment or nation before it preaches Christ. John probably has in mind those in his own churches, like the Nicolaitans and Jezebel, who are anxious to justify compromise. Perhaps the church's greatest sin has been when it has allowed itself to be part of the system of government to the exclusion of criticizing the world.

In a similar way, secular ideology speaks the seductive words of the false prophet. In today's Western culture, it is normal, reasonable and sensible to assume that Christian faith has nothing to offer. The church and its leadership are portrayed as either bigoted and intolerant or ridiculous, mostly harmless and quite irrelevant. No good reason is given, but then there need be no reason: as long as the words of the dragon are heeded, the false prophet has done its work well.

The only cure is to keep our eyes fixed firmly on Jesus Christ, and to follow closely in the steps of the Lamb; to speak out against all that opposes God, and to proclaim the gospel of Christ before all else.

PRAYER

*Lord, forgive us for those times when the Church
has mistaken earthly power for your kingdom,
and thus compromised with the beast.*

HOLY WAR

Satan's trinity of evil presents a formidable force, but ranged against them is a greater one. John next sees the Lamb standing on Mount Zion, the symbolic place of God's presence and salvation (Joel 2:32; Micah 4:6–7; Isaiah 24:21–23; Psalm 2:5–6). With him are the 144,000 who make up his holy army.

Most commentators assume that this vision refers to the final triumph of Christ over the beast, but this is unlikely. The Church that stands with him is described as the numbered host of the fighting people of God (7:4–8) rather than the countless multitude of the final kingdom (7:9). Moreover, they are the firstfruits—the first instalment of the harvest to follow (see Deuteronomy 26:1–11). Through their witness many more will be brought into the kingdom of God (11:13). This is not a vision of the end, but of the status of the persecuted, witnessing Church.

Heartland

In opposition to the followers of the beast, the people of God are marked with his name (v. 1). They belong to him and are safely installed on Mount Zion. They are not literally in Jerusalem, of course, any more than they are literally in heaven. They are all over the world, and they are encouraged and buoyed up by a voice from heaven (v. 2). It is the voice of God that they hear, sounding like that of the risen Christ (1:15) mingled with the thunder of the presence of God (4:5) and the music of heaven (5:8–9). They sing already the song of heaven (v. 3), although it is meaningless to the world that follows the beast. It is a song that comes from the knowledge of God, who has gained their salvation at great cost and will not let them go.

The fact that the praises and the song of Christ's army take place before the heavenly throne shows where the heart and true life of God's people lie. In fact, in Revelation, the praises of God always take place in heaven, until heaven and earth are made anew (chs. 21—22). This is not to suppose that John thinks worship can't take place on earth; indeed, some commentators see the whole book as a liturgical act of worship! It is rather that all worship joins the worshipper with the praises and prayers of heaven. Worship launched from earth lands in the presence of God himself.

Like a mighty army

One of the most misunderstood verses in Revelation is surely the description of the 144,000 as virgins who are undefiled by women (v. 4). Is the Church really only made up of men? Are women defiling? In fact, this is an image taken from the regulations for holy war in the Old Testament (1 Samuel 21:5; compare Deuteronomy 23:9–10). Sexual intercourse, while good, was seen as making the participants temporarily unclean as far as participation in worship was concerned. Therefore, those who went to fight God's wars were expected to abstain from sex during the time of their holy military service. John's description of the Church as celibate adult males is purely symbolic, intended to drive home the picture of a holy army. It conveys his views neither on sex nor on women.

All the same, 'virgins' is a strange term for celibate males, and in John's time the word had the same sort of association with women that it has in English. John is looking ahead to another image for the Church, that of the bride of Christ—a female image that balances the all-maleness of the army. The 144,000 fight now, but the time will come when they are wedded to their long-awaited lover (19:6–9), and so they keep themselves pure from the temptations offered by the world.

While it is an army, the host on Mount Zion does not conquer by force of arms. It conquers by following the Lamb wherever he goes—even to death. Once again, John uses the language of combat to describe the reality of sacrifice. The Church conquers through its willingness to die for Christ. The conquest lies in the success of its witness, which brings in the rest of the harvest of salvation.

That witness is honest and truthful, in contrast with the lies of the beast and the false prophet, for the people of God are 'blameless' (v. 5). This last word translates a term that can mean both 'morally upright' and 'physically unblemished'. John surely intends the ambiguity. The Church is called to be morally pure, but also to be a sacrifice, if need be—and in the Old Testament, sacrificial victims must be spotless.

PRAYER

Cleanse us by your Spirit, Lord, that we may serve you.
Open our ears, that we may hear your voice and join in the
worship of heaven.

ETERNAL GOSPEL

As a counterpart to the three woes come three angels, proclaiming the gospel (v. 6), which is the weapon of witness wielded by the army of the Lamb. It is a call to recognize God the creator and bow before him in worship and repentance. At the same time it is a proclamation of judgment. The gospel is not an optional extra for those whose religious taste runs that way. It is a stark choice with eternal consequences. All the earth faces the decision of whether to acknowledge God or to follow after the beast.

The beast is now revealed in its incarnation at the time that John was writing. It is the great city Babylon (v. 8), which John's readers would have easily identified, since the term had become a standard Jewish name for Rome since the destruction of Jerusalem and its temple in AD70. Already Babylon is personified in female form, but stands in stark contrast to the virgin Church of 14:4, a picture that will be painted more fully in chapter 17. Babylon, the great imperial power of the Old Testament, had become a byword for corruption and evil power. Its destruction could only be good news. The gospel is the good news that God comes to tear down the structures of evil and oppression, and to remove the source of evil's glamour.

Cup of wrath

Babylon does not have the appearance of being entirely evil. She holds a cup from which all the nations have drunk (Jeremiah 51:7). Power, glory, pomp and success make a heady and seductive brew. Why do people choose to reject God? Because the alternative offers real pleasure. No one would ever sin if sin was not enjoyable and desirable. It is in its long-term consequences that it is destructive. Adultery is enjoyable—until it comes to light, and trust and love perish. Power and wealth bring security and pleasure, but at the cost of the security and pleasure of others, and in turn that spells the lessening of the one who has paid such a price.

The intoxicating brew that Rome offers is also a cup of wrath (v. 8). The judgment of God is built in to sin, and sin becomes its own punishment. The destruction of the power of Babylon, then, is the removal of the seductive glamour. The gospel comes to shed a new light on the glory of Rome (and all its successors). In its light, the true picture emerges, and those who have been made drunk have the chance of recovering from their addiction if they heed the call to repentance (v. 7).

If they do not, proclaims the third angel, then they will share the fate of Babylon (v. 11). Those who have worshipped God will find his eternal presence a blessing and a joy. For those who worship the Babylon-beast, the presence of the Lamb and the holy angels is no joy at all; it is eternal torment.

Verses 9–11 are the most terrible in the book of Revelation. The point of them, though, is not to describe the literal fate of those who reject God, any more than any of the other images are literal. For instance, in 20:10 the devil and the two beasts are thrown into a lake of burning sulphur and tormented for ever, yet one cannot literally torment a political system or a false religion, which is what the beasts, at least, represent. John uses such language to point to the horror of rejecting God's offer of eternal life. The essence of eternal life is a relationship with God (John 17:3). Those who have placed their love, trust and worship in the passing powers of this world have no foundation for the life of eternity.

On the face of it, this is hardly good news. The third angel, though, is merely spelling out the fate that is the alternative to the gospel. The good news is that this need not be the final consequence. The light of the gospel still shines, Babylon is doomed, and her cup may be rejected.

Holding fast

As we have seen, Revelation is a book for the Church. John is aware that the brew of Babylon smells good to Christians too. They must hold firm to the faith, and remember whose mark they bear. Verse 12 echoes 11:10. There the Church was to endure in the face of persecution and suffering. Now the call is for endurance in the face of the world's beguiling glamour and riches. Arguably, it has been the soft attack that has proved the more dangerous. Pain and threat breed resilience and courage; luxury and power corrupt and lead astray.

PRAYER

Lord, it's not easy to ignore the lure of things we know to be wrong.
Keep us firmly in your grasp when our grasp of you grows weak.

The COMING LORD

The saints who obey the call to endurance are promised eternal life, in one of the best-known verses from Revelation. Verse 13 is often quoted at funerals, where, appearing out of context, it reinforces the popular non-Christian view that salvation is on the basis of good works. The deeds that accompany the saints into heaven, however, are their acts of faithful witness, which grow out of their faith in the God who brings redemption. In John's vision of total commitment, this witness has led to their martyrdom. John, of course, characterizes the whole Church as martyred, so in reality this promise applies to all Christians, no matter how they may die. The blessedness, or eternal joy, that they are promised is because they have died 'in the Lord'. This is one of Paul's favourite terms for Christians (Romans 6:3; 8:1), and here it has the same meaning. It refers to a relationship of faith and love that unites the believer with Jesus Christ, a relationship that is mediated by the Holy Spirit. It is the indwelling Spirit who transforms the lives of God's people and brings the presence of Christ into their lives. Hence, it is the Spirit who now announces the promise of eternal life, for he is the one whose presence guarantees that life and brings it to fruition.

The faith and love that the Spirit brings can be shown as genuine only when they flow out in the life and actions of his disciples. As often in the New Testament, John ties together the faith that saves with the works that demonstrate the reality of faith. At the same time, there is a sense of reward for work well done. The efforts of those who labour to serve God will not go unrecognized, and the accolade of 'good and faithful servant' (Matthew 25:21, 23, NIV) awaits those who persevere in faith and witness.

Being ready

The term 'labour' is used by Paul to describe missionary work, and has a similar sense in John 4:35-38, where the task of making disciples is likened to a harvest of ripe fields. Revelation 14:13 leads into the first of two harvest images. John sees the Son of Man, Jesus himself, seated on a cloud, which indicates the glory of God and reminds us of the cloud that marked the triumph of the two witnesses who are the Church (11:12). The image of a son of man on a cloud draws on Daniel 7:13, where a human figure takes dominion from the beasts of empire. This, then, is Christ coming in his final glory and judgment (Mark 13:26–27; 14:62). The saints have borne witness, the gospel of hope and judgment has been proclaimed, and now judgment falls. Once again, the story of the world has been told in terms of witness, salvation and judgment.

Yet another of the angels of Revelation appears to relay God's command to Christ (v. 15), for the time of his coming is known only to the Father (Mark 13:32). It is a strange fact that many clever and impressive interpretations of the Bible rely on the ability to ignore simple and straightforward statements. Here John accepts Jesus' own clear word that the time of the end is known only to God the Father. Throughout the Church's history, though, interpreters of Revelation have sought to find a clearly documented prediction of the final coming of the kingdom of God. They have taken John's numbers literally, combined them with those of Daniel, Ezekiel and who knows what others, and drawn up detailed schedules as though the second coming were being planned like a railway timetable.

All this runs in quite the opposite direction from John's meaning. The reason for his call to endurance and perseverance is that the time of the end is not known. The Church must be ready at any moment for the coming of its Lord. The task of bearing witness will not wait until tomorrow, because that may be too late. On the other hand, endurance is necessary because the time may yet be distant. All the time of the Church is the last days, and it lives its life in hopeful expectation of the coming one.

In this twofold emphasis on urgency and perseverance, John is strictly faithful to the teaching of Jesus. None can tell when the bridegroom may arrive (Matthew 25:1–13), for he comes like a thief in the night (Matthew 24:43; 2 Peter 3:10). The task of his followers is to be ready, and to be found at their labours when he comes.

PRAYER

Lord, thank you that we will one day meet you face to face. Until that time comes, let us learn to be your people on earth.

GRAIN *of* JOY, GRAPES *of* WRATH

The Son of Man comes with a sickle in his hand to reap the earth (v. 16). Then comes an angel who also harvests the earth, this time under the guise of gathering grapes rather than reaping grain (vv. 17–18). Why the two harvests?

John's harvest image reflects Joel 3:13, where God's judgment of the wicked is likened to a grape harvest: 'Put in the sickle, for the harvest is ripe. Go in, tread, for the wine press is full. The vats overflow, for their wickedness is great.' John has reinterpreted the two stages of vine harvesting as two harvests which are strongly contrasted.

The first, a grain harvest, is reaped by Christ in person and its result is not immediately made clear. The second is carried out by an angel who comes from the presence of God (in the heavenly temple). It is trodden—presumably by Jesus as judge, for the use of the passive, 'was trodden' (v. 20), indicates divine action. The second harvest, then, like Joel's, is one of judgment.

Bloody vintage

The angel who carries out the harvesting of the grapes is one with 'authority over fire' (v. 18), the image of destruction (20:15). The fact that an angel is involved stresses the distance between those judged and the God they have rejected. So too does the fact that the vintage is trodden 'outside the city' (v. 20). If we have to ask what city this is, the answer must be the city of God. The image is drawn from the Old Testament, however, where death sentences are carried out beyond the boundary of the community as a sign of the offender's expulsion from the people of God (Leviticus 24:14; Numbers 15:35). For the same reason, Jesus was crucified outside Jerusalem, but there is no suggestion in verse 20 that the treading of the second harvest has any saving significance.

The gruesome image of blood flowing for hundreds of miles and several feet deep is one of total destruction. It is 'as high as a horse's bridle'. In fact, the Greek says 'the horses' bridles', although no horses have so far been mentioned. The reason is probably that John is using a stock image taken from apocalyptic writings, which he knew his readers would recognize as an image of judgment. They would also know the treading of blood as God's judgment from Isaiah 63:1–6. The grape harvest is the destruction of those who reject God. By distancing themselves from him, they find themselves outside the city, in the place of destruction. It is also a universal destruction. The angel swings his sickle 'over the earth' (v. 19) to gather 'the clusters of the vine of the earth' (v. 18). It is a terrible vision of judgment on a world that has rejected God.

Reaping the earth

At the same time, however, the grain harvest is also a harvest of all the earth (vv. 15–16), yet it is carried out by Christ seated on the cloud that is the vehicle of the Church's salvation (11:12). Moreover, the actual act of reaping is almost never used in the Bible as an image of punishment or destruction (Hosea 6:11 may be the only exception). Threshing certainly is, but this harvest is not threshed; it is merely gathered in. It stands therefore as an image of salvation, and, like the judgment, it is a salvation that encompasses the whole earth. It is this harvest of which the saints were the firstfruits (14:4).

John is not really presenting two harvests at all, but giving us two alternatives. The destiny of the earth may be destruction or salvation. Which it will be depends on the response of the peoples of the earth to the witness of the suffering Church. In turn, that witness depends on the faithfulness and steadfastness of God's people.

These verses present an immensely important point. Revelation is not setting out a blueprint for the development of history and beyond. It is declaring that the future remains open to various possibilities, which depend (at least to some extent) on the ministry of God's people here and now.

PRAYER

Lord, inspire your Church to witness lovingly and faithfully, so that the final harvest will be one of eternal life for your world.

EXODUS SONG

The two contrasting images of the harvests dominate the rest of Revelation. The judgment of Satan, the beast and Rome is the main theme of chapters 16—19. The victory of the saints and the entry of the nations into God's salvation close the book in chapters 20—22. The present chapter prepares us by combining the two themes. Seven angels appear with the plagues that will spell out final destruction. At the same time, the martyred Church, now in heaven, sings a song that celebrates the salvation of the nations.

Conquering Church

With his typical method of overlapping images, John first introduces us to the seven angels who will deliver the deadly payload of the seven bowls (v. 1). These are the last judgments, for after them comes the kingdom of God. They are another image of the grape harvest, bringing God's judgment to its completion. We know that they are waiting in the wings, but first a more joyful vision is presented. The Church, having won its victory over satanic opposition, now stands with the company of heaven, singing God's praises. In the Greek, 'conquer' (v. 2) is in the present tense: they are those who are con-quering the beast and its helpers. The vision is at the same time one of the final triumph and of the present reality of the suffering Church. To bear faithful witness to Christ is to be already part of the heavenly host. To be in the Lord (14:13) is to be already sharing in the worship of angels, archangels and all the company of heaven. It is to be already granted a foretaste of the final victory celebration.

The victorious Church stands on (not beside, as NRSV has it) the crystal sea, which is now shot through with flames. It is the symbol of chaos, and now carries the flames of judgment, as evil bears within itself the seeds of its own destruction. The victorious people of God can place it beneath their feet, for victory is arriving. It also stands for the Red Sea, the barrier through which God brings his people to safety by fire and water. So the assembled martyrs sing the song of Moses (v. 3), for a new exodus has taken place, and God has rescued his people once again through the decisive act of Jesus, the Lamb of God.

King of nations

The song of verses 3–4 includes no direct quotations from the Israelites' victory song in Exodus 15:1–18, and at first sight it seems strange to call it the song of Moses. It contains references to other Old Testament passages that deal with similar themes, and is in fact a careful reworking of the song of Exodus 15, using methods of interpretation that were common among Jewish scholars of John's day. Like the original song of Moses, it celebrates God's victory over the might of earthly kings, and his great act of deliverance. At the same time it is a new song, celebrating a new creation. It is typical of Old Testament hymns that they call for a new song to celebrate God's new victory (Psalm 98:1; 144:9), and this passage rejoices in his greatest triumph. The victory is, however, very different from mere destruction.

For the God who desires the salvation of the world, there is no true victory in wiping out opposition. The real success lies in bringing the nations of the world to repentance and worship. Therefore God is celebrated as the king of the nations—not their nemesis but their true ruler. All now fear him and glorify his name. This is the language of worship, not of defeat (11:13). Indeed, all the nations now come before their true king, not in grief and terror but in worshipful awe and reverence because his judgments have been revealed.

While, in Revelation, judgments (v. 4) usually mean the destructive consequences of sin (which still wait as a dreadful alternative), here they refer to God's righteous acts, by which he justifies those who turn to him. This picks up a strong Old Testament tradition in which the downtrodden can turn to God for support and vindication (see Psalm 7:8). Through the sacrifice of the Lamb, whose song this is, God has declared in favour of those who put their trust in him. This judgment, which results in acquittal for the faithful, is open to all who turn in repentance. Therefore the song envisages a new exodus in which God has not only saved his people, but has also demonstrated his might by drawing all the nations to himself.

PRAYER

Thank you, Father, for your promise that, as the people of Israel passed through the sea to safety, so we too will pass through the chaos of the world into eternal life.

FINAL PLAGUES

Having presented the possibility of salvation's triumph in the grain harvest and the song of the new exodus, John turns back to the possibility of widespread disaster contained in the vision of the harvest of grapes. Once again the heavenly temple is opened (v. 5; see also 11:19), but this time the reason is not to demonstrate the accessibility of God. It shows that God is the author of the doom that is to fall on the earth: the temple is obscured by the cloud of his presence (v. 8). The seven angels who emerge from the sanctuary are robed in priestly garb (v. 6) as the mediators of God's will. While the bowls, like the other judgments, are the result of human wickedness and spiritual corruption, it is God who allows them full play, so that they may burn themselves out in self-destruction, and bring the obliteration of all who cling to them. The plagues which are to come are the wrath of God (v. 7).

At the same time, there is a positive purpose to this judgment. God is to remake creation, and before the new can come, the old must be destroyed. Therefore no one can enter the temple, the presence of God, until the seven bowls have been emptied: the presence of God among his people is a characteristic of the world to come. In John Donne's words, 'that he may build, the Lord casts down'. What is a painful but necessary experience known to all Christians is also the necessary fate of creation.

Safe in heaven?

We have seen the martyr Church singing praises in heaven (15:2–4), and the coming plagues affect only those who have followed the beast. Some interpreters argue that this should be taken to mean that before the final doom of the world, Christians will miraculously be taken up into heaven to avoid the sufferings of the world. This idea of a 'rapture' of Christians is based on 1 Thessalonians 4:17. It is never mentioned in Revelation, however, and Paul's purpose is to reassure his readers that all Christians will be reunited at Christ's return, not that some will escape suffering. There is no hint in 1 Thessalonians of any delay between the snatching up of living Christians and the resurrection of the dead. And there is no suggestion in the Bible that Christians will ever be spared the consequences of living in a fallen world.

We need to remember that John is not interested in providing a chronological picture of the end times. The song of Moses and the Lamb is part of the alternative to the plagues—salvation of the nations as a preferred option to their destruction. Whichever it is to be, the Church is called to be in the thick of it, serving Christ and witnessing to his saving grace.

The final plagues affect only the worshippers of the beast (16:2) because they are a symbol of the results of rejecting God. We should no more assume that they are a literal description of how the world will end than we should interpret literally any other image in Revelation.

Realism

At the same time, there is a realism to these verses, despite the fantastic setting. Like the earlier plagues, they reflect what actually happens in the world. The first four in particular reflect and intensify the effects of the seven trumpets. Whereas the earlier seven-series were limited in their scope, giving time for repentance, the final seven are unlimited, and the image is of universal devastation.

Since all the series of judgments ended with the final judgment of the world, and are therefore different ways of looking at the same events, we are given a sense of increasing urgency in the face of the troubles of the world. It is not that there will be various series of judgments, but that the reader of Revelation is expected to become more and more convinced of the need for faithful, uncompromising witness. The judgments, which are consequences of the world's sin, may lead, with the witness of the Church, to repentance, or they may not. The seven bowls show what happens in a world that adamantly refuses to acknowledge its creator.

PRAYER

Father, as we live in a world of turmoil, give us the faith to see in the suffering around us the birth pains of your new creation. Give us strength to witness by word and deed to your truth, and to see your love and goodness among the sorrows of the world.

NATURE *in* TORMENT

The voice of God gives the command for the final onslaught, and the bowls are emptied. Like the other seven-series, the bowls are divided into sets of four and three. The first four strike at the created world and echo the plagues of Egypt. For all their disastrous consequences, these terrible events are the precursors of the new exodus, as God prepares the new creation as the promised dwelling of his people.

The world's disease

The plague of sores (v. 2) marks those who have the sign of the beast. What had been seen as the symbol of security and power turns out to be the symptom of disease. The trust in something other than God is revealed as illusory.

The seas and the fresh waters become fetid blood (vv. 3–4), in ironic punishment for those who have themselves shed the blood of God's people. At last the martyrs are vindicated, and they call from the altar (vv. 5–7; compare 6:9–11) that God's judgment has shown itself to be just.

The heat of the sun becomes unlimited (v. 8), and is no longer the source of life-giving warmth, but of punishment. The end result is not repentance, as it was at the fall of the city (11:13), but rejection of God. Instead of giving him the glory, the afflicted curse God; they choose not life, but death (Job 2:9).

All the plagues are symptoms of the world's disease. It is a spiritual illness that springs from the desire of human beings to be their own god, not realizing that by doing so they are worshipping something far worse.

Eco-disasters

As we have seen already, it is a mistake to suppose that Revelation is intended as a literal prediction of future events. By the same token, it is foolish to try to relate specific aspects of John's prophecy to particular events in a given age. It is equally foolish, though, to try to pretend that what he has to say must therefore apply to someone other than ourselves. He paints a picture of a world turned deadly by the results of human sinfulness and pride. It fits our present age perhaps more closely than any other.

We are rapidly coming to realize that the human race is part of a vast and delicate system, which we have the power to uphold and nurture or to destroy. The biblical images of humans as the caretakers and gardeners of creation (Genesis 1—2) stand in stark contrast to the way we treat the world.

Through human pride and power, technology pollutes the sea and the fresh waters with toxic effluent, sewerage, radioactive waste and excess fertilizer. It strips away the delicate protection of ozone to let the sun scorch human skin. It tears away the forests that generate oxygen, in order to make way for cash crops and herds to satisfy the Western world's craving for meat. Meanwhile, the poor and dispossessed cut down the same trees for fuel, allowing farmlands to erode. They crowd into shanty towns where disease takes daily toll, while new untreatable diseases emerge and excess use of antibiotics creates resistant bacteria. As our waste gases heat the world, unprecedented storms tear into coastlines, deserts expand, and thousands of species face extinction. In addition to the problems created by human technology, nature itself is far from benign, as the tsunami of Christmas 2004 demonstrated to terrible effect.

In the face of such disasters, we often hear the word 'apocalyptic', and it fits well.

This is not to claim that we live in imminent expectation of the end of the world, or at least no more so than at any other time. It is to claim that Revelation's picture of a world that brings disaster on itself by ignoring the creator and the very fact of creation, with all its attendant responsibility, is grounded in reality, not in fevered imagination.

We have seen this warning once already in the first four of the trumpet judgments. Now it is repeated—and so is the challenge to us. Judgment knocks at the door, God calls for repentance, and who will listen?

PRAYER

Lord, we mistreat what you have made and suffer the consequences because we do not acknowledge that you have made it. Open our eyes to you, the creator, that we might see your creation and take our proper place within it.

GLAMOROUS DARKNESS

Darkness, another Egyptian plague, continues the exodus theme (v. 10). It is also symbolic of the continuing irony in God's judgment. Those who have lived in spiritual darkness under the rule of the beast are condemned to it for ever, and find it to be a torment; aware of their need, they nonetheless reject its only cure. Still there is no repentance but only blasphemy, for these are the ones who have given their souls to the blaspheming beast, and there is no room left in their hearts for repentance.

We frequently say that it is never too late to repent. In this world at least, that is surely true. We have to recognize, however, that repentance comes less and less easily to those for whom sin has become habitual. There comes a point where light is too painful even to contemplate for those who dwell in darkness (John 3:19–21).

Defiant forces

The sixth bowl seems almost out of place. Instead of bringing suffering and destruction, it allows the forces of the world to regroup (v. 12). But of course, it is disaster. The forces of the east reflect the same Roman paranoia about the armies of Parthia as we saw in the four horsemen of chapter 6. It also carries ideas of the myth of the returning Nero. Most of all, though, it was from the east that the armies of Babylon and Assyria marched on Israel. These are the forces of chaos and destruction.

Instead of repenting, the armies of the world take to the battlefield (v. 14). No doubt they do so under proud banners, beating the drums of patriotism and just warfare. They are ready to fight for their homeland, their way of life and their friends and families. Above all, they sharpen their swords and slap home the magazines of their rifles in the name of religion, spurred on by words of prophecy and the sight of miracles (v. 14; compare 13:13). Faith is a great incentive to death. The hidden force behind their battle preparations is demonic, however. They have worshipped the beast, the force of military might, the apparatus of statehood. They have listened to the false prophet, and now it calls on them to make the supreme sacrifice. The Egyptian plague of frogs becomes symbolic of the lying words that seduce them (v. 13). The devil has his martyrs too, and they call themselves crusaders, but their death does not lead to eternal life. It is not offered in glad sacrifice to the truth, but comes in the attempt to bring destruction on others. It is a glamorous delusion, and a powerful one. Over the centuries it has seduced Christians into the belief that faith in the God of love and sacrifice can be spread by the sword and the rack, the stake and the gun.

Then the voice of Christ breaks in (v. 15). This is Jesus as he spoke to the seven churches, calling them again to be awake, to be clothed in faith and righteousness, lest they be taken in by the false prophets and bogus messiahs (Mark 13:21–22). The image of keeping clothes on is obviously one of staying awake and prepared; only by constant vigilance are the white robes of victory finally attained.

Last battle

The forces of chaos take their stand at Har-magedon (v. 16), 'the mountain of Megiddo'. The town of Megiddo was the site of several major battles (Judges 5:19; 2 Kings 23:29; see especially Zechariah 12:11) and so would have been readily associated with conflict for Revelation's original audience. It is in a plain, however, and while the nearest mountain is Mount Carmel, the site of Elijah's confrontation with the prophets of Baal (1 Kings 18:20–40), it is not really close enough to be known as the mountain of Megiddo.

Rather than predicting a literal battle in a real place, John may be characterizing the site of battle as a mountain to symbolize the beast's parody of Christ; or reflecting Ezekiel 38:8 and 39:2, where the nations do battle on the mountains of Israel. The last battle has already been fought on a lonely hill outside Jerusalem, and it was won on the cross.

As the Lamb and his army stand on Mount Zion (14:1), the beast's army assembles to oppose them. In the Old Testament, the sacred hills ('high places') of Canaanite religion came to symbolize false worship, and were a constant temptation to worship other gods. The 'mountain' of the kings of the east is the mere might of the world's corrupt systems and can offer no eternal security and no hope of victory. Hence their mountain has no real existence. Like the emperor's new clothes, it exists only as a delusion to fool the gullible.

PRAYER

Forgive your Church, Lord, for the times it has tried to impose faith by force and used the gospel to oppress rather than liberate.

67

The WEIGHT *of* JUDGMENT

Unlike the first two seven-series, the bowls contain no interlude between the sixth and seventh judgments. The picture of the heavenly reality in which the Church shares is now complete. All that remains is to describe the coming of God's kingdom in its fullness. For that to happen, the destruction of the sinful systems of the world must be brought to completion.

City of evil

The seventh angel pours out the bowl that signals Satan's downfall (v. 17). The air, the area of the heavens below the moon, was held to be the sphere of the devil's influence (Ephesians 2:2). Now that region is judged, and the voice of God declares the completion of the victory that was won by the cross of Christ (see Jesus' cry of 'It is finished' in John 19:30).

The great city, which is Babylon and Jerusalem, Egypt and Sodom, is destroyed by earthquake (v. 19). This is the same earthquake that we saw in 11:13. There it only destroyed a tenth of the city, while here its ravages are total. It is still the same one because it is not a literal earth tremor, but it includes the response to God's judgment. In chapter 11 there was repentance, but here there is none, and the destruction is total. Once again we are presented with the alternative outcomes that spring from the gospel's call to decision.

The cities of the nations fall with the great city, for they all partake of it. All cities embody to some degree the corruption of Babylon, and in so far as they share its characteristics, they must share its fate.

The fate of the cities also embodies an economic and political reality that John will explore more fully in the next two chapters. Those kingdoms and cities which have tied their fortunes to that of Rome cannot stand when the central pillar of the empire is removed. Present-day readers should have no difficulty with this idea. We live in a world that is intimately interconnected through trade, politics and rapid communication. What affects one city or country can strike at others in distant continents, through political repercussions and, above all, economic consequences.

In preparation for the next section, Babylon is mentioned again by name and singled out as the recipient of God's wrath. All cities share in the great city, but Babylon/Rome embodies it most fully. Babylon is made to drink the cup of God's wrath, for it has made others drink its own cup of corruption (14:8). Once again, the irony of judgment, in which punishment fits the crime, points to the idea that sin is its own reward: its results are its own sentence.

The cup/bowl image is a recurring theme in the later chapters of Revelation and helps to tie them together, forming another of the strands that would have aided John's readers in understanding the structure and themes of the book.

Final destruction

Like the sixth seal (6:14), the seventh bowl removes all hiding places and destroys all the false security of the world (v. 20). The mountains may also symbolize false religion, like the mountain of Megiddo. There is no refuge in misdirected faith, no safety in the isolation of islands. All stand exposed to the wrath of God, which falls like a ton of bricks—or a hundred pounds of hailstone (v. 21), in yet another allusion to the plagues that prepared the way of the exodus from Egypt. In Exodus, the plague of hail is not the final one, but here it is treated as such since it fits with the thunder and lightning of God's appearance, which in turn recall the presence of God on Mount Sinai.

The tragedy is that judgment need not fall. It is open to people to acknowledge God, to turn away from their own insecure bastions of faith and power, and be accepted. Instead, they curse God.

In a lesser way, we see a similar choice in daily life. Sometimes, in the midst of affliction, a person may find God and the compassion of a Lamb who also suffered, and as a result they receive the strength to cope. Yet others may look for strength in bitterness and rejection: 'What has God ever done for me?' John calls us to the first option. He does not promise an avoidance of suffering—far from it; but he does offer a share in the life of the Lamb that was slain.

REFLECT

All cities share to some degree the character of Babylon.
How may we help ours to become signposts to Zion?

BEAUTIFUL EVIL

As the seventh bowl brought final doom to the sinful world, special mention was given to Babylon, the city that sums up all evil. Now, the camera zooms in closer, as it were, for a detailed look at the fall of the great city, as chapters 17—19 spell out the contents of the final bowl. In actual fact, the destruction of Babylon is simply described by the angel. What John sees is the city in all its glory, as his readers would have seen Rome. John must persuade them that the glory is false, and the splendour is that of an expensive whore.

There are three figurative women in Revelation. The first we have already met, the woman clothed with the sun (12:1). She is the people of God, through whom God enters the world in Jesus Christ, and she is kept safe by the power of God. The third is the bride of Christ, who is both the first woman transformed—the people of God as they yet will be—and the city in which God dwells (21:2). The second, the harlot Babylon, is the devil's counterpart to the others. She is both a people and a city, and she is dressed so splendidly that even John is amazed (v. 6).

Occasionally, readers of Revelation assume that John's use of female imagery for Rome/Babylon reflects his view of women, but the fact is that in the ancient world, cities were commonly characterized as female, much as ships are called 'she' by sailors. The particular image of the city-harlot has a long history in biblical imagery (Tyre, in Isaiah 23:16–17; Nineveh, in Nahum 3:4; and, above all, Jerusalem herself in Isaiah 1:21; Ezekiel 16:15). The Babylon persona in Revelation goes no further than this, but we will consider it in more detail in the next section.

Rome the seducer

The woman of chapter 12 was kept safe by God in the wilderness, like the tribes of the exodus. The biblical image of the wilderness is also the place of temptation, rebellion against God, and the haunt of dangerous beasts, so it is there that John is taken in his Spirit-given vision to see the whore (v. 3). Over-dressed in the richest clothes and jewels (purple and scarlet were the most expensive dress), she is the picture of the costliest courtesan (v. 4). She offers pleasure and delight, the opportunity to forget the cares and responsibilities of everyday life. No wonder that the kings of the world (and their subjects with them) have given themselves to her (v. 2). Drunk in her embrace, they have indeed forgotten the God who calls them to responsibility before him, who demands their worship and offers them everlasting love.

Sexual promiscuity or unfaithfulness is a standard image of idolatry (Hosea 3:1), which is the basic sin of turning away from God and offering his due to something that is other than him and therefore cannot be worthy of it. Rome, the great ruler of the world's mightiest empire, seems to offer much but has taken even more. She has demanded the worship due to God, and she has removed the dignity of nations and people who should stand before God as his responsible servants.

She is therefore not only Rome, but all cities which suck their inhabitants into a culture that has no room for God, and demand a compliance which leaves no space for the free service of the creator. She is not only the seducer of kings; she is the bright goal to which the poor and desperate flee, only to be swallowed up. She sums up all that is evil in the city, and so represents in 'a mystery' (v. 5; that is, a symbol visible to those with discernment) all cities and nations that rebel against God and practise idolatry.

Violent temptress

Babylon may be a seducer, but she has no soft words for those who reject her blandishments. The people of God who stand against her are murdered, because, for all her charm, she is still founded on the power of violence and its intoxicating allure. Hence she is seated on the beast (v. 3), which represents the military might of the empire and the power of naked strength. She has become so used to violence in opposition to the people of God that death has become an addiction. Her beauty is a velvet glove over the iron fist of the legions.

REFLECT

Many of us live in a world of affluence and comfort, for which we can give thanks; but it can also cushion us against the challenge of discipleship. Have we the courage and will to examine critically that which makes us feel well?

VICTIM *or* OPPRESSOR?

John is undoubtedly using traditional language when he describes Rome as an alluring prostitute, and, for him, the image is therefore firmly one of a city that will meet a devastating fate under the judgment of God. For some present-day interpreters of Revelation, this image raises disturbing questions about the attitude to women that Revelation could be seen as fostering.

For all that it is a stock picture, does it not encourage us to see the female as the tempter, the corrupter of virtue? And if woman is also the image of the people of God, is she not a passive one, kept safe in the desert while her children (all male virgins) war against the devil until she can be transformed into the virgin bride, passively prepared for her husband, the conquering Lamb (12:6, 17; 14:4; 21:2)? The image of womanhood therefore must be one either of seductive evil (Eve collaborates with the serpent!) or of helpless subjection before the onslaught of the dragon and the Lamb. The (probably) real woman, Jezebel (2:20), is herself characterized as a seducer of God's people, and the fate of the Old Testament Jezebel may have inspired that of Babylon (1 Kings 21:23; 2 Kings 9:36), for it gets worse. The terrible fate of the Babylon whore is to be stripped naked (an image of abuse of the female) and literally devoured—her flesh eaten—by her rebellious lovers (17:16).

To our age, which is rightly sensitive to the attitudes that can be expressed and fostered by careless language, this imagery may speak of a casual acceptance of the wickedness, passivity, weakness and legitimate victimhood of women. Of course, John is not explicitly fostering such an attitude, but he was undoubtedly a man of his time, and that was a time in which women were severely disadvantaged economically, politically, socially and religiously.

We also need to be sensitive to the nuances of the picture-language, however. The male virgins, as we have seen, are being characterized as female in preparation for their role as part of the bride of Christ. The woman who is kept safe in the desert represents both the male and female people of God, and the nakedness of the harlot is a symbol of shame and exposure to judgment rather than victimization of the female.

Unwilling whore?

Another problem with the Babylon image is that of prostitution. For John, the harlot who rides the beast is a figure of power, splendour and desire, yet the reality of prostitution is far from such a fantasy. In the Roman world, prostitutes were generally slaves, who had no say over their employment and whose fate was often squalid and miserable. Their earnings went not towards their own finery but into their owners' coffers. Moreover, many would have been non-Roman, victims of imperial power who had been bought or captured in subject provinces and transported to pleasure their new overlords.

The case is not much different in the 21st century. In the developing world, prostitution is often little more than slavery (and sometimes that very thing). In the West, it is usually the resort of the desperate and impoverished, the homeless and the dispossessed. For those who willingly embrace it, it is frequently the end product of manipulation and misplaced affection. The powerful, independent and wealthy courtesan is a rare creature indeed. Is John, then, consciously or otherwise, simply asking us to buy into an abusive male fantasy?

We need to realize that the origin of his image lies in the Old Testament, where the metaphor of prostitution is borrowed from the Canaanite fertility cults and, as such, becomes an image of wilfully turning away from the God of Israel in order to follow ways of worship that belonged to other gods. John is not, at this point, interested in social reality, which will come later.

All the same, an awareness of that reality lends a richness to the imagery here, and points up the tragedy of the whore who rides the beast. Like the slave-prostitute, Rome is the victim of her own imperial power, and will be destroyed by it. She wears finery, but it is bought by destruction not only of others but of her own potential for good. Babylon is a city, and could have been the city of God, but instead panders to the beast and is trapped in the path of futility. For all her power and bloodlust, she is doomed by the very oppression that she metes out to others. The slave owner has become the slave of her own power and is as trapped within it as any struggling subject nation.

PRAYER

Father, for all victims of abuse, by others or themselves,
we pray your mercy.

MYSTERIOUS BEAST

John is amazed, presumably at the beauty and magnificence of Babylon (17:6), but he should not be. Evil, as we have seen before, may be beautiful and attractive but its beauty lies in the fact that it is almost always a perversion of something good. Promiscuity and adultery are wrong because they are a wrong use of the bright gift of sex, which itself is good and beautiful. Wealth and prosperity are not in themselves evil, for they bring comfort and security and the ease that is necessary for the growth of culture. At the same time, they come at the cost, all too often, of the suffering and poverty of others who have as much claim on comfort and security as the wealthy. It is not wrong to celebrate one's homeland and culture, to be proud of the traditions and self-identity of one's nation. Yet we can all too easily see the way in which nationalism and tribalism spill over into contempt for others and a belief in the right to conquer and subdue.

The angel therefore explains the glorious harlot by pointing to the beast on which she rides (v. 7). It is here that her power is found, and it is this naked oppression that has made her the whore she is.

The sleeping beast

In a parody of God and his Messiah (4:8), the beast is described as the one who was, is not, and is to come (v. 8)—but its coming will be to defeat, not victory. There is also a warning here to those who see little sign of the beast on their horizons. The churches of Asia Minor may well have felt that the terrifying, anti-God power that John ascribes to Rome was hardly matched by the reality. Nero did terrible things to the church in Rome, and there may have been sporadic acts of persecution elsewhere, as at Pergamum when Antipas was killed (2:13). In these churches, though, for those with a little discretion, life was not so difficult.

For those of us today who live in relative freedom, in lands where Christianity is respected or tolerated, the bestial picture of the state belongs to another age. We put across our point in polite debate and have our say in the democratic process.

John's answer is that the beast does not die so easily. It does not disappear with the death of Nero, the defeat of Hitler or the overthrow of Saddam Hussein. It is always ready to rise again, for it lies sleeping in the very structures of the world in which we live. In fact, it *is* those structures, which are never purely good, even if they are rarely purely evil. All too easily they may change, the balance of justice may tip, and the beast ascend from the pit to roam free once more. Its ultimate defeat is certain, but for those who are not attuned to God, who fail to see the world from the divine perspective, it is a seductive power and will be worshipped. Thus Rome, the manifestation of the beast in John's time, is only one example of its perennial incarnation in oppressive governments and systems throughout history.

The sixth emperor

John sees his churches as being poised at the threshold of the beast's reawakening; it is not, but will soon arise. The seven heads of the beast (v. 9) represent seven kings (and hills, just to make the identification with Rome quite clear). Five have gone and the sixth is now reigning (v. 10). Many commentators have seen this as a sure way of working out exactly when Revelation was written: all we have to do is to decide which of the preceding emperors are the five who have fallen. But it is impossible to do so. There were five emperors before Nero, and Nero was already in the past. In fact, the seven emperors are symbolic. They are the total, complete list of the rulers who will hold sway before the end comes. John's churches are in the time of the sixth simply because they are in the end times, waiting for the return of Christ. All churches, at any period of history, stand in the time of the sixth emperor. Those who have wisdom recognize this, and live their lives with one eye on the coming kingdom of God, trusting in the power of the Lamb.

Like all the references to the imminence of the end, the list of emperors is a call to the churches to be ready for their coming Lord. The corruption of the empire in which they live is itself a sign of the end times. There is no place or time for complacency and compromise.

PRAYER

Give your people open eyes, Lord, to see the beast even when it appears to sleep, and to bear witness against it.

The BEAST DECODED

The difficult and complex explanation of the beast in 17:9–14 has been a fertile ground for all manner of strange theories. For those who see Revelation as a coded description of the course of future history, the heads and the horns have been seen as world empires and coalitions of nations, including even the European Union. Verse 9 suggests that the meaning is one that John expected his readers to know, which rules out a literal futuristic interpretation.

In fact, he is once again using the myth of the return of Nero, which had two forms. According to the first, Nero was in hiding but would return to reclaim his throne and take the empire on to greater glory. This is the form of the legend that lies behind chapter 13, where the beast parodies the resurrection of Jesus by surviving a mortal wound and carrying on. The mythical Nero is seen as the one who typifies the beast's ability to return from the dead.

A second version had Nero returning at the head of an army to wreak destruction on his faithless empire. This is the form of the myth behind the present passage. Here the same beast is itself one of its own heads, which is both one of the seven and yet an eighth. In other words, Nero, a fallen emperor whose time appears to have passed, returns as an extra and final ruler, who embodies the nature of the beast itself. The coming of this ruler spells the end, the destruction of the beast.

John's readers were surely familiar with the Nero legend in both its forms and would have recognized the images here. In chapter 13, the return of Nero formed a handy symbol to show how secular power apes the resurrection by appearing indestructible. Here in chapter 17, a version of the myth that has an emphasis on judgment is brought into play. The beast has not only a mocking form of resurrection but also its own second coming for judgment.

That judgment recoils, however. Those who give their allegiance to the beast, who place their trust in earthly might, will find that their names are not in the book of life that represents God's eternal desire for the salvation of his creatures (17:8). They may have set themselves up as the world's arbiters, but discover that they themselves are judged by the Lord of lords and King of kings (v. 14).

Historical reality

This passage does far more than play with images; it presents a powerful analysis of the Roman empire and of secular power itself. The whore who is Babylon is sustained by a sea of nations and peoples whose ambitions and hopes cannot be thwarted for ever. Their rulers exercise power under the oversight of Rome, but they will want their turn at the top (v. 12). In the end, the empire must fall, torn apart by the subjects whose strength she milks for her own ends.

Nero will return, turning the power of subject armies against Rome itself, and tearing down the glorious edifice which is built on fear and oppression (v. 16). An empire built on injustice and power will eventually fall prey to the very forces that sustain it. Of course, John knows there is no real chance of Nero's return. The point is the instability of a rule based on injustice. If naked power is the way to rule, then anyone can seize that power, so we see the subject nations, the ten horns, turning against the rider of the beast and consuming her.

Judgment comes

The inevitable shift of power between the rider of the beast, Rome borne up by its military and political might, and the subject nations is seen as God's process of judgment (v. 17). He has given up his opponents to the results of their own chosen way, and they destroy themselves. They may believe that they are seeking to further their own ends, but in fact they have fought against Christ and his saints, and, through the self-destructiveness of evil, the Lamb has prevailed.

Of course, none of this will happen overnight, and the pattern will recur throughout history. Here John sees these events as the precursor of the final judgment, but once again the vital message is that God's kingdom alone is eternal, and final victory awaits those who remain loyal to Christ.

PRAYER

Lord, open the eyes of the rulers of the world to your rule,
that they may turn from the way of force and discover
the rule of your kingdom.

The STATE of the BEAST

Chapters 13 and 17 of Revelation, the images of the beast from the sea that serves Satan and wars against the people of God, give one of the most radical criticisms of the secular state in the Bible. The beast represents the military might of Rome, and reaches beyond that into a timeless representation of all secular authority and power. As such, these chapters appear to stand in direct opposition to the other biblical passages that have formed the basis for most Christian political thought.

Servant of God?

For Paul, writing to the Roman church, the state was God's servant, expressing his desire for order and good behaviour. It wielded the power to punish transgression on behalf of God himself (Romans 13:1–7). This view is echoed in 1 Peter 2:13–17, while in 1 Timothy 2:1–2 the rulers are presented as those who provide the peace in which a godly life might flourish (1 Timothy 2:1–2). In the Old Testament, the state of Israel and the people of God are effectively indistinguishable, and even pagan kings may unwittingly carry out God's purposes (Isaiah 45:1–7).

In Revelation there is no mitigating view of the state at all. The beast, like its master Satan, may ultimately fall into God's plan, but only in a negative way. It promotes no good, and is the opponent of God rather than his servant.

Redressing the balance

It has been argued that John's pessimism is the result of the situation in which the churches found themselves, although we have seen that there was probably no widespread persecution at the time of Revelation's writing. Perhaps the memory of Nero's bloodbath was sufficient to remove any rosy view of the state from Christian eyes, or at least from the less complacent, more perceptive, prophetic vision.

John's analysis, however, runs deeper than that. Paul had already hinted at limits to the goodness of the state. By characterizing it as the servant of God (Romans 13:4) he had used a term which, in the Old Testament, carries the weight of responsibility rather than privilege. John sees an empire that promotes the worship of false gods and rewards wealth to the detriment of the poor. It has rejected its responsibility to God, and can no longer claim to be his servant. The whore Babylon is dressed in the most expensive finery because it is a city for the rich and powerful, not for the downtrodden and despairing. It seeks to control the distribution of wealth (13:16–17) and is the arbiter of human worth.

It is no accident that the two churches that receive uncritical praise, Smyrna and Philadelphia, are notable for their poverty and powerlessness in worldly terms (2:9; 3:8). Their very weakness has prevented them from being sucked into the system of the beast.

Revelation's judgment of the state, then, has two main components: the false worship it promotes and the unjust society it embodies. Paul's implicit criticism, which is overlooked by most commentators on Romans, is made the focus of John's picture. His viewpoint redresses the balance in the biblical view of secular politics and provides a warning for all who would seek to promote a Christian political understanding. It cannot be taken alone, or made to bear the full burden of a theology of political power, but it must, like the whole of Revelation, be taken into account in a Christian understanding of the world.

A truly biblical view of secular power will indeed seek to see, and to foster, the state's service to God. It will look for that which promotes well-being and good living, and will hope to bring to bear the values of God's kingdom on the kingdoms of this world. It will seek signs that point to God as the true source of salvation and it will seek justice and equality for all.

Above all, it will never be complacent. It will always be honest and courageous in its criticism of the world. It will never mistake even the best earthly society for the kingdom of God, for beneath the surface of any state, the beast slumbers lightly.

PRAYER

Encourage our prayer, Lord, for those who rule, that they may seek justice based on the knowledge of your love. Enable us to discern where your Spirit is at work in the systems of the world, and to speak prophetically when he is ignored.

LUXURY & DESOLATION

The prediction of Rome's destruction at the hands of the very forces that have raised her to greatness might seem to be the last word on the city that has brought so much misery and sin to the world, but John has not finished. Chapters 18:1—19:8 present a dirge for the death of Babylon and a celebration by those whom it has oppressed. The aspect of lament draws on the doom songs of the Old Testament prophets, where the fall of the city is foretold in the form of a song of grief, often written as though it had already happened: Babylon (Isaiah 13; Jeremiah 51), Tyre (Ezekiel 26:1–6), Edom (Isaiah 34) and Nineveh (Nahum 3).

By using these diverse sources, John reinforces his conviction that Rome embodies all the evils of the infamous cities of the past, and allows us to see her as the embodiment of the wicked city that may be manifested anywhere, in any age. He creates a masterpiece of prophetic poetry, and sums up all that calls for God's judgment on the city that has opposed him. It is not simply a triumphant gloating over the downfall of wickedness, but presents a detailed analysis of what is wrong with Rome. It has, in fact, been termed the most trenchant critique of the Roman economy to come from the time of the early Roman empire. As we shall see, it is also a critique of all major empires and economies, including our own today.

Desolation

An angel shining with the glory of heaven (v. 1) announces the fall of Babylon (v. 2). In earthly terms, there was nothing to compare with the splendour of the great city, and it has seduced many to false worship. Yet it is nothing to the glory of heaven, which is promised to the saints, and in which they have a share already, through the life of worship and prayer. The glory of heaven stands in opposition to the splendour of earth, and it proves to be the lasting glory. This is not simply a test of strength, with the greatest winning; it is also a contrast of the basis of splendour. The glory of God lies in his giving, and in the sacrifice of the Lamb. The glory of Babylon is taken from others, and is essentially parasitic. Now the brilliance and wealth of Rome lie desolate, with unclean spirits and beasts lurking in its ruins (Baruch 4:35; Isaiah 13:21–22).

The demons, perhaps, are those that were once worshipped as gods in the temples of the empire (compare 1 Corinthians 10:20; Deuteronomy 32:17). Now their followers are gone, the rich offerings rotted, and nothing remains but haunted desolation. It is worth noting that in the New Testament, while demons and their satanic ruler are taken seriously, they generally seem to lack power without human vehicles. Once cast out of their hosts, they are mere haunters of the desert (Luke 11:24–26). Even Satan himself operates through human agencies, summed up in Revelation as the beast and the false prophet. The point is that we confront the demonic in the institutions and actions of everyday life, not in some abstract world of the 'spiritual'.

Luxurious lies

Babylon seduced the rulers of the world by the offer of power, and drew in the wealthy by the promise of riches (v. 3). Those who were powerless may have been forced to worship the beast simply in order to survive in a world dominated by the power of Rome. Those with wealth and strength have followed her willingly, ready to seize the opportunities of privilege, 'the power of her luxury'.

Luxury is, of course, the sign of power. It is the powerful who can afford what is unnecessary, and it is frequently gained at the expense of what is necessary for others. In our age, we hear much (though unhappily to little effect) of the impact of the wealthier nations on poorer ones. Coffee and carnations are the main exports of nations that desperately need to grow food for consumption at home, but wealth lies abroad, and the power of wealth dictates what will be grown, rather than the needs of the growers.

Rome too sucked luxuries out of the lives of its subjects, creating a life of splendour for the powerful and rich. In the first century, the wealthy were a much smaller group than they are today, and a harder one to break into. Babylon therefore lied to most in its promise of prosperity, but created a culture of greed and envy. In return, the true riches of heaven were ignored, and so judgment falls.

REFLECT

'The wealthy' are always someone other than us—
but almost everyone in the Western world is rich compared to the
rest of the world.

In the WORLD, NOT of the WORLD

The doom of Babylon will be shared by all who share in the life of Babylon, so a voice (presumably of an angel, since it refers to God in verse 5) tells the people of God to leave the city, lest they share its fate (v. 4). The image is a reminder of the return of the exiles from historic Babylon (Isaiah 48:20) and of the exodus theme that runs through Revelation. Does it mean a literal removal of the saints from contact with the sinful world? Many have taken it to mean that, and the Church's history is littered with the stories of sects who have declared themselves separate from 'the world'. There have been those who have attempted to build their own towns and nations, un-polluted by Babylon. Others have lived in secular communities while building separation into their religious and social lives. Examples of both still exist, drawing their inspiration from the present passage and others, such as 2 Corinthians 6:14—7:1, which seems to call for some kind of divorce between Christians and the world.

It is unlikely that this passage is calling for physical separation, since the witness of the Church must be carried out in the streets of the city itself, and it is there that martyrdom awaits (11:8). Paul, too, explained that his talk of separation was a moral and spiritual refusal to identify with the existing system of values, not a call to live within the boundaries of a ghetto (1 Corinthians 5:9–10; 7:29–31). The separation that should mark the life of the Church is a separation of morals and spirituality, and this makes it all the more difficult to achieve. It is easy to be a devout and faithful follower of Jesus while singing a rousing hymn on a Sunday morning. It is another matter to make even a simple choice between a football ticket and a charity collecting tin on a Saturday afternoon.

Challenging heaven

Such choices are the stuff of Christian witness, and they are rarely clear cut, yet if there is no difference between the lives and values of Christians and those of the city in which they dwell, then Babylon has indeed triumphed.

Its triumph remains temporary, though. The achievements of the great city may indeed be towering (v. 5), but, like the tower of Babel

(Genesis 11:1–9), it is an edifice of sin, challenging heaven to act.

Judgment comes as the city receives the treatment it has meted out to others (v. 6). The double measure of judgment (see Jeremiah 16:18) may reflect a Hebrew manner of speech, meaning 'duplicate' rather than 'twice as much'. The judgment gives measure for measure; once again we will see evil being its own punishment.

Call for judgment

The voice that began with a call for the moral and spiritual separation of the saints continues with a call for vengeance on the wicked city. This is not addressed to the people of God: their role is suffering witness, not judgment. Despite all its violent and military imagery, Revelation never calls on believers to take up arms against the evil power. Christian opinion is divided over the question of pacifism, and any discussion of it must take into account the whole of scripture. There is, however, no support for violence in Revelation.

The call for judgment is therefore possibly aimed at the beast and its ten horns of chapter 17, or, more probably, is a general command to all the powers that combine, willingly or otherwise, in bringing the judgment of God to fruition. In this sense, it paradoxically does include the people of God, for the proclamation of the gospel is itself an act of judgment. Those who hear the word are given an insight into their own situation, and so may choose either darkness or light (John 3:19–21).

However this may be, the judgment of God brings about a great reversal (vv. 7–8). The harlot who called herself a queen is suddenly a widow, the status that was proverbial for its powerlessness and poverty. Like all earthly riches and good fortune, her position can be overturned in a single day. Her self-sufficiency is not sufficient at all.

PRAYER

Father, we so often unthinkingly accept the way of the world in which we live. Give us a critical faith, that we may know when to accept the world and when to resist it.

SELF-PITYING MOURNERS

The voice from heaven continues its prediction of judgment against Rome. (Although the speech marks end at verse 8 in NRSV, Greek does not have them, and there is no good reason to suppose that the angelic announcement ends before verse 20.) The city will not go altogether unmourned to its doom. Three classes of people will raise a lament: the kings who shared its rule and luxury, the merchants who grew rich trading in its luxuries, and the sailors whose livelihood was in the transport of its commodities. God's judgment is couched in terms of economic disaster, for it is the economy of Rome that embodies its wickedness.

Loveless lovers

The kings of the earth (v. 9) join in mourning at the loss of the might of Babylon, yet the suggestion is not that they mourn the city for itself. They are the ones who have identified themselves with its idolatry (fornication) and have shared in its riches. The doom of Babylon spells the end of their own wealth, the loss of their luxuries. Hard times are ahead, and their sorrow is for all that they have lost.

The city has encouraged its hangers-on to seek their own gratification and enrichment. It has therefore earned no love for itself, but only fostered a love of wealth, which in the end is a love of self. It has encouraged selfishness, and so is left with no true lovers, but only paid customers who see the whore's death as a loss of their own pleasure. The essence of sin is that it turns in on itself, seeking neither God nor anyone else.

Mingled with their sorrow and self-pity is fear, which causes them to watch from as far away as they can (v. 10). They are right to be fearful, for the judgment of Babylon is also the judgment of those who have shared her lifestyle and power. The destruction they observe is also the fate that awaits them.

Self-destructive sin

Just who are these wailing kings? If they are the same subject nations represented by the ten horns in 17:12 and 16, why do they mourn, since they themselves have destroyed Babylon? For this reason, some commentators believe that the horms represent neighbouring kingdoms, and that Babylon is to be destroyed by invaders while the subject nations mourn. This misses John's point, however. Since the harlot rode the beast, its horns must be the subject kingdoms of the empire.

These are indeed the very nations that have destroyed Rome. Turning on their former provider in an ever greater lust for wealth and power, they have destroyed their own corrupt benefactor, and now see their ambitions go up in smoke. Like so many who have set out on a course of destruction and self-aggrandisement, they stand appalled by the consequences of their selfish actions. They are appalled, though, not at the fate of Babylon/Rome, but at the self-destruction that their actions have wrought. Babylon was their power base and the source of their wealth. Without her, even though their own envy has destroyed her, they find themselves to be nothing; and, instruments of judgment though they unwittingly are, they find themselves to be subject to the same judgment.

A startling aspect of the judgment of Babylon is the speed at which it comes. 'In one hour' (v. 10) God's judgment falls. John is pointing to the unexpectedness that marks God's final judgment on the evil of the world, which here is represented by Rome/Babylon. The unlooked-for nature of judgment is a theme that runs throughout the New Testament and marks Jesus' own teaching (for example, Matthew 25:1ff). Like Jesus' parable, the catastrophic destruction of the evil city is a call to believers to be constantly vigilant. No one knows when the end may come. Christians must be about their task of faithful witness with a sense of urgency.

PRAYER

*Father, the pursuit of self-interest often damages others
and ruins ourselves. Give to all who suffer the consequences of their
own actions a desire for repentance and forgiveness,
and a concern for the needs of others.*

CARGOES *of* OPPRESSION

The second group that will mourn the passing of Rome will be the merchants. Once again, it is self-interest that weeps. The city that rode the beast has none who truly mourns for her—at least, not within her own sphere of influence. The loss the merchants have suffered is immense: their great cargoes of luxuries and bulk necessities were worth uncountable sums of money. In one hour (the refrain for all three mourners: vv. 10, 17, 19), their security has been swept away. There is a greater security, one that will last for eternity, but it has been ignored for the illusory safety of wealth and prestige.

Hungry city

It is worth looking in more detail at the list of the goods that will no longer be traded. John has provided an accurate reflection of the sort of materials that flowed into Rome by sea (vv. 12–13). Gold and silver from Spain, precious stones from India, pearls from the Red Sea and the Persian Gulf, fine linen from Egypt and silk from China (though its source was unknown to the Romans, who believed it came from India), purple and scarlet dyes from Asia Minor, are just the start of the list. Fine woods, materials for artisans, spices, all were the epitome of expense. In Rome itself, the wealthy vied with one another in their pursuit of expensive furniture and clothing, the elaboration of their cuisine and the brilliance of their jewellery.

All this represented a vast flow of money from Rome, but little of it went to the people of the empire. The wealth garnered from the subjects of Rome went into the luxuries of her ruling classes.

Only towards the end of the list do normal foodstuffs make an appearance, and even then their mention is barbed. The oil and wheat consumed in vast quantities by Rome itself indicate the dependence of the great city on the production of its empire—and drained the resources of those who produced it. Rome, of course, would have argued that in return it produced the intangible assets of empire, stability, peace, government and easy communication. Of course, it gave less of these than its propagandists would have had people believe, and in return demanded not only material but spiritual tribute. It usurped the role of God in claiming to give meaning, purpose and salvation to its subjects.

The very last item is a telling one. The Greek literally says, 'bodies and human lives (or souls)'. 'Bodies' was a common term for slaves. John has presumably added the rider that these are indeed human lives. To the empire, people are merely commodities, to be dealt in along with clothing and livestock.

Weapons of trade

John is doing much more than condemning conspicuous wealth. The trade of Rome was one of its weapons of oppression. There were those throughout the empire who benefited from it, but those who produced the goods consumed by the city saw little of the profits. It is hard to estimate how wealth was distributed in the Roman world, but it seems probable that the truly rich comprised no more than two per cent of the population. The lot of peasants and artisans was not significantly improved by the immense consumption of the imperial city. As in today's world, the demands of the consumer, rather than local needs, dictated what was produced. Imperial tax and imperial trade worked in the interests of the rulers, but little trickled down from their coffers to the common folk of the empire.

There were few who saw this, however. The dazzle of Rome blinded the poor as well as the rich. The imperial cult encouraged the view of Rome as divinely favoured, the imperial propagandists promoted a worshipful view of the benefits of Roman rule, and a popular belief in ineluctable fate discouraged thoughts of changing the *status quo*. The institution of slavery, for example, which for John is the crowning sign of economic and moral corruption, was never questioned, save by a radical Jewish group, the Essenes—and some Christians such as John himself. It took another one and a half millenia before Christians turned against slavery. We need to be able to question, in the light of God's kingdom, the things we take for granted; the results could be very disturbing.

PRAYER

Father, there are still those who treat people as commodities,
as units of trade or consumption, production or resources.
Help our world to see people as your great treasure,
infinitely loved and divinely desired.

IDOLATRY & JUSTICE

The importance of John's criticism of Roman economics can be seen by looking at the structure of the threefold lament by the kings, the merchants and the mariners. If we were to take out verses 11–14, we would be left with three short dirges sung by those who will 'stand far off' (18:10), ending with the refrain, 'in one hour...' (18:9–10, 15–17a, 17b–19). John has broken into this pattern with the extra verses 11–14 on the disastrous trade of Rome, showing that this is a major reason for the coming of God's judgment.

Soul thirst

The worship of luxuries is a form of idolatry. The exotic fruits and dainties which were the hallmark of the lives of the privileged had become the focus of their souls' longing (v. 14). Where the psalmist longed for the spiritual refreshment of the living God (Psalm 42:1), the heart-sickness of Rome's élite turned to the next morsel that might titillate the jaded palate.

The economic sins of Rome are driven home as her dress is once more described (vv. 16–17). It is her wealth that has made her a whore, and she has sacrificed honour, integrity and life itself in the pursuit of further riches. In our own day, we see how the richest individuals rarely seem to be satisfied with even incalculable wealth, and the most powerful nations run the world's economy in a way that is calculated to bring them more.

Sailors' lament

The third group to mourn the passing of the city is the seafarers (vv. 17b–19). Ship owners, captains and hands alike see the passing of their livelihood. The vast commercial fleets that bore the lifeblood of Rome are no longer in business.

Most of the sailors would hardly have been wealthy, yet they too praise the great city for its unique majesty. The seductive splendour draws rich and poor alike to worship, for it contains the false promise that this wealth may somehow be available to the worshipper. Like a modern-day lottery, the prize glitters but remains at odds of many millions to one. To the Christian reader of Revelation, the contrast with God's free gift of life and love cannot be greater—unless one is also seduced by the glory of Babylon, which is the danger John seeks to avert.

Every city

John grounds his visionary foretelling of the judgment of God in a realistic assessment of the economics and politics of his day. Amid the strange creatures and celestial portents is a keen awareness of the sins of the imperial system within which he and his churches are called to live and serve God.

By identifying Rome with Babylon, the archetypal wicked city, John demands that his readers look at their own city, their own political, social and economic system. There they will be able to see both signs of the grace of God and traces of Babylon. The temptation to believe that Revelation is concerned only with Rome, or the first-century Church, or a safely distant future, is denied by this use of universal symbols.

At the same time, we have to resist the temptation to make naive equations. John's condemnation of Rome's imports does not mean, for instance, that all international trade is sinful. On the other hand, we cannot assume, simply because our present economy makes no use of slaves, or because empires are no more (at least in name), that all is well with our present world.

Trade is still a powerful force for maintaining inequalities in the world. International loans ensure that poor nations remain in debt, no matter how hard they may work; import tariffs make it difficult for Third World nations to compete with wealthier ones; enforced competition between poorer countries ensures that prices are kept unprofitably low. All these factors work together to ensure that the poorer nations remain poor, and the weak remain powerless.

PRAYER

Father, uphold and strengthen those who work in our world for the spread of justice, for fairness to the weak and mercy to the poor. Give to us, who consume the produce of the world, an awareness of the true cost of our luxuries.

SAD JUSTICE

In contrast to the mourners, the angelic voice exhorts the people of God to rejoice at the ending of the harlot's reign (v. 20).

Many of John's readers would have been tempted to wonder what they had to rejoice about. The churches of the trading cities of Asia Minor would contain many who were involved in the empire's commerce. They would find it only too easy to identify with those who mourned the fall of Babylon, which is no doubt what John intended.

He challenges his readers to ask where their heart really lies. Are they servants of Christ, soldiers of the kingdom who stand against the injustice and idolatry of the beast? Or are they victims of the harlot's seduction, so caught up in the values and promises of the corrupt world system that they can no longer divorce themselves from it? Is the longing of their hearts met by the love of God, or is it slaked by the material promises of the passing age?

The vision of Babylon's ultimate judgment is a call to John's readers to reject its values now, and to find true riches and real hope in the love and service of God. It is a frightening demand, both for the first-century churches of Asia Minor and for readers today. Both are firmly embedded in their culture of material prosperity and financial security, which are bought at the expense of others. To break free demands courage to swim against the stream, and faith in God who comes to give the victory.

Rotten foundations

Those who belong to God look on Babylon and rejoice at its downfall, for they can see beneath the glitter to the reality. In the foundations of the great city lie unspeakable sins. Economic oppression through the merchants who maintained a stranglehold on the empire (v. 23c), and the ruling system's bewitchment by idolatry (v. 23d), have been made perfectly clear in this chapter. There are other factors to be taken into account, however.

The harlot has drunk the blood of the people of God (v. 24a; 17:6), for she can brook no opposition. There is no room for those who question her ways, and God's ways are a continual challenge to the world. She has made war on the followers of Jesus, and must answer for that.

Persecution of the Church by no means exhausts her violence. The empire exists by conquest and the rule of the armies. Local rebellion and dissension were punished by extreme measures, and so Babylon is charged with the death of 'all who have been slaughtered on earth' (v. 24b). The charge may be extreme, but then, Babylon is not Rome alone, but every state, past and future, that builds its power on the corpses of its victims.

God's justice is called down by the victims of Rome, but also by those of Spain, France, Britain and all later empires. Aztecs and Incas, natives of India, Australia and North America, to name but a few, have been victims of imperial expansion. Today, justice continues to be demanded by Serbs, Bosnians, Croats, Russians, Chechens, Sudanese, Iraqis, Palestinians...

As the angel hurls his symbolic millstone (v. 21), it would seem that there is little to mourn in the passing of Babylon.

Silent harps

Strangely enough, there is mourning. Judgment may seem long overdue, but when it falls, it will silence the musicians and the lovers, the craftsmen and the millers (vv. 22–23). Have these people deserved their fate? Perhaps not individually, but they are caught up in the system that seduces humanity away from God. They have dwelt in Babylon, choosing it over the city of God, and so their beauty and their art vanish into darkness.

There is surely a note of sadness here, not at the ending of evil, at which heaven rejoices, but at the loss of what could have been. There was real beauty in Babylon, but it was used not for the praise of God, but for the adornment of corruption. Yet, despite the words of the earthly mourners, which are laments for their own loss, the only sense of loss at the death of the great city comes from the one who pronounces judgment on her. God allows human freedom, even the freedom to reject him, but it is still a defeat of his love, and a sorrow in his heart.

PRAYER

Thank you, Lord, for your promise of mercy and justice, and your sorrow at all that evil destroys.

WITNESS

In his call to faithful witness, John has been careful not to provide a detailed checklist of how that witness will be carried out. We know that it leads to persecution and even martyrdom. The Church is called to be faithful to the point of death itself, and it is in seeing the triumph of Christians over death that the world's hope of salvation lies.

At the same time as he refuses to give instructions on how to bear witness, John does provide very good pointers as to where that witness will be brought to bear.

Evangelism

In those sections of today's Church where 'witnessing' is rightly emphasized, there will be little doubt of what John means. Witnessing involves telling others about Jesus, as believers chat about their faith, answer the questions of the curious and make a defence against the scornful.

It will also include more structured evangelism: the setting up of opportunities to hear the gospel in small groups, by home visiting and by community-wide mission. All these were practised by the early church, and John would no doubt have been familiar with them.

These techniques for mission reflect an essential part of Christian discipleship (Matthew 28:19–20), but do not in themselves encompass all that Revelation presents about being a witness to Jesus.

Soldiers and servants

Along with the emphasis on the role of the Church as God's witnessing army, we have seen a detailed condemnation of the forces that oppose God. They are the idolatry, violence, injustice and exploitation characterizing the social, political and economic system that is the beast, and the city of Babylon.

Once these two ideas are put together, it becomes clear that witnessing to the truth of God involves active opposition to the forces of corruption in the world. The Church is called to witness by modelling an alternative view of community, with an alternative set of values: love, worship, equality and justice. This is what it means to be called to separation from Babylon.

That separation of values will go hand in hand with exposing the corruption and injustice that masquerade as reasonable and necessary. True witness will include the struggle for justice and the demand for equality. It will not be content with the explanation that the world must be as it is, for it has seen a better vision in Jesus Christ and his kingdom. It will expose the oppression that is inherent in much international trade. It will point up the injustices in societies that see divisions between rich and poor as an inevitable by-product of economic 'progress'.

Keeping faith in its place

This 'implied text' of Revelation may well be as uncomfortable to today's readers as it would have been to John's first hearers. Many of us have been taught that there is a world of difference between 'spiritual' matters and the 'secular' world. The task of faith, it is said, is to inspire and motivate people in their daily lives, but not to challenge the nature of those lives. In fact, that was the task of the state religion of Rome, and from time to time the Church has succumbed to its lure.

For others of us, the task of faith is to bolster the way things have always been done, and to defend traditional morality, family structures and social groupings. But that too was the task of the Roman state religion, and it was Christianity's very threat to these traditional values that earned Christians the title of atheists! Christians offered an alternative family of God and threatened to break barriers between men and women, slaves and free. The very reason why Revelation can brook no compromise with the beast is that the Lordship of Christ reaches into every corner of life and questions the allegiance of every aspect of living. Much that we hold to be 'Christian' may turn out to be no more than an attempt to convince ourselves that the values of Babylon are acceptable. John calls us to look at all of life and question it in the light of the gospel.

REFLECT

Do we allow the gospel to challenge what we have always taken for granted about witnessing and mission?

HALLELUJAH!

There is another response to Babylon's fall: heaven rings with the praises of God. In chapter 4 we met the four creatures, the elders and the great multitude who form concentric circles around the throne of God. Now a liturgical hymn of praise moves like a Mexican wave from the multitude (v. 1) to the elders and the creatures (v. 4), is answered from the throne (v. 5) and bounces back to the multitude (v. 6). The voice from the throne is not identified, but it is probably a fair assumption that it is Christ's. He shares the throne of God and receives worship with him, but is still the mediator of worship, which is offered to the Father through the Son.

There is a constant command to 'praise God', both in Hebrew ('Hallelujah': vv. 1, 3, 4, 6) and Greek (v. 5). Interestingly, this is the only New Testament passage to use the Hebrew word *hallelujah*, which was preserved in the Church's worship as a liturgical term. It occurs here probably because John sees this song as echoing the so-called 'Hallel psalms' (Psalms 113—118) with their refrain of 'praise God', which were sung in the temple at times of pilgrimage and celebration. Another influence may be Psalm 104:35, where *hallelujah* is the response to God's judgment of the wicked.

Grim vengeance?

To some commentators, the song of praise is a grim sequel to the appalling scenes of destruction at the fall of Babylon. The apparent exultation over death and destruction seems to be a far cry from the Christian values of love and forgiveness. What is being celebrated, however, is not the destruction of rebellious people but the end of a system that has opposed God and has itself brought about the destruction of its followers. God has now acted to clear away all obstacles to the vision of divine glory.

While this is indeed vengeance for the deaths of his saints, it is first and foremost the revealing of his salvation. The necessary removal of opposition, of judgment on sinful Babylon, is the other side of salvation. God has waited a long time for the repentance of the world through the witness of his Church (6:11). Now salvation is revealed, and judgment with it. God's vengeance is never a petty reaction: this is no ancient despot indulging in a fit of rage, but the God of justice at last declaring that the time has come for the final reckoning.

A major argument in theology is about whether God can allow any of his creatures to be lost. Surely anything other than the salvation of all is a defeat for his love and power? The other side to this argument is that love demands a limiting of power. If God creates people to be truly free agents, they must have the power of defying him to the end. In loving, God chooses not to overpower his creatures, even though it may end in their destruction and his own pain.

In a grim counterpart to the incense of heaven, the smoke from burning Babylon ascends for ever, a statement of the finality of God's judgment (v. 3).

Just God

The conflict that many see between the mercy and justice of God is a false one, arising because we tend to think in legalistic terms of transgression and punishment. On this view, forgiveness is simply deciding to overlook sin. The question then becomes, why overlook sin in some, but not others? Moreover, it calls in question the whole process of salvation. Why must the Lamb be slain, the Church witness and suffer, if all that is to happen is that God decides to ignore sin?

Part of the answer at least lies in the biblical emphasis on relationships. Forgiveness is not simply what God does; it is part of an overall process of reconciliation, in which a mutually loving relationship between God and his people is restored. Forgiveness is one-sided, affecting only the forgiver. It must be accepted by the one who is forgiven for the relationship to be healed. Judgment, as we have frequently seen in Revelation, is ultimately the consequence of refusing a relationship with the source of eternal life. Cut off from that which holds all creation in being, there is only destruction; the smoke of the burning goes up for ever.

PRAYER

We praise you, Lord, for your justice, but even more for your love.

PRE-EMPTIVE WORSHIP

Heaven's song of praise ends with a declaration of God's reign, and declares the arrival of the marriage feast of the Lamb (vv. 6–7), although neither of these has actually taken place yet.

The banquet of the kingdom, which both Jews and Christians expected as the victory celebration of Messiah's coming, has not quite arrived. The people of God stand ready to be united with their Lord, like a bride awaiting her husband, but he is not yet here. They have prepared themselves by remaining faithful to him, and await the white robes of victory (v. 8), which will also be the bridal dress as God's people finally enter into intimate and eternal communion with their Lord.

This touches on one of the central aspects of worship. When we praise God, we do so not only for what he has done, but also for what he will do. Much of the church's liturgy is a celebration of promise. At baptism we thank God for a person's new birth in Christ, but only time will tell whether they will go on to live a life of faith. In the celebration of the eucharist, we thank God for all the benefits of Christ's death and resurrection, although final salvation still lies in the future.

Like Revelation's heavenly worshippers, we feel it is inappropriate to put conditional clauses into worship: 'we praise you, God, that you have delivered us from the powers of darkness—provided that we do indeed put our faith in you, and everything goes as it should…' It is inappropriate because there is a sense in which worship reaches beyond the present moment to claim not only the promise, but the reality of the future. Worship lifts us into the timeless presence of God, where the marriage supper is not a distant promise but a present reality. The eucharist is both a foreshadowing, and a present experience (albeit very diluted) of the final victory feast.

Self-examination

This is probably why John is told to write down the rather obvious beatitude on those who are invited to the marriage feast (v. 9). The Greek makes it plain that the reference is to those who have not only received the invitation but have also responded. As Revelation was read out in the worship of the churches of Asia Minor, it would have come as a call to self-examination. Have you indeed responded to the invitation? Are you here to receive the blessing of God? Are you indeed one of the faithful witnesses who hold fast to the testimony about Jesus Christ?

When John falls in worship before the glorious angel who speaks to him, the rebuke is aimed as much at his readers as at him (v. 10). Whom do you truly worship? You must worship only God, for he alone is worthy, not because of his beauty and wonder but because of what he has done as creator and redeemer (4:11; 5:9–11) and what he promises to those who remain with him (v. 9). Similarly, the gospel you preach must be only the gospel of Jesus, brought to life among you by the Spirit of God. Any other revelation, even if it came from an angel, is false (Galatians 1:8).

Divine Christ

The term 'angel' does not actually occur in the Greek of verse 9, but it is obviously implied. His rebuke to John is entirely consistent with Jewish and Christian thought. Worship may never be offered to anyone other than God, even to an angel whose appearance radiates glory and whose words bring the promise of God. It is the maker of the promise, not the bearer of the message, who is to be worshipped. This makes it all the more significant that worship in Revelation is offered to Jesus. There is a clear division between the divine receiver of worship and all his creatures; Jesus stands on the divine side of that division.

Once again we see the almost trinitarian linking of God, Jesus and the Spirit in verse 10. 'Spirit' here is taken in many English translations in a sort of general sense: those who bear witness have a prophetic spirit. It makes more sense, however, to see a reference to the Holy Spirit, who is closely linked with prophecy. John and the angel are both servants who worship God and bear witness to Jesus in the power of the Spirit. From the earliest days this has been the centre of the Church's worship and mission.

PRAYER

Praise you, Father, Son and Holy Spirit, for you have redeemed us from the world and promised us your kingdom.

The COMING *of* CHRIST

Several times we have been brought close to the coming of Christ and the final moment of this age. In the sixth seal (6:12–17), the seventh trumpet (11:15–19), the two harvests (14:14–20) and the seventh bowl (16:17–21), we have arrived at the end of history. Each time we have backtracked as John showed us in ever greater detail the conflict in which the Church is involved as it seeks to bear witness to Jesus before the nations of the world.

Now the final moment arrives. John once again sees heaven opened, indicating a new set of prophetic visions; from now on we will gaze into an eternal future beyond the bounds of history. We are taken back, in fact, to Harmagedon, where the forces of the antichrist, the beast who embodies the sinful systems of the world, wait for the final conflict with God (6:16).

The first vision, though, is of a rider on a white horse. It is Christ, coming in glory as he has promised. Behind him stream the armies of heaven, the faithful witnesses (v. 14; see 14:1), dressed in the white robes of victory. He wears many crowns (v. 12), for he is the Lord of lords and King of kings, whose rule far surpasses any dominion claimed by the seven-crowned dragon or its beast-servant with its ten diadems.

Suffering king

He has his titles written on his robe and his thigh for all to see (v. 16), and he is acclaimed as Faithful and True (v. 11). He has promised that his rule will come, that evil will be defeated, and his people vindicated. Now he comes to put those promises into deeds—yet for all that he has a name written on him, it is insufficient to sum up his full being.

In the ancient world, it was held that a name embodied a person's true nature. Jesus is indeed faithful and true, the ruler of all, yet these attributes are not all that he is. He has a name that only he knows (v. 12), for his true being lies far beyond human comprehension. Having told us so much, John cannot state the name, but there is a transparent clue. When Moses met God at the burning bush, he asked God's name. 'I am who I am,' was the reply (Exodus 3:14).

God is the self-sufficient being, the one who alone can fully know what and who he is, and Jesus too has a name and nature that only he can comprehend. The secret name is surely the name of God. Its secrecy is not that no one knows it (though the divine name, YHWH, was considered by Jews to be too holy to be spoken) but that it represents something beyond human understanding. That name is also revealed as the Word of God (v. 13). Though God's being is hidden in mystery, he has communicated something of himself to us in Jesus Christ (see John 1:18). Jesus is God's self-expression, showing in human form the key to his nature (see Colossians 1:19). That nature has revealed itself in self-sacrifice as the slaughtered Lamb, and is now revealed in judgment as the one who vindicates his saints and passes sentence on those who persist in evil (v. 15).

He appears wearing a robe dipped in blood. Some commentators see this as the blood of his enemies (Isaiah 63:1–6) but in this vision the winepress has not yet been trodden (v. 15), and the blood is surely his own, shed for the sins of the world. We have seen that the martyrs washed their robes in the blood of the Lamb (7:14) as they shared in Christ's sufferings (12:11). Now John shows us the original blood of redemption. The one who comes as conqueror and as judge has first shed his blood to be the Saviour.

Victorious judge

Although much of the imagery of this vision is of conquest and military might, it is no more than imagery. Jesus comes not to fight but to judge, and the weapon he wields is the word of judgment, the sword from his mouth. The victory is that of truth over deceit, not simply of great power over lesser might.

The judgment will be pronounced on the nations of the world. They have followed the beast and been seduced by the whore, rejecting the witness of the saints and the offer of salvation. Now they are left only with their own pride and power. Once again Jesus is pictured as coming to rule (literally, 'shepherd') with a rod of iron (2:27; 12:5). If only the nations had repented, it would have been the shepherd's crook.

PRAYER

Lord, we praise you for your glory,
and for the love and suffering it reflects.

The LAST BATTLE

The final conflict begins with a grisly invitation to the carrion birds (vv. 17–18). The coming of Christ is the prelude to the marriage feast of the Lamb, the celebration of salvation. The invitation to the birds is a ghastly parody of the heavenly banquet—another great supper of God.

It is only at this point that we catch sight of the beast and his armies. The vision of Christ has captured the eye and rendered the great power of the world irrelevant.

Anti-climax

And then it's all over: no gargantuan struggle, none of the heroic trappings of mythical conflict. The last battle turns out to be no battle at all. The beast and the false prophet are captured and thrown into a burning lake, their followers wiped out by the sword of Christ (vv. 20–21). The armies of heaven do not lift a finger, for they have already won their fight, in the long struggle of the martyrs against the beast.

All the army language is imagery, after all. This is not a battle but a judgment. There is no literal beast or lake of fire. This is an important point, for there are aspects of John's imagery that have been hallowed by centuries of literal interpretation. The two beasts, and later the devil (20:10), are thrown alive into the fire (v. 20) and tormented for ever. This is not a statement about the eternal torment of those who are not saved. The two beasts are metaphors for political and religious systems, not actual people, and systems cannot be tortured. Like the smoke of fallen Babylon, the eternal torment of the unholy trinity is a statement of the eternal triumph of God's kingdom.

What is happening is that Christ pronounces his judgment on the military and political systems of the world, and they are destroyed. There is no place in the kingdom of God for corruption or for oppression. It spells an end to the rule of fear, the favouring of wealth and power, the inequity of trade between rich and poor.

The kingdom brings to a close a system of values based on what people do or have. They are no longer judged on what they make, on their 'contribution to society', on their faithfulness to the party line or any other of the myriad ways in which we are tempted to judge our fellow human beings. All that is left is the single question: have they given themselves body and soul to the way of the world, or have they reached out in desperate trust to the open hand of God?

False prophet

With the political and social structures of the world go the ideologies and propaganda, the religious justification for idolatry and rebellion against God. The beast from the land (13:11), the false prophet, also perishes in the flames. The call to worship that which is less than God cannot survive the burning vision of the coming of God himself.

It remains true in this present age that the best argument against false religion is to present the best example of true worship. Faith which results in changed lives, reborn hope and renewed relationships presents a vision of God that overwhelms the lesser gods, be they those with an overt religious claim or the petty gods of materialism.

House on sand

For those who have invested their very selves in the values and structures of this world, there is nothing left. They have built their lives on a foundation without strength. The word of judgment is spoken, and the sword of the rider mows them down.

To say that this world is a preparation for the next is a cliché, but then, clichés are born because they are true. Revelation presents a consistent call to decide between what is offered by this world and what is offered by God. To follow the beast is to have no foundation on which to build the life of heaven. Without that, would heaven even be recognized as such?

PRAYER

Lord, give us such a vision of you that when the time comes,
we will recognize you gladly.

MILLENNIUM

Probably the most puzzling section of Revelation is 20:1–10, dealing with the thousand-year reign of the martyrs with Christ (the 'millennium'). More has been written on these verses than on any other section of the book. Basically, there are four ways of approaching the passage, and three of them have been given technical names which describe the viewpoints of those who hold them.

Premillennialism

'Premillennialism' is the oldest way of interpreting the text, and is sometimes called 'chiliasm' from the Greek for 'thousand'. ('Millennium' comes from the Latin for 'thousand'.) On this view, the passage follows in a simple narrative from chapter 19, and the second coming precedes the millennium, which is a literal rule of Christ over the world, prior to the last judgment. It is a period of peace and prosperity in which the newly resurrected Christians run the world under the authority of Jesus. There are several variants of the general idea, but they need not concern us here, since all are based on the same premise—that Revelation offers a literal schedule for the future.

To make matters more complicated, there are some who hold a premillennial view (or, rather, believe that John did), but suggest that it need not be taken literally.

Postmillennialism

On the second interpretation, 20:1–11 is a separate vision, more or less retelling the tale of chapter 19. It adds the idea that as the gospel spreads throughout the world, a period of justice and faith develops, which will last for one thousand years (or at least a long time, since the number may be symbolic). Then comes a final period of rebellion and tribulation, followed by the coming of Christ and the last judgment.

This view allows an optimistic picture of the results of the Church's witness, and gives hope to those involved in the struggle for justice in the present time. It fits poorly with the overall message of Revelation, however, and few hold it today.

Amillennialism

On this interpretation, the 'a-' means 'no' millennium (compare atheism: belief in no god), which is rather misleading, because in fact the millennium is held to happen, but is seen as going on now. The reign of Christ is a present reality, and the saints share it with him. The resurrection of the martyrs (v. 4) is a reference to their 'born-again' status as Christians, and Satan is bound by the preaching of the gospel. The millennium is therefore the period of the Church, and is apparent only to the eyes of faith.

This view owes much to the teaching of the great theologian Augustine of Hippo, who advanced it as a counter-measure to what he saw as the over-enthusiasm of premillennialists who seemed more concerned with the second coming than with discipleship here and now.

Pure symbolism

The most recent approach, which is truly 'amillennial' in that it regards the passage as pure symbol or metaphor, suggests that, like much of Revelation, none of the passage should be taken as a literal description of actual history. The purpose is simply to make an important theological point—that the martyred Church will be vindicated and seen by all to be blessed by God. John did not intend a reference to any specific events in the history of the world. This interpretation allows us to see that many of the unanswerable questions raised by more literal views are pointless.

The approach we will take comes close to this one, but recognizes that the amillennial view grounds the passage in the life of the Church. Pre- and postmillennial interpretations depend on seeing Revelation as sketching, at least broadly, the future history of the world. So far, we have seen the book to be concerned with the current mission of the Church in any age—a mission that is carried out in the light of God's coming kingdom. The passage is symbolic, offering encouragement to believers, who are assured that they are united with Christ, the Lord of lords, and will ultimately be vindicated and share in eternal life.

PRAYER

Lord Jesus Christ, open our eyes to see you reigning now,
in our lives and over the world.

BINDING SATAN

John records another vision ('Then I saw', v. 1), which does not follow on directly from chapter 19. Instead, as he has so often done, he is telling the same story from another angle. We have seen the last battle twice, in chapters 16 and 19 (see commentary on pp. 153–155 and 184–187). In 20:7–10 we will see it again as Gog and Magog oppose God. These figures are taken from Ezekiel 38—39, where the last battle between God and his enemies is told twice over.

Following the victorious return of Christ, an angel is sent from heaven to bind the dragon (v. 2). Here the devil is given all of Revelation's titles for him: he is Satan, the devil, the dragon, the great serpent. It is as though John wants us to see the full force of the power of evil. The force that opposes God is not to be taken lightly. As Satan, he is the accuser of God's people, the one who points out their sins and proclaims that such have no place in the kingdom of God. As the devil, he is the personification of evil, the focus of all malignity. The dragon, the archetypal monster of chaos, is the opponent of all that stands for order and creation. He is that which seeks only to destroy and finds his strange fulfilment in the ending of all things. The serpent is the tempter, the one who brought sin into Eden and turned humanity from its first intended destiny.

Evil is no paper tiger. It must be faced as the great and terrible force it is. In the end, though, the dragon is seized by an angel of God and almost contemptuously disposed of. Cast into the pit, the abyss of chaos, he is triply imprisoned: bound, locked and sealed away (v. 3). Great though evil may be, it is nothing in the face of God. All its despair, destruction and corruption are unable to quench the life-giving force of the creator.

Satan unbound

In retelling the story, John takes us back to chapter 12, where the devil was cast out of heaven by the coming of Christ, and robbed of his rule (vv. 2–3; compare 12:9), but the victory has not yet been completed. The struggle goes on for a while, and so Satan must be released for a short time—the end times in which the saints witness to the gospel (20:7–9; compare 12:17).

The binding and release of Satan demonstrate two important truths. Firstly, even the forces of evil work God's will. He does not wish them, but since they are there, they will serve his purpose. They must be tolerated as a painful consequence of human freedom. As long as the world remains in its present state, evil is a possibility which is all too often realized, yet it may drive people into the loving arms of God, and it stands as a permanent warning of the dreadful consequences of rebellion.

Secondly, for these same reasons, evil is resilient. It can never be truly locked away. Sooner or later, no matter what good resolutions or how just a society human beings may make, evil will return. In this world, all our victories over it are temporary. The final abolition of sin can only come when the world itself is remade and humanity enters fully into the life of the new creation. Satan will run free again for a while, but will perish entirely in the new world, which has no place for him (v. 10).

Strong man preaching

The image of the binding of Satan was a common one in the ancient world. Magical texts and exorcism formulas frequently sought to invoke greater powers to subdue demons by 'binding' them, either to the will of the magician, or to keep them away from their victims. (Significantly, in Jesus' exorcisms, he invokes no greater power than his own.) According to Jesus, it was in his ministry that Satan was bound (Matthew 12:29). The devil is the strong man who is rendered helpless by the coming of the kingdom, and whose goods are plundered. He stands by helpless whenever the gospel is received in faith and sinners are freed from his power. Similarly, Jesus saw the preaching of the disciples as casting Satan out of heaven (Luke 10:18). It is the liberating power of the gospel that binds Satan, and what is now visible only to the eye of faith will one day be apparent to all, as Christ returns in majesty.

PRAYER

Father, at times it is hard to believe in the triumph of good over evil, and light over darkness, yet the world is shot through with signs of your love and power. Give us eyes to see you at work, and faith to know that you will triumph and that we will share in your victory.

Church Triumphant

John's next scene relies on the book of Daniel, where the prophet saw thrones set up, and books opened (Daniel 7:9–10). He made no mention of who sat on the thrones or what was in the books, but John is a little less cryptic.

The figures on the thrones (v. 4) are almost certainly the martyr Church, which remains faithful to Christ even to the point of death.

Outlasting the beast

The martyrs who share Christ's rule are not just those who have literally been beheaded. That is a figure of speech (perhaps indicating the manner of death of the martyrs known to John's first readers). Indeed, they are not only those who have literally been martyred, but include all the members of the Church, which John characterizes as martyred (compare Ephesians 2:6). They are the faithful witnesses who have not been seduced or bullied into worshipping the beast.

This is the real point of the millennium. In this world, the beast appears triumphant. The true witnesses of Christ are judged by it and (in the terms of John's story) put to death. The power of the godless structures of the world seems irrefutable and irresistible, yet in the final analysis it is the beast that perishes in flames, and the martyred Church that rises triumphant.

We have already seen this 'first resurrection' at 11:11. The martyred witnesses triumph over death, and, through their life, bring the nations to faith. It is the figurative resurrection of those who have put their faith in the risen Christ, and live in newness of life (Romans 6:4, 10–11). Those who live in that resurrection life need not fear the ultimate 'second death' of final judgment. The new life of the Church is shown as a part of Christ's rule and judgment on the beast and the nations.

The description of the martyrs in the millennium passage is entirely in terms that contrast them with the beast. The Christians to whom John writes might well be tempted to wonder whether their resistance and witness are worthwhile. The temptation to compromise with the beast might seem even more appealing when set against the alternative of martyrdom. The millennium passage exhorts them (and us!) to open their eyes to the reality of the rule they share with Christ, and assures them that this reality will not remain hidden for ever. They are now priests of God, mediating his reality to the world (1:6; 5:10). This too will be acknowledged by all when the end comes.

Now and not yet

The image of the millennium therefore faces in two directions in time. It looks forward to the new creation, the final judgment and the resurrection of all the dead (v. 5). At the same time, the role of the Church remains what it is now: to share the rule of Christ, to be his priests and to affirm the truth of its testimony to Jesus.

The millennium confirms the role of the martyr Church in living out, in the presence of the beast, the values of the coming kingdom. Through the death and resurrection of Jesus, and the witness of the Church, the kingdom has a foothold in the world. Those who share in the work of the kingdom here can be assured of a final glorious outcome (v. 6). The fact that the Church currently shares in Christ's rule and judgment will be clear at the end, but is now grasped only by faith. Similarly, the future will reveal the full extent of judgment, but its presence is shown by the world's response to the gospel. By the acceptance or rejection of the message of Christ, the world prepares itself for the final outcome.

Because of his stress on the call to witness, and to suffering as necessary for the truth of the gospel, John may seem to have little to say about any present blessings that Christians may experience. By stressing the coming and present share in Christ's reign, he points to the real strength of Christianity in the present age. To be a Christian is to know God and to experience, in however limited a way, his presence, his love and the empowering of his Spirit. Against this, the beast has nothing to offer.

PRAYER

Father, thank you for your promised victory. Help your people in this world to see that they already have a share in it and to know your blessing now.

ETERNAL CONSEQUENCES

Once the thousand-year reign of Christ is ended, Satan is set free (v. 7), and the nations rebel (v. 8). The devil has been restrained by the preaching of the gospel, but now, in a last act of defiance, he deceives the world with his myth of human self-sufficiency. The nations will seize the power that belongs to God and remove the troublesome saints. John is telling again the story of the last battle from chapters 16 and 19. In Ezekiel 37—40 John found a similar pattern of resurrection, the restoration of God's people under the rule of the Messiah, invasion by the forces of Gog, and the coming of the new Jerusalem.

The point is that in this world, there will always be Satan, for he represents the human tendency to sin. There will always be 'the nations', for they represent the human tendency to set up systems and structures that oppose God. Nothing less than a new creation will see an end to this pattern.

Dwelling of God

Once again, the armies of evil surround the camp of the saints (v. 9). The term 'camp' brings us once again to the exodus theme that runs through Revelation. The people of God in this world are on a journey which will lead to the new Jerusalem. This has not yet come into being, so the 'beloved city' is a reference to the camp of God's people.

Wherever a church is gathered, there is the dwelling of God, and there is the city of God. Like the tabernacle of the wilderness wanderings, the presence of God moves with his people as protector, teacher and guide. At the same time, as the wilderness wanderings were a time of trial and the painful shaping of the people of Israel into the people of God, so the Church's time in the world is one of testing and suffering, of perseverance and the building of faith. It may often be hard for us to recognize the city of God in the midst of our world, and in the midst of our local congregation, but then we rarely see things as God does.

Gog and Magog descend on the saints. In Ezekiel 38:2, Gog is king of the mythical land of Magog, while in Revelation they are both either lands or kings. In both books, the names are simply symbols for the enemies of God.

Once again, there is no battle but only judgment. Fire falls from heaven and destroys the attackers (v. 10).

Lake of fire

Satan is now finally destroyed, heralding the coming of the new age, the new creation. He is destined to an eternity of torment in the lake of fire with the beast and the false prophet.

This again raises a rather important question, especially since they will shortly be joined by those human beings who have rejected God (14:10; 20:14–15). Does John truly envisage an eternity of suffering for those who are not saved?

To be sure, the Church has taught this for a long time (though never without dissent), but as far as Revelation is concerned there are good indicators that we are once again reading the language of symbol rather than fact. Firstly, the beast and the false prophet are abstractions, symbols themselves, as indeed are Death and Hades (20:13). It is impossible to speak of these symbols being eternally tormented, though for sinners and the devil it may make more sense. Secondly, the lake of fire is described as the second death, which is the language of final ending. The eternal torment, like the smoke of fallen Babylon, which goes up for ever (19:3), is better taken as a figure of speech, indicating the eternal and irrevocable consequences of rejecting God's offer of salvation.

A third point that we need to bear in mind in making doctrine, if not in reading Revelation, is philosophical. God is the creator and sustainer of all. To have an eternal hell of torment, with no remission or hope of repentance, is to have God sustaining, in his perfect new creation, a part of it which will always be in rebellion against him, and which can only be described as evil. It would also make nonsense of the promise in 21:4 that there will be no more mourning, crying and pain. It would be sensible to go with those parts of the book that indicate a final ending, an annihilation, of those who are not redeemed.

PRAYER

Father, let the seriousness of rejecting you
give urgency to our witness.

BOOK *of* LIFE

After the millennium and rebellion comes the last judgment. God appears seated on a throne, which is now the white of victory, and creation dissolves at his appearing (v. 11). Both the earthly world and the spiritual dimension that lies behind it are stripped away. All that remains is God, and those he is to judge.

The disappearance of creation is not a great act of destruction like the fall of Babylon. It is simply a clearing of the site, ready for God's re-creation of the new heaven and earth. It has served its purpose. It has brought forth creatures who can know and love God and so find an eternal destiny with him—or be lost for ever.

Deeds and destiny

All the dead are raised for judgment, even those with no grave save the depth of the sea (v. 13); no one is beyond the reach of God. Resurrection is the Christian doctrine of life after death—a statement that God is the giver of eternal life, rather than its being a sort of natural process in which the souls of the departed drift off into a new existence. Of course, it may well be that the soul or personality, or whatever, does not die at death. Paul, for instance, thought of death as going to be with the Lord (Philippians 1:23). In 20:4 the souls of the martyrs were seen sharing in Christ's rule, which is probably both an image of the suffering Church on earth (as we have argued), and also a statement that those who die are in Christ's safekeeping till the resurrection. The fullness of eternal life remains an act of new creation, however, in which the present life can be thought of as providing a basic blueprint; the outcome of resurrection is governed by the life lived in the present world.

Twice John stresses that judgment is on the basis of deeds (vv. 12, 13: the books represent God's unfailing knowledge of human thoughts and actions), yet at the same time it depends on the book of life. The implication is that the deeds, in their earthly life, of resurrected humanity reflect their status before God. Actions spring from faith—faith in God or faith in something else. Can it be that there are some who do not count themselves as believers, whose deeds are nonetheless the deeds of faith in God? The answer would seem to be yes, or otherwise the books of deeds need not be consulted. Jesus hinted at just such a scenario when he envisaged those at the last judgment who would be surprised to find that they had welcomed him (Matthew 25:37–40).

Open verdict

In the crucial section of Revelation, 11:1–13, we saw the witness of the suffering Church resulting in the salvation of the majority of those who had followed the beast (11:13). In the image of the two harvests (14:14–20), we saw two possible results of the world's judgment. It may lead either to salvation or to destruction. There is no attempt to bring together these two images. They are left side by side, for the task of the Church is not yet ended, and even the prophet John cannot tell us how it will be resolved.

From chapter 15 onwards, the descriptions of judgment on the beast and Babylon have had the grape harvest in view. God's vintage of wrath is trodden, and the consequences shown in detail. Now the picture is more ambiguous. We are told that judgment takes place. Some suffer the second death. But how many? Exactly who? We are not told. The thrust of Revelation as a whole forbids a belief that salvation is given without repentance and faith on the part of the saved. John's ambiguity here is a way of saying that repentance and faith may belong to more than we suspect. We are not given the right, as yet, to judge any. All we may do is proclaim the gospel, joyfully welcoming those who respond visibly, and leaving the final decision to God.

Harvest of life

From now on, the first harvest, the gathering in to eternal life (14:14–16) governs the visions. Judgment is past, for good or ill, and a new creation is about to begin.

PRAYER

Father, protect us from the temptation to pass the judgment that is reserved for you. Instead, show us such a vision of your love that we will desire nothing more than to share it with others.

New Creation

Judgment gives way to the new world, as another vision unfolds before John's eyes. This new creation has been the goal all along. History and faith have been directed towards it, and the newness of life, the Spirit-given 'first resurrection', has been its foreshadowing. Now John sees it, although, like the rest of Revelation, the description that follows is symbolic. There can be no literal description of something that no one living has experienced. At the same time, there are hints of what it will be—hints found in worship and prayer, in the beauty and harmony of the present creation, and hints found in the present possibility of a relationship with God, for the centre of the new creation, like the centre of present reality (4:2–4) is God himself. Where he is presently hidden from sight, he will be in plain view (which is, of course, also a metaphor for something we can barely imagine).

Renewal

In his depiction of the new creation, John draws on the old. He is not describing a total replacement, but a renewal (21:5). What is to come is based on what already is, but it will be greater, purer and more fully itself. The Greek word John uses for 'new' (*kainos*) tends to carry a connotation of newness of quality, of feel, rather than complete replacement—a hint perhaps that the new life in Christ which begins in this world forms the link with the next, and brings renewal to all creation.

So John sees a new heaven and a new earth. Heaven too must be renewed, since it stands for the spiritual reality of the present age. As such, it had a place for the devil, who is no more. The sea, too, is gone. For those who think of the seas as the greatest beauty of the earth, this is at first a startling image. A new creation without the thunder of breakers, the rich diversity of the ocean deeps and the haunting cry of gulls seems strangely impoverished. It is not the physical sea of earth that is in view, however. The crystal sea before the throne of God (4:6) has gone. It symbolized the forces of chaos, which have their spiritual as well as earthly counterparts. Towards the end of the book, it became the lake of fire (15:2), symbol of eternal destruction and separation from God. It stood for the Red Sea, a barrier to the people of God, and for the abyss out of which evil comes, and which must be overcome by the creative power of God. The sea, in short, stands for all that has opposed God's will and persecuted his people: it is the dragon, the beasts, Babylon and their temptations to turn away from Christ. In the new creation, these are things of the past. The spiritual realm is purified of chaos, and it becomes the source of harmony and peace.

Goal of creation

If this is the final destiny of creation, we might ask why God did not just create it straight away. It might have saved a lot of trouble, after all! For all that God created a good world (Genesis 1), it came with the possibility of sin and failure (Genesis 2—3).

This is not a question that John is concerned to answer, nor does it appear elsewhere in the Bible. The scriptures start where we are, in the here and now, and address what it means to know God in the real world rather than in a fantasy realm. All the same, the question is a fair one, and the answer is in fact implied throughout the Bible and especially in Revelation.

God's desire is for people who will freely love and serve him. In the world at large, there are certain values that he treasures, such as love, honesty, integrity, faithfulness, compassion and mercy. The processes by which such values may come about can only be found in a world such as ours. They need a world where there is the possibility of disobedience, so that obedience can be freely offered; where love is given against the potential for hatred; where service is a real alternative to selfishness. Only if sin is a real possibility can virtue be meaningful. Honesty, integrity and faithfulness demand the possibility of falsehood; compassion and mercy need cruelty and legalism as real options. God does not desire that any of these bad things actually happen, but they must be real possibilities. Only when love and virtue have been freely offered can they be preserved for eternity in the new creation. Revelation is a call to us to be faithful witnesses of God's love and mercy, which will one day be seen by all.

PRAYER

Father, in the storms and tempests of our lives, when chaos seems to rule, keep us true to the vision of the world to come, when the sea of troubles will be no more.

CITY of GOD

It has been said that Revelation could be subtitled 'A Tale of Two Cities'. All that can be said of the two sides in the conflict between the purposes of God and of Satan is summed up in their representatives, Babylon and the new Jerusalem.

For the Christians of John's churches, as for most inhabitants of Greek and Roman society, life outside the ambit of a city was unthinkable. Their identity was formed by the city in which they lived, by its culture, its social life, its local politics and its religion. This was what made the claims of Christianity so difficult for many believers. The call to dissociate themselves from much that their neighbours took for granted—the trade guilds, the social and religious life of the pagan temples, the enthusiastic support of the empire itself—led to a sense of being outsiders in their own home community.

The same can apply to Christian minorities today, especially in countries where the dominant religion is ardently held (and, of course, for any cultural minority in any part of the world). Even in more 'liberal' Western nations, those who take their faith and witness seriously can feel that they have become to some extent outsiders in their workplace, their local pub or even their family.

For John's readers, then and now, the city of God, a place where they would truly feel at home, belonged to the future. In some sense, as we have seen, it is present wherever God is acknowledged and worshipped. The community of believers becomes itself the dwelling place of God (13:6). The only tangible city, however, tends to be Babylon and its satellites, the great whore who is the mother of whores (17:5)—that is, the other cities of the empire or of the world.

In the climactic visions of Revelation, John assures us that the time will come when the city of God, the new Jerusalem, will be a reality—the only reality.

City of hope

The fact that John's hope is couched in terms of a city should counteract one false impression that Revelation can give: that the city must always be a symbol of evil. In the ancient world, the city was the symbol of order and dignity, of art and culture. It was the city that enabled the flourishing of law and art, of philosophy and religion. It is a view that has passed into our language: politics, police, policy and polite are a few of the words we draw from *polis*, the Greek word for city. The Latin equivalent is *civitas*, from which we get city itself, along with civilization, civility and a host of others.

The vision of the new Jerusalem confirms this idea, that human beings are intended to live in communities where all that is good may flourish, where they may interact for their mutual benefit and share love, understanding and faith. Without the city, much that we call civilization could not exist, and in the new creation all that is good in the city will be preserved for ever.

Witness

With the vision of new Jerusalem before it, the Church's witness must surely include working to make the cities of the present world reflect to some extent the world that is to come. We cannot wash our hands of the cities in which most of us live, for God has decreed that we will live in a city for ever. Like the Jews who were exiled to Babylon, Christians must work for the good of their present city, bringing to it the values and faith of the city of God (Jeremiah 29:1–14). There will always be much of Babylon in our cities, but there can be something of Zion too.

The new Jerusalem appears as glorious as any bride on her wedding day, radiant in splendour, and yet not standing alone but prepared to be joined with her partner. John's image is influenced by Old Testament pictures of the earthly Jerusalem (for example, Isaiah 62), and their development in the Christian churches (Ephesians 5:25–33). The bride, however, has not prepared herself. It is God who, through grace, has created people for himself, for a relationship of love and intimacy of which marriage is the best, but still a poor, analogy.

REFLECT

Think of your own city or town. Pray for its troubles and give thanks for its virtues. Pray for its transformation into a reflection of the city of God.

ETERNAL LOVE, ETERNAL LIFE

The new Jerusalem comes down from heaven, for it is the gift of God. The God to whom all history is moving, the God who is coming to meet his people, is a gracious God. He is the giver of eternal life, and the one who has prepared a place for his people.

The city of God is more than a place; it is the presence of God himself. He is the dwelling place of his people. His presence surrounds and protects, sustains and nourishes. He is the source of all true hope, all life and all meaning. Therefore the voice from the throne (v. 3), like the voice in 21:5, is probably that of God himself. He announces that his promised presence among his people has now come about. The words translated in NRSV as 'home' and 'dwell' (v. 3) are literally 'tent' or 'tabernacle' and its related verb. They call to mind once more the story of the exodus, as God dwelt among his people in the holy tent and led them to the promised land. More than that, the Greek words used are the ones normally used to translate the Hebrew *shekinah*, the glowing cloud that shows the presence of God's glory (Exodus 40:34; 1 Kings 8:10–11). That luminous glory is now to be among his peoples for ever (see Ezekiel 37:27–28; Zechariah 2:10–11).

The many peoples of God

The various early manuscripts of Revelation are divided as to whether God promises that those among whom he will dwell are to be his 'people' or his 'peoples'. Each is found in English versions, so that, for instance, RSV has 'people' and NRSV has 'peoples'. The plural is the best one to go for, since rather more of the earliest and most reliable manuscripts favour it. It is also easier to see how a puzzled scribe might change it to the singular, so that it would refer to the single people of God, rather than the other way round.

This is an important point, because it shows the breadth of the vision of the city of God. It is the presence of God with all the peoples of the earth. Once again we are brought to the hopeful vision of the grain harvest of chapter 14. John's picture of eternal life includes the vast numbers who have responded to the witness of the suffering Church and have been brought into the everlasting kingdom of God. If the vision of the world to come is meant as an inspiration to the

Church, it is a vision that includes the salvation of the majority rather than a select few. We are called to witness in this hope, not in a sense of pessimism or despair. It is also important to note that there is no distinction here between those who have suffered and died for their faith, and the greater host of peoples who enter because of the martyrs' witness. All are God's peoples, whether they come early or late to receive his grace (Matthew 20:1–16).

Loving God

Three times we hear that God will be with his peoples, and, in words of tender intimacy (see Isaiah 25:8), are told that he will wipe away every tear from their eyes (v. 4). It is the image of a caring parent bringing comfort to a bruised child. It is also a picture of direct action. This is something that God will do. It will not be delegated to angels, to saints, or even to Jesus himself. There are no barriers or intermediaries, but only the living presence of the loving God himself. All those who have reached out in faith and hope, in despair and powerlessness, to the often distant possibility of God, find themselves now surrounded with his presence and held in his arms.

John uses the word 'love' very little. It is significant that the book as a whole is bracketed with images of love. It begins with an assertion that salvation springs from God's love (1:5) and ends with the personal presence of that love.

This is a love that banishes death itself and spells the end to all its associated misery. The results of human sinfulness (Genesis 3:16–19) have been undone. The first world, in which we now live, is a necessary prelude to the new creation. But it is a prelude only. The eternal love is the eternal reality.

PRAYER

Father, as history is bracketed by your love, may it also be the beginning and ending of our lives, and the chief characteristic that marks us as yours.

GOAL *of* CREATION

At various points in Revelation, a voice has been heard from the throne. The context has sometimes suggested that the speaker is God. Now, for the first time, it is clearly stated that God speaks. The direct speech, neither mediated by an angel nor coming as a distant voice, is another indication of God's dwelling with his people.

He is making all things new, and, as we saw earlier (21:1), the idea is of renewal rather than simple replacement. Creation is God's handiwork, and so it is valuable and worthy of preservation. The new creation is a fulfilment of the old rather than a simple replacement of it. Paul, writing to the Romans, saw the whole of creation as being involved in God's plan of salvation. All that God has made awaits a final transformation (Romans 8:22).

Message of hope

The message that a new creation awaits, that there is hope and purpose for the world, is worth sharing. John is told to write it down, so that it can be spread to many. Christianity is not a mystery religion, whose teaching is accessible only to those who have been initiated; neither is it a form of the ancient religion of gnosticism, where salvation was thought to come through arcane teachings. There have been times in the Church's history when both these mistakes have been made. They have usually been condemned as heresy, although occasionally the official attitude of the Church has been to keep the deep teachings of the faith restricted to a chosen few. By ordering that it be written down (and read aloud: see 1:3), God himself declares that his word is for everyone.

It is a message to be shared, a vision to be spread abroad, so that all may hear and receive God's gift of salvation. It is a message to be trusted, as it comes from the one who is himself steadfast and trustworthy. Nor does it lie entirely in the future. Although John's vision is of the final completion of the new creation, God's work of renewal begins in the here and now, with the gift of his creative Spirit to his people. The Spirit who roams through all creation is the Spirit who dwells among and empowers the Church.

In his vision, John hears the fulfilment of the promise. God declares his purposes to be complete. Creation has reached its final point and achieved what God has desired. He has a people—many diverse peoples—who acknowledge him freely, offer their worship and service as loving children, and receive his own eternal love and blessing.

Precious creation

We cannot begin to understand the form that the new creation will take, any more than we can imagine what life will be like after resurrection. The nearest we can come is through imagery and analogy (for example, 1 Corinthians 15:35–44). We have the promise, and that must be enough. At the same time, the fact that the promise of renewal is for all creation has a definite significance for the present. It reinforces the biblical doctrine that human beings are a part of the whole of creation.

That may sound so obvious as to be trite, yet the way we use our world—destroying resources, plant and animal species, polluting air and seas—suggests that we see it as an entity apart from our selves. It is approached as something that we can manipulate and use for our own ends, without consequences for us.

There is certainly something unique about human beings, of course. We have the capacity for moral action and the ability to relate to God. In the Genesis stories of creation, this uniqueness is described as being in the image of God (Genesis 1:27) and being animated by his spirit, or breath (Genesis 2:7). At the same time, humans are called into being by the same creative command of God as all other things (Genesis 1) and are formed from the same earth as all other animals (Genesis 2:7).

We are made to be part of a universe which affects us as we affect it, and on which our lives depend. We damage ourselves when we do it harm. For this same reason, we are destined for ever to be part of a greater creation. Our ultimate destiny is connected with that of the world, and vice versa.

PRAYER

Thank you, God, that we are part of a greater whole. Instil in us a respect and a sense of wonder for all your works.

BEGINNING & END

All this is the work of the God who is the beginning and the end of creation. He has made it and he will bring it to fruition. The description of God as beginning and end, Alpha and Omega, is more than a statement of the origin and destiny of the universe. By encompassing the start and the finish, it describes in shorthand the biblical doctrine of God as sustainer and guide of all that he has made.

The Bible has no concept of a God who winds up the universe like clockwork and then leaves it to run along on its own. God is intimately involved in his works, a part of the system he has made and the motive force behind it.

To say this does not imply that we have to accept a view of creation which states that the biblical stories of origins are literally true. It does say that all the complex processes of evolution and development, from the formation of stars and galaxies to the appearance of life on earth, has a purpose and goal.

Chance and purpose

There is a fashionable strand of thought which claims that the discoveries of scientists working on the origins of the universe, or on the processes of evolution, have left no place for belief in a God who is the creator. Even less place, it is claimed, is left for the notion of purpose in a mechanism that depends on random events.

This book is not the place to start arguing against such views in detail, but no discussion of creation can afford to ignore them. Suffice it to say that there is a vast difference between what science actually says and what some of its interpreters claim for it. We can say that modern research suggests a process of development and a mechanism by which it (at least in part) comes about. What we cannot say is that these mechanisms are purposeless. The only world where we have studied the development of life suggests very strongly that it is oriented to the production of complex, conscious, moral and spiritual beings.

We may choose to see the world as a vast battleground in which the fittest survive and the rest go to the wall, an amoral jungle of competing species and individuals. In such a world, it is hard indeed to see the hand of God. But we may choose instead to see the world as a vast and complex system of interlocking relationships, engaged in the quest for greater and more wonderful forms of life, which brings forth the beings God desires. On such a view, the reality of death and decay is a necessary part of the process that continually refines and develops the world. In such a world, there is every evidence of a sustaining and directing creator.

To speak of God as the beginning and end of creation gives us a new way of looking at the idea of causation. We think of a cause as something that lies only at the beginning, but it could also be at the end of a process, drawing things towards their final goal. As well as a spring that sets the ball in motion, there is, you might say, a magnet that draws it towards the target. Christians can look at the vast processes of the cosmos and the minute mechanisms of genetics, at the diversity of living things and the many ways of overcoming obstacles demonstrated by different species, and see them as creation's groping towards its final goal of producing beings who are able to relate to God, who draws all things to himself.

Life giver

It is this God, creator, sustainer and saviour, who gives the promise of eternal life. It is he who is able to satisfy the soul-thirst that leaves us seeking more in the presence of plenty, which declares that there must be hope in the face of despair, and meaning when all seems pointless. In him alone is true satisfaction found.

In the new creation, the living water promised by Jesus (John 4:10; 7:37–38), which is fulfilled in part through the gift of the Holy Spirit, becomes an eternal reality as we find our true purpose and destiny in God.

PRAYER

Lord, you have made us for yourself,
and our souls are restless till they find their rest in you.

St Augustine of Hippo

CHILDREN *of* GOD

The messages to the seven churches each ended with a promise to 'the one who conquers'. We have seen that conquering means being faithful in witness even to the point of death. The promises to the churches referred forward to the last two chapters of the book, and now all is made clear. What is promised are the wonders of the new creation, the new Jerusalem, which await those who remain faithful to Christ.

By now it should be clear that this promise is not 'pie in the sky when you die'. The vision of the world to come is a driving force behind the Church's present witness and worship. It is foreshadowed in our experience of the Spirit of God and tasted in the believer's relationship with Christ. Above all, it is presaged by the present privilege of being called God's children.

Children were one of Jesus' favourite images for his disciples (Matthew 7:11; 18:2–6; 19:14; John 13:33; 21:5). It was an image of trust and dependence. Children rely on their parents for their very lives, and so Jesus' disciples were to rely on God (v. 7). Furthermore, it was an image of love and acceptance. The followers of Jesus are servants of God, his slaves (Romans 1:1; Revelation 1:1). They are ambassadors of God (2 Corinthians 5:20) and his stewards (1 Corinthians 4:1). All of these can be positions of responsibility and privilege—or they can be positions of fear and unease. To be children of God, however, is to be welcomed into the family circle, to know love and peace, safety and well-being. As a valued child, even rebuke and punishment are given with love in mind, and with proper growth as the goal (1 Corinthians 4:14). In the new creation, the goal has been achieved, and there remains only the eternal welcome home.

Cast out

It comes as something of a shock suddenly to be confronted with a reminder of those who are not to share in the new order (v. 8). Surely judgment is now past, and only glory remains? True enough, as the order of John's story goes. It is written, though, as an encouragement and challenge to the churches. The promise has been given to the conquerors, but a warning is given to those who are tempted to compromise with the world.

The first on the list of Christians who may be in danger of failure are cowards: those who are put off from the life of faithful witness by fear, and so prove faithless to Jesus. We might expect some mention of the loveless and the hypocrites, those who were most roundly condemned by Jesus himself. There is also the nagging thought that courage is not a virtue that most people would claim with any certainty! John, however, is writing from a particular viewpoint. He wants to call the churches to be witnesses who will remain true to their Lord in the face of the persecuting beast. In times of strong opposition, courage is the cardinal virtue. Fortunately it is also a gift of God, given to those who seek to be faithful.

The rest of the list reflects the charges brought against the whore Babylon and the beast on which she rode. To compromise with the forces of the world is to be identified with the sins of the world. Few members of John's churches are likely to have been murderers or sorcerers, but if they tried to steer a quiet middle path of compromise, they were tacitly siding with the power that kills the saints of God and claims an authority which is his alone.

Some interpreters argue that this passage must be about unbelievers, since no Christian can truly be lost. In the present context, it must refer to members of the churches, for only they have been called to conquer, and the very call itself presupposes the possibility of refusal. On the other hand, it is probably fair to suppose that John has in mind those whose lifestyle is adamantly non-Christian rather than those who occasionally lapse. Hence the list continues with idolaters—those who worship something other than the true God—and liars, who claim the name of Christian but whose life denies that claim.

John is saying no more than that the Church on earth undoubtedly contains those who are not genuine disciples. Jesus said the same (Matthew 13:24–30). What both Jesus and John affirm is that the judgment of who is or is not a true disciple will be God's, not ours.

PRAYER

Father, in your love you have called us to be your children.
Help us to rely on you for the courage we sometimes need
as members of your family.

BELOVED BRIDE

The theme of warning to the churches continues in the appearance of one of the angels of the seven bowls. It is the instrument of God's wrath who invites the prophet to have a closer look at the city of God. The presence of the judging angel points up the choice that faces the Church and, through the Church's witness, the nations of the world. They may belong to Babylon or to the city of God. Here and now, they may, by their choice of god (the beast or the true God), make their own dwelling resemble either Babylon or new Jerusalem.

The use of the destroying angel to point to God's dwelling place is also a reminder of the purpose of judgment. It is not simply divine vindictiveness, but a necessary outworking of redemption and the new creation. Right up to the end, we have seen judgment as a call to repentance. Now the final judgment is once more shown as a preparation for renewal and remaking.

Intimate love

We have seen the city of God represented as a place in which the peoples will dwell (21:3). In that sense, it stands for God's new creation, the remade universe which will be the environment for the redeemed. We have also seen it shown as the presence of God himself, his being and love that will surround and sustain his creation. Of course, it already does, but the spiritual reality that underlies all things will be a tangible experience in the age to come. Now, in this verse, we are shown the city as people, the redeemed of God. John will go on to describe the city in detail, but we need to keep in mind that this is a metaphor for his people, who both constitute the dwelling place of God and are contained by his new creation. Hence, new Jerusalem is both city and bride.

This has been hinted at already in the promise that the victors will be God's children (21:7). Now another image of intimate love is brought into play. The city of God, whose beauty is like that of a bride in all her finery (21:2), turns out in fact to be the bride, the one who is married to the Lamb. This image has been slowly built up since chapter 17, with the contrasting images of the harlot city in chapters 17—18 and the introduction of the bride in 19:7, and it now comes to fruition. Here in verses 9–10 John uses the pattern of hearing one thing and seeing another, which we first met in 5:5–6 where the lion turned out to be the Lamb.

The image of God's people as his wife has a long history in the Bible. Hosea had likened the love of God to his own experience with a faithless wife. The people had turned away and worshipped other gods, just as Hosea's wife, Gomer, had been a prostitute in the Canaanite fertility cults (Hosea 1—3). God would nonetheless bring his people back to himself, a process that would be painful to both God and Israel. Now the new Jerusalem appears as the bride of the Lamb, the one who has brought them back to God at great personal cost. The reconciliation has been achieved through the shedding of blood—the blood of Christ and the blood of the martyrs.

The picture of God's search for his faithless wife (for example, Jeremiah 3:20; Ezekiel 16:32) led to the image of a relationship of intimacy and love between God and his people which is as deep and passionate as any sexual relationship. Jews and Christians came to read the Bible's great love poem, the Song of Songs, as an allegory of the love of God for his people. It was read particularly at Passover, the festival of God's rescue of his people. The same image is used of the relationship of Christ to the Church (Ephesians 5:28–32).

Divine longing

Such an image does much to dispel the notion of God as a distant and probably angry figure of power. It is the language of passion, of a longing which is as intense as pain. God is no calculating cosmic architect but the father who sees his children on the path to ruin, the lover whose bride has left him at the altar to seek a road to self-destruction. It is this divine pain that finds expression on the cross and shows itself as redeeming love. It is this heartfelt desire for the good and the love of his creatures that lies behind the language of jealousy that sometimes describes God in the Old Testament (for example, Exodus 20:5).

This rich tradition is now applied to Jesus and the people he has redeemed. Once again, he is worthy to be addressed in terms befitting God, for he is indeed God, come to be one of us. To woo his bride, God has put on human garb and suffered human pain.

PRAYER

Eternal God, we cannot measure the depth of your love. We can only wonder at its immensity and lose ourselves within it.

MEETING PLACE

By now we should not be surprised to find John describing afresh something he has already shown us. Following the pattern we met at 5:5–6 and 7:4, 9, he hears of a bride and sees a city. The city explains the meaning of the bride.

Spirit of prophecy

Once again, the Spirit of God whisks him away on a visionary trip. The footnote in NRSV ('in the Spirit') is a better translation than the main text's 'in the spirit'. This is not something that happens in John's spirit, dredged up from the fevered depths of his subconscious, but is the work of the Holy Spirit. The phrase 'in the Spirit' occurs four times at significant points in the book. It introduces the whole work as a visionary experience that brought the words of Christ to him (1:10), and it begins the series of visions of heaven and the reality that underlies the world (4:2). It is the Spirit who opens his eyes to the spiritual significance of Rome (17:3) and now shows him the meaning of the new Jerusalem, the city which is the pattern of all true cities, and of which Babylon is a poisonous travesty.

The Spirit is not the one who speaks and gives the revelation. He is a chain of communication that leads from God, through Christ to the angel of chapter 10. The work of the Spirit, as the inspirer of prophecy, is to grant John the visionary experiences through which such communication becomes possible. This is a view of the Spirit's work that we find elsewhere in the New Testament. The Spirit is the one who makes Christ real to us so that we can hear him speak, the one who opens up a relationship with God that makes worship possible (Romans 8:15; Galatians 4:6), who forms a channel for our prayer (Romans 8:26–27) and who carries the revelation of God himself (1 Corinthians 2:10–12).

These four references to the Spirit's visionary inspiration may perhaps point to the original visions on which John has reflected and prayed to produce his book. (The finished work, of course, is a piece of carefully written theological literature.)

Mountain of God

The mountain to which John is carried is not merely a vantage point from which he can get a better view. It is the mountain to which the city itself descends (Ezekiel 40:2), and it is full of symbolism. In primitive thought, mountains are likely to be holy places, since they are nearer to the gods. The gods of Greek myth dwelt on Mount Olympus, and, closer to biblical home, the Canaanite gods dwelt on a mythical mountain to the far north of the world. This myth is hijacked by the writer of Psalm 48 and applied to Zion, the mountain of Jerusalem where the true God dwells in his temple (Psalm 48:1–2). It was at Mount Sinai that God revealed himself to the Israelites (Exodus 19:9–18). It was to Sinai (also called Horeb) that Elijah fled to meet with God (1 Kings 19:8) after showing the supremacy of YHWH over the gods of Canaan on Mount Carmel (1 Kings 18:20–40).

The high mountain of new Jerusalem signifies once again the meeting of God and his people. It is the place where God is encountered, the final reality of God's dwelling with his people. In the present age this is a spiritual truth, recognized only by faith. God is with his people, and they are securely kept by the Lamb on his holy mount (14:1). In our worship and prayer, we can meet consciously with God and sometimes catch a glimpse of his reality. In the age to come, there is no distinction between spiritual and physical. There is one reality, apprehended by those who are called to spend eternity in the presence of God, whose reality suffuses the new creation.

The city of God is seen coming down from heaven, because it is God's creation and gift. Standing here for the people of God, it is a reminder that they are brought into being by him. He calls them by the preaching of the gospel and draws them close to him in prayer. He teaches and cares for them, equips them with spiritual gifts, and challenges and transforms them by the work of the Holy Spirit. He strengthens them for service, lending courage in persecution and patience in adversity. What we are now is part of the process of formation that leads to the unimaginable gift of what we will be in the fullness of God's kingdom.

PRAYER

Lord, thank you for those moments when your Spirit grants us a vision of your constant presence. May we always be aware of you, until the time when we meet you in your new creation.

SHINING CITY

The detailed description of the holy city combines the themes we have noted so far, although the central one remains that of God's abiding presence. The city shines with the glory of God, the glowing cloud of the *shekinah* that showed God's presence in the temple of old. It is translucent, so that the glory may shine from it, and its appearance is like jasper—the precious stone to which God himself is compared (4:3). Once again, the dwelling of the saints is seen as within the presence of God.

Priests of the king

The walls are adorned with jewels, as prophesied in Isaiah 54:11–12. These are no random selection of trinkets, but the jewels found in the breastplate of the high priest (Exodus 28:17–20). (There is a slight difference between John's list and that of Exodus, but it is hard to be sure exactly what the names of precious stones in Hebrew refer to, and they had no fixed Greek equivalents.) Like the high priest's breastplate, the city is square, the geometric shape symbolizing perfection, and bears twelve jewels. In fact, the city is a perfect cube (or perhaps pyramid, although a cube is the more obvious interpretation), symbolizing its absolute perfection (perfection in 3D). It therefore has a priestly function, since it is also the people of God, his royal priesthood.

In the new creation, there is no need for a priesthood to mediate the presence of God to the nations (v. 22). The witnessing task of the Church is ended. It is the other task of a priesthood, that of offering worship, which goes on eternally. The city symbolizes the worshipping community of the redeemed.

A brief warning may be in order at this point. We must not think of the life of the new creation as one of an eternal church service! No matter how enjoyable our worship may be, the thought of doing it for ever without a break makes the age to come thoroughly unattractive. To speak of the new creation as eternal worship is to speak of an eternal awareness of the presence and worthiness of God, rather than an endless liturgy or prayer meeting or whatever. It is better, in fact, to see that eternal awareness as the goal towards which all earthly worship aspires.

Paradise regained

The city is also the place that God has prepared for his people to live in. It symbolizes the whole of the new creation as the habitat of the redeemed peoples. In this sense, it is paradise restored. According to Jewish interpretation, Havilah, the land adjacent to Eden (Genesis 2:11–12) was counted as part of paradise. It was there that gold and precious stones were to be found in abundance. The new Jerusalem is thus built out of the materials of Eden, and is a fulfilment of the glory God originally intended for his creatures. The angels at the gates are a further indication that the holy city is a kind of return to paradise. When God cast Adam and Eve out of the garden, he set the cherubim (an order of angels) to guard the way back (Genesis 3:24) so that sinful humanity was barred from the presence of God. Now the angels stand at the gates to open them in welcome.

Better than Paradise

The city, while it reflects the restoration of the glory lost at the fall, is not Eden remade. The garden that humanity was to till has been replaced by the community centred on God. Even God cannot undo what has been done. Innocence has been lost and cannot be restored. The way is not back but forward, through the consequences of sin, the cross, resurrection and judgment, into a creation which takes account of all that has happened and, by the grace of God, transforms the world's pain into the world's joy.

Seen in that light, the path of Christian discipleship is a reflection of the history of creation and of all humanity. The way through failure, repentance, forgiveness, death and resurrection is the way to eternal life in the presence of God.

PRAYER

Father, thank you that you can take Edens that are devastated and build on the site of our destruction a shining city.

The NEVER-ENDING STORY

The gates of the city bear the names of the twelve tribes of Israel (v. 12). The last time we heard of the tribes, they stood for the Church (7:4–8). This time, they stand for historic Israel, which becomes clear when we see that the foundations of the city are inscribed with the names of the twelve apostles (v. 14). The city, then, represents the whole people of God. It is founded on the gospel proclaimed by the apostles (Ephesians 2:20), and entry into it is also entry into the covenant people of God.

The new Jerusalem is the culmination of a process which has its origins in the call of Abraham, the rescue of the Israelites from Egypt and the forging of God's people in the desert of Sinai. Indeed, it goes back further, to the first human choice of sin, lost in the mists of pre-history, and shrouded in the Hebrew story of Eden and the serpent. It was the goal of the people of God, symbolized but never realized in the historic city of Jerusalem, the temple, and the dream of Messiah. It was made possible by the coming of Christ, and is partially realized in the worship and witness of his people. It is the promise and goal of his Church.

The story of the people of God is the story of the outworking of his salvation, and we are as much a part of it as any character in the Bible. The call to witness that forms the backbone of Revelation is a call to all Christians to take their place in the story that leads from Eden to the new Jerusalem.

Heavenly surveyor

Once before, we have seen measurements being taken. John was told to measure the temple of God (11:1) as a sign of God's protection of his people. Now the measurements are carried out because suffering is at an end (v. 15). There are no more foes to conquer the outward aspect of the people. The victory has been won and God's peace rules over his people, encompassing their every dimension.

The measuring angel finds the dimensions of the city to be multiples of twelve, the number of the people of God. It is a cube, sign of perfection, and also the shape of the holy of holies, the innermost sanctuary of the earthly temple built by Solomon (1 Kings 6:20), where the presence of God dwelt. The city is found both to represent the people of God and also to be his dwelling place. When John first measured the temple, the outer court was left unprotected (11:2): God's people would be trampled underfoot, though their relationship with God was safe. Now there is no outer court; the whole is the holiest of holies.

Temple city

There is no temple in the city to symbolize the presence of God, for all of it is filled with the glory of God. There is no central place of worship, for all the inhabitants are priests who see God face to face (22:4), and the character of their very existence is worship and service. In fact, it is the people themselves who form the temple, as promised to those who overcome the time of trial faced by the witnessing Church (3:12).

A similar thought lies behind the wall of jasper (v. 18). It is built of the stone that represents God. Zechariah had prophesied that in the restored Jerusalem, God himself would be its wall of fire (Zechariah 2:5). No wall is really necessary, and its height is ridiculously small compared with the size of the city (v. 17), but the presence of a wall was what defined a city in John's day. The city of God is defined by his presence, and he is its eternal security.

Living in the midst of the divine glory, there is no need of external illumination (v. 23). The sun and moon are rendered redundant by the light of God himself (Isaiah 60:19–20: we hear echoes of Isaiah 60 in verses 23–26). In fact, the light of glory comes from both God and the Lamb. Once again we see the divine terms in which Christ is described. He shares the throne of God and shines with the same light. It is hard to imagine a clearer statement of Christ's divinity, and therefore of the eternal nature of the trinity. Because of the coming of Christ, God himself must be seen in new terms, both of his inner nature and of the sacrificial quality of his love.

PRAYER

Lord, in this world we often grope in darkness. Thank you for the promise of a day when your light will illumine all we see.

SAVIOUR *of the* NATIONS

The city of God lies open to the nations of the world and their kings. There is no indication that these are any other than the ones who trampled the outer court of the temple (11:2) in their persecution of the Church, who were seduced by the whore (17:2; 18:3, 23) and who were destroyed in their final rebellion by the returning Christ (19:15). In the present scenario, they have repented and entered into the promised salvation (11:13; 15:4). John's picture of the new creation builds on the possibility held out by the harvest of grain (14:14–16). He does not set before us a corresponding image of a city peopled only by the martyrs.

If John does not explicitly choose between the two possibilities, his final vision is the optimistic one. He has majored on the vision of judgment because his aim has been to convince his readers of the danger of compromise and the underlying sinfulness of a world that may look all too attractive. Human beings are indeed free to reject even the love of God, but they do so in the face of the faithful proclamation of the gospel. John knew that the word of God does not go out in vain (Isaiah 55:9–11), and so shows God's ultimate triumph—the conversion of the nations.

Redeemed creation

The nations and their kings bring their 'glory and honour' into the city (v. 26). These terms can also be translated as 'treasure and wealth', and that is how they should be understood. In Isaiah's vision of the restored Jerusalem, the kings come in homage to Zion, bringing offerings of all the treasures of the earth (Isaiah 60:8–12). In John's vision, they do not come to the new Jerusalem as servants of the saints, but as equal sharers in its glory. (They come also, of course, to be a part of it. The image of open gates is symbolic of the openness of God's kingdom; it is not a statement that the new creation will be in two parts, dividing the city from the nations around it.) What the nations bring is all that is good in the earth. Only those things that are unacceptable to God are excluded (v. 27).

Those who once brought their goods to adorn the whore now bring them into the city of God. For those who seek to live their present lives in the light of the coming city of God, there is a challenge here. It is not enough to say that one day all wealth will be offered in worship to God. We need to ask whether it is used in that way here and now. Riches that are used to combat inequality, to aid the downtrodden or to alleviate suffering are surely riches that are offered to God. Those that bolster oppressors, widen the gap between rich and poor and bring violence and misery are paid in tribute to Babylon.

At times, Christians have embraced a very negative view of the material world, scorning earthly pleasure as sinful, and earthly riches as wicked. John does not share this view. The wickedness of Babylon did not lie in the existence of wealth and splendour, but in the use to which they were put, and the human cost at which they were obtained.

Salvation is not a freeing of the soul from material being, but a transformation of the material into an eternal form. This is why the distinctively Christian view of 'life after death' is resurrection, not simply survival of the soul.

The Bible does not present us with a world-denying form of spirituality. In John's vision, the new creation is not a place of austerity, but of richness and splendour. Nothing that is good in the present age will be lost, but it will be transformed into greater wonder. The Bible begins with the assertion that what God has made, he pronounced good (Genesis 1). If the world lay under his curse through human sin (Genesis 3:17; Romans 8:20–22), it was through no failing in creation. There is much that is good in the world, and it is the gift of God. In the new creation, the curse is removed and the goodness remains.

PRAYER

Father, thank you for the wealth and treasure of the world,
and for your promise of their redemption. Here and now,
may we learn to use them to your praise and glory.

WATER *of* LIFE

The theme of paradise restored continues with the river of life (v. 1),
which runs through the streets of the city like the river that flowed
out of Eden (Genesis 2:10), and is bounded by the tree of life (v. 2).
The image is hard to imagine visually, but its message is clear. Jesus
had promised eternal life, the life of the Spirit, as refreshing water
(John 4:14; 7:38). In turn, he drew on the Old Testament images
that inspire Revelation. Ezekiel had pictured a river flowing from the
temple of restored Jerusalem, and bringing life to the land. There is
no temple in the new Jerusalem, but the river still symbolizes the
same thing, that life flows from the presence of God. Where he is, the
world bursts into flower and fruitfulness. Beside Ezekiel's river stood
trees that bore fruit all year (Ezekiel 47:1–12; compare Zechariah
14:8). For John, the trees are the tree of life (Genesis 2:9), which was
denied to humanity by sin (Genesis 3:22). Now all may eat of it; all
may be refreshed by the waters of eternity. Most particularly, the
leaves of the tree are for the healing of the nations. Again, there is
no indication that these nations are different from those that have
opposed God in earlier chapters. Nor is there any qualification, suggesting that they are a converted remnant from the nations. John is
sticking with his optimistic prediction that salvation will come to the
rebellious world, and that all (or at least most) will be gathered into
the city of God.

Eco-city

If the city of God is the ideal city, it is worth noting that it does not
form a bastion against the encroachment of nature. Its central feat-
ures are a river and a tree. The human struggle against unrestrained
nature is seen by the Bible as a result of sin (Genesis 3:17–19). In the
new creation, civilization and the natural world flow in harmony.
Even in our world, a city with no parks and trees is considered a bare
and arid place.

One to one

The most staggering feature of the city, however, is that the people
will see God's face (v. 4). In the biblical tradition, to look on the face

of God was more than human life could bear (Exodus 33:20–23). In the new creation, there will be no barrier of fear between God and his creatures. In their worship, they will gaze on his reality.

The people bear the name of God on their foreheads (v. 4). They have already been marked as his (7:3), though here the thought may refer to the high priest's headpiece, which was said in later Jewish sources to bear the name of God, YHWH. The priestly function of the people of God continues in the age to come, as worship is offered to God and to the Lamb.

As his servants, the people of the city share in the reign of God. This does not mean that there are some other people who are ruled by them. The martyrs, the nations and their kings have all entered the city, and all are now God's. To say that they share his reign is a way of saying that they share his glory and dwell within it.

Eternal journey

John has now brought his description of the coming age to a triumphant conclusion, but it is not the end of the story. In fact, it is the beginning of the tale, but it is one that cannot be comprehended by those who are not yet in the new city. The journey of the Church and the nations moves towards the climax that John foretells. After that, who can say? Perhaps the journey continues in an ever deeper exploration of God, his love and his new creation. The infinite God can never be exhausted, and his wonders can never come to an end. There will always be more to be discovered, and more service, worship and love to encounter.

John's vision is no more than the title page of the second volume in the story of creation and redemption. For those of us who are still in the first part, it is enough to know that there is a sequel, and that it is even better than the first.

PRAYER

Father, thank you for your promise of eternity.
May we journey in faith, hope and love until we know
even as we are known.

TRUE PROPHET?

John begins his final section, an epilogue to round off the book. Although he does not describe himself as a prophet, he announces his book as prophecy, he describes his calling to prophesy, and he is described as one of the brotherhood of prophets (22:9). Perhaps he avoided the word because he was in conflict with others, such as Jezebel of Thyatira (2:20), who were ready to claim the title while delivering false teaching.

Was John right? It is easy to say that one's own words are prophecy, but how does the hearer know? The angel asserts that the words of God delivered by John are trustworthy and true. Of course, God's words always are, or he would not be God. But are the words those of God? There are some who would want to argue with John's views on compromise with Roman culture and religion, and with his assertion that blessing follows the readers and doers of his teaching (1:3; 22:7, 9), that cursing will fall on its detractors (22:18–19), and that he has received it as divine revelation (1:1; 22:8). To say that it is the word of God is not a definitive response to such criticism.

Testing the spirits

In the early church, prophets played an important role in both leadership and teaching. This meant that an equally important emphasis was placed on the testing of prophecies (1 Corinthians 14:29; 1 John 4:1). It is hard to be sure exactly what criteria were used, but the main one was surely how well the prophecy conformed to the teaching of scripture (Deuteronomy 13:1–3). John goes out of his way to demonstrate that his prophecy is not only in line with scripture but also ties the prophecies of the Old Testament together.

From our point of view, the answer has already been given, since the Church as a whole has agreed that Revelation has a place in holy scripture. That place did not come easily, and there was a lot of debate before it was accepted, but accepted it was.

Even that does not solve the issue completely, however. We still have to ask whether this portion of the Bible is prophecy, as far as we are concerned. For instance, Leviticus, with its detailed laws relating to the Jewish temple's sacrificial worship, is scripture, but much of it cannot address Christians (or even modern Jews) directly, however useful it may be as a testimony to God's working in the past. Is Revelation a book of the past, or is it still speaking to us?

The answer will depend on whether it challenges us to follow Christ, to witness to him and stay loyal to him come what may. It will depend on whether it challenges us to worship God, Father, Son and Holy Spirit, and to worship him alone. It will depend on whether it sets before us a vision of heaven, of the new creation, that inspires us, draws us to it and provokes our worship.

From the point of view of the present writer, it does all this and more. It challenges our assumptions about the role of the Church and the acceptability of today's culture, society and politics. For those of us who worship with a written liturgy, Revelation is the source of many of the praises we sing to God week by week. It challenges us to use our imaginations in our telling of the gospel story. John takes a literary form of his day, apocalyptic, and bends it to his own purpose of challenging the discipleship of his readers. In doing so, he challenges today's readers to find their own imaginative vehicle for teaching and evangelism. Perhaps above all, John shows a way of thinking that is steeped in knowledge of the Bible. It informs his thinking in a way that questions the extent to which we ourselves engage with scripture and allow it to inform our way of seeing the world.

Of course, the book of Revelation can be misused, promoting fanaticism and bigotry, and it can bolster a religious escapism that is far from its original intent. While John uses the language of violence and warfare in a subversive way, undermining the literal meaning, and replacing it with the idea of suffering and self-sacrifice, the strength of that language can still be disturbing for present-day readers. But Revelation is a fitting climax to the canon (the accepted list) of scripture. It is indeed a message from the God who sets the spirits of prophets on fire with his word.

PRAYER

Father, set our spirits on fire with your Spirit of prophecy, that we too may speak your words of inspiration, to you in worship, to each other in encouragement and to the world in witness.

COMING SOON?

A voice breaks into the angel's speech—that of Jesus (v. 7), affirming that his appearance is at hand. The immediate meaning is of his final coming in judgment of the world, and the consummation of the kingdom of God. We have also heard his promise (and threat) to visit his churches before then, to come in judgment and encouragement to his worshipping communities (chs. 2—3). For John's readers, and for us, the promise operates on both levels. Christ's judgment will be apparent, both on the last day and in the outworking of the Church's life and mission, and we need to be ready.

It is not clear whether John saw the coming persecution of the Church as a sign of the imminent return of Christ. His letter to the seven churches was written in a spirit of urgency, which may indicate that he did, but at the same time he makes it clear that for the Church all times are the last times, and the mission of the Church is never a task to be postponed.

Whatever John may have expected, we have to accept that it is nowadays impossible to feel the same emotional urgency as many of the first Christians did, and which we find reflected in much of the New Testament. One answer is to try to whip up such a sense of expectation by interpreting Revelation as a literal prediction of our own times. Then the return of Jesus can be seen as truly about to happen. Unfortunately, this is not what Revelation is about, and throughout history those who have taken such an approach have been disappointed. John was wiser, and knew that what really counted was not when these things would happen, but how Christians were to live, worship and witness before they come about. John's message is mainly concerned with how the Church is to behave before the day of judgment. Blessed (now) is the one who keeps (now) the words of the prophecy in this book. That should be our concern as well.

True worship

As once before (19:10), John gives way to the temptation to fall in homage at the feet of the great angel who has opened his visionary eyes (v. 8). He is rebuked in the same terms as before. The angel is a creature, made, like human beings, to serve God. The very term 'angel' simply means 'messenger', and as such the purpose of the angel is like that of the prophets. He is there merely to bring God's message, and the only true object of worship is God (v. 9).

In John's world, it might not have seemed strange, at least outside Christian and Jewish circles, to offer worship to an angel. Pagan thought was happy with the notion of many beings who were in various degrees divine. For Jews and Christians, however, divinity was absolute and belonged only to God (with whom Christians also identified Jesus). John's mistake still stands as a warning to any who are tempted to place that which is not God at the centre of their lives.

The fact that John mentions this error twice is a sure sign that he saw it as important. It is significant, too, that he is tempted to worship the bearer of the word of God. It is hard to tempt Christians to worship something that is overtly labelled as a god, but to worship the messenger is a subtler temptation. A popular preacher, church leader or Christian writer may gain a following that has more to do with his or her personality or style than the God to whom they point. Perhaps John is aware of the pull of 'Jezebel' and fears a personal following of his own.

Open book

Most apocalypses were written in the name of a famous person of long ago, and were presented as though they were prophecies by that person, but John writes under his own name, for his contemporaries, and the book is to remain unsealed (v. 10; compare Daniel 12:9), its contents open to all.

It is not a book of secret wisdom for the chosen few, or a book for a distant time, but a book of encouragement and challenge for the churches of the present—a book for the Church in all ages. It is a book for good and bad, pure and impure, at all times as they go about their daily lives. Verse 11 reflects Daniel 12:10 and Isaiah 6:9–10, reminding John's readers that his prophetic word is a book of promise and hope to the righteous and a call to repentance to the evildoer. For both, it is a call to be prepared (Matthew 24:37–39).

PRAYER

Lord, give us a desire to know you and to serve you,
not at some time in the future, but now.

Yours Faithfully

John's visions reached their climax in verse 5. Then, as it were, he was left standing with the angel, who assured him of the truth of the visions and their message. Into this broke the voice of Jesus, promising his coming. Now Jesus speaks again, saying that he is coming to bring his reward to those who have done the work of God (vv. 12–13).

That Jesus is coming 'soon' (NRSV) could indicate that John sees the second coming as lying close to his own time, but the Greek word (*tachys*: 'quickly') can also mean 'suddenly', and might refer to the unexpected suddenness of his coming, as in 16:15, where he is described as 'coming like a thief'.

Once again, we need to stress that the language of reward and works goes together with the language of faith. The works referred to in verse 12 stem from faith in God. For the Church, they are the work of faithful witness, in all its far-reaching meaning. Those who have stood firm against the beast, who have spoken the words of the gospel boldly, who have lived out the values of new Jerusalem in the midst of Babylon, will receive their reward. Christ is coming to pronounce to his faithful servants that they have done well.

Lord and God

Jesus' promise is trustworthy, as the words of God are trustworthy (22:6), for Jesus is God. The promise is bolstered by another of Revelation's clear statements of the divinity of Christ. Earlier, God has been described as the Alpha and the Omega, the beginning and the end (1:8; 21:6). Jesus has been called the first and the last—the same sense, but different words (1:17). Now all three titles are claimed by Christ (v. 13).

He is the Alpha and the Omega, the first and the last, the beginning and the end. It is from him, as from God, that all things come. He is the creative principle of God, which brought the universe into being (John 1:1–5). He is the goal of creation, which finds its meaning and fulfilment in him, the one who is again coming to bring salvation to the world. John, who had been tempted to fall in worship before the angel, now hears the words of the one who truly is worthy of worship, for he and all creation was created to give glory to the one who now speaks.

Final greetings

Revelation is a book in the form of a letter. It is a letter from John, but it is even more a letter from Jesus. Verses 14–18 formally end the letter, and it is signed with the first-century equivalent of 'yours faithfully, Jesus'.

Like most of the New Testament letters, there is a closing exhortation to live out the Christian life. Here it takes the form of a repetition of the basic warning of the book (vv. 14–15). For those who are faithful—if need be, to the point of death—and wash their robes in the blood of martyrdom, which is the blood of the Lamb, there is life. For those who reject the offer of salvation, there is nothing. They are outside the city, which is the new creation, and being outside they are separated from the source of life itself.

'Dogs' was a Jewish term of abuse for Gentiles, signifying that which is unclean, for dogs are among the unclean animals in Jewish law (Matthew 7:6; 15:26). Here it probably refers to false Christians, like the ones listed in 21:8, for it replaces the cowardly and faithless in the earlier list. Paul had used the same derogatory term for Christian teachers who undermined his gospel by insisting that Gentile converts obey the full Jewish law (Philippians 3:2–3). It may be possible, though, to see a deeper meaning. 'Dogs' are combined with sorcerers, fornicators and so on. Those who seek their salvation, their personal fulfilment, in self-gratification, the abuse of power and the pursuit of illusion, become less than truly human. Humanity is created to find itself in God, and only in him can ultimate fulfilment be found.

PRAYER

Lord Jesus Christ, in your word you call us to follow you to glory.
As we read your message to us, open our ears to your voice, so that
your word may not return empty to you.

COME, DESIRE *of* NATIONS

John, who has been the recipient of the visions and the messages, has now disappeared from his own book. The last word belongs to Jesus who has sent his angel (via John) to the seven churches (in Greek, the 'you' is plural in verse 16) with a message for all the churches.

John shows by example what it is to proclaim the gospel. The message is about Jesus, not about the speaker. Those gifted with fine oratory or other means of witnessing need to remember that they are drawing attention to Jesus, not to themselves. Those who feel that their speech is poor, and their deeds unworthy, can draw encouragement from the fact that it is Jesus, not they, who is the attraction of Christianity.

Promised one

Jesus is the one promised by scripture, the king of David's line (Isaiah 11:1), the glorious ruler from Israel (Numbers 24:17). He is the one whom the Church desires as a bride looks forward to her wedding. He is the one to whom the Holy Spirit, inspirer of worship and prayer, points his Church. His coming is the consummation of human hopes and desires, a release from longing and spiritual thirst, the realization of eternal life.

That eternal life is not just a future event but a present experience for those who come to him. Eternal life is not just a quantity, an endless existence, but a quality, a richness of life, an exuberant overflowing of life that comes from knowing God and being joined to him through Christ (John 17:3; 10:10). The call of the Church, inspired by the Spirit, is addressed both to Christ as a prayer for the hastening of the kingdom, and to the thirsty as an invitation to come now for satisfaction of their deepest longings. The description of the Church as the bride in verse 17 is a reminder of the present state of God's people. Although the final victory has not yet arrived, they already live in its light and strive to show something here and now of what they eventually will be.

Sacred book

Verses 18–19 are frequently held up as a warning to those who would tamper with scripture as a whole (and by that is often meant a particular interpretation of scripture). John intends it more specifically, addressing it to those who are tempted to soft-pedal the challenge of the gospel. It is because the offer is so wonderful that the warning to those who adulterate it is so terrible. If the book is accepted as true prophecy, then there can be no watering down either of its promises or of its warnings. There is a strong temptation to feel that the gospel should be 'nice', whereas it is a two-edged sword (1:16). It brings the good news of God's stupendous love, and also the terrible news of human sinfulness. It shows a God whose love reaches beyond human imagining and yet is still all too resistible by human beings. Such resistance is self-destruction, and that too is part of the gospel. Let the message stand, says the prophet, and let people make their choice of life or death.

Make it so

The final word is Christ's, and it is a word of encouragement (v. 20). He is coming. There is hope for a beleaguered church and for weary witnesses. In the darkest moments of life and faith, there is light on the horizon that shines from the city of God, the destination of the saints and the goal of all true human aspirations. He will triumph, and all things will be well, and all manner of things will be well.

What can we say to that? Only amen, let it be, make it so.

Until then, we are borne by the grace of God (v. 21). He has come to the world in Jesus Christ to give himself freely, for that is the meaning of grace. May it be with all his people and, through them, flow into the world.

PRAYER

Amen. Come, Lord Jesus.

NOTES

NOTES

NOTES

NOTES

NOTES

NOTES

NOTES

Guidelines is a unique Bible reading resource that offers four months of in-depth study written by leading scholars. Contributors are drawn from around the world, as well as the UK, and represent a stimulating and thought-provoking breadth of Christian tradition.

Instead of the usual dated daily readings, *Guidelines* provides weekly units, broken into at least six sections, plus an introduction giving context for the passage, and a final section of points for thought and prayer. On any day you can read as many or as few sections as you wish, to fit in with work or home routine. As well as a copy of *Guidelines*, you will need a Bible. Each contributor also suggests books for further study.

Guidelines is edited by Dr Katharine Dell, Senior Lecturer in the Faculty of Divinity at Cambridge University and Director of Studies in Theology at St Catharine's College, and Dr Jeremy Duff, Director of Lifelong Learning in Liverpool Diocese and Canon at Liverpool Cathedral.

GUIDELINES SUBSCRIPTIONS

❏ I would like to give a gift subscription
   (please complete both name and address sections below)
❏ I would like to take out a subscription myself
   (complete name and address details only once)

This completed coupon should be sent with appropriate payment to BRF. Alternatively, please write to us quoting your name, address, the subscription you would like for either yourself or a friend (with their name and address), the start date and credit card number, expiry date and signature if paying by credit card.

Gift subscription name _____

Gift subscription address _____

_____ Postcode _____

Please send to the above, beginning with the next January/May/September* issue.
(* *delete as applicable*)

(please tick box)	UK	SURFACE	AIR MAIL
GUIDELINES	❏ £11.70	❏ £13.05	❏ £15.30
GUIDELINES 3-year sub	❏ £29.25		

Please complete the payment details below and send your coupon, with appropriate payment to: **BRF, First Floor, Elsfield Hall, 15–17 Elsfield Way, Oxford OX2 8FG**

Your name _____

Your address _____

_____ Postcode _____

Total enclosed £ _____ (cheques should be made payable to 'BRF')

Payment by cheque ❏ postal order ❏ Visa ❏ Mastercard ❏ Switch ❏

Card number: ☐☐☐☐ ☐☐☐☐ ☐☐☐☐ ☐☐☐☐

Expiry date of card: ☐☐☐☐ Issue number (Switch): ☐☐☐☐

Signature (essential if paying by credit/Switch card) _____

NB: BRF notes are also available from your local Christian bookshop.   **BRF is a Registered Charity**

REVELATION

THE PEOPLE'S BIBLE COMMENTARY

VOUCHER SCHEME

The People's Bible Commentary (PBC) provides a range of readable, accessible commentaries that will grow into a library covering the whole Bible.

To help you build your PBC library, we have a voucher scheme that works as follows: a voucher is printed on this page of each People's Bible Commentary volume (as above). These vouchers count towards free copies of other books in the series.

For every four purchases of PBC volumes you are entitled to a further volume FREE.

Please find the coupon for the PBC voucher scheme opposite.

All you need do:

- Cut out the vouchers from the PBCs you have purchased and attach them to the coupon.

- Complete your name and address details, and indicate your choice of free book from the list on page 240.

- Take the coupon to your local Christian bookshop who will exchange it for your free PBC book; or send the coupon straight to BRF who will send you your free book direct. Please allow 28 days for delivery.

Please note that PBC volumes provided under the voucher scheme are subject to availability. If your first choice is not available, you may be sent your second choice of book.

THE PEOPLE'S
BIBLE COMMENTARY

VOUCHER SCHEME COUPON

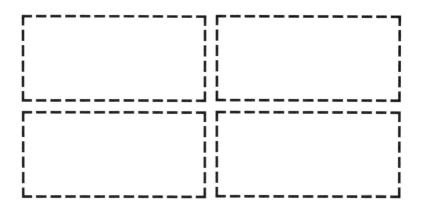

Customer and bookseller should both complete the form
overleaf.

TO BE COMPLETED BY THE CUSTOMER

My choice of free PBC volume is:
(Please indicate a first and second choice; all volumes are supplied subject to availability.)

❑ Leviticus and Numbers
❑ Deuteronomy
❑ Joshua and Judges
❑ Ruth, Esther, Ecclesiastes, Song of Songs, Lamentations
❑ 1 & 2 Samuel
❑ 1 & 2 Kings
❑ Chronicles to Nehemiah
❑ Job
❑ Psalms 1—72
❑ Psalms 73—150
❑ Proverbs
❑ Jeremiah
❑ Ezekiel
❑ Hosea to Micah
❑ Nahum to Malachi
❑ Matthew
❑ Mark
❑ Luke
❑ John
❑ Romans
❑ 1 Corinthians
❑ 2 Corinthians
❑ Galatians and Thessalonians
❑ Ephesians to Colossians and Philemon
❑ Timothy, Titus and Hebrews
❑ James to Jude

Name: . . . .

Address: . . . .

. . . .

Postcode: . . . .

TO BE COMPLETED BY THE BOOKSELLER

(Please complete the following. Coupons redeemed will be credited to your account for the value of the book(s) supplied as indicated above. Please note that only coupons correctly completed with original vouchers will be accepted for credit.)

Name: . . . .

Address: . . . .

. . . .

Postcode: . . . .

Account Number: . . . .

Completed coupons should be sent to: BRF, PBC Voucher Scheme, First Floor, Elsfield Hall, 15–17 Elsfield Way, Oxford OX2 8FG.

Tel 01865 319700; Fax 01865 319701; e-mail enquiries@brf.org.uk Registered Charity No. 233280

THIS OFFER IS AVAILABLE IN THE UK ONLY
PLEASE NOTE: ALL VOUCHERS ATTACHED TO THE COUPON MUST BE ORIGINAL COPIES.